CHINA LAKE

CHINA

WINNER OF THE IOWA PRIZE
IN LITERARY NONFICTION

LAKE

A JOURNEY INTO THE CONTRADICTED HEART
OF A GLOBAL CLIMATE CATASTROPHE

WITHDRAWN

BARRET BAUMGART

UNIVERSITY OF IOWA PRESS | IOWA CITY

University of Iowa Press, Iowa City 52242
Copyright © 2017 by Barret Baumgart
www.uipress.uiowa.edu
Printed in the United States of America

Design by April Leidig

Image credits: page 38, re-creation of *Westward the Course of Empire Takes Its Way* by Emanuel Leutze; page 87, copyright David S. Whitely; page 160, photo by the Great March for Climate Action; page 197, photo by Kevin S. O'Brien, U.S. Navy; all other photos are from author's personal collection.

No part of this book may be reproduced or used in any form or by any means without permission in writing from the publisher. All reasonable steps have been taken to contact copyright holders of material used in this book. The publisher would be pleased to make suitable arrangements with any whom it has not been possible to reach.

The University of Iowa Press is a member of Green Press Initiative and is committed to preserving natural resources.

Printed on acid-free paper

Library of Congress Cataloging-in-Publication Data
Names: Baumgart, Barret, 1987– author.
Title: China Lake : a journey into the contradicted heart of a global climate catastrophe / Barret Baumgart.
Other titles: Journey into the contradicted heart of a global climate catastrophe
Description: Iowa City : University Of Iowa Press, [2017] | "Winner of the Iowa Prize for Literary Nonfiction."
Identifiers: LCCN 2016040706 | ISBN 978-1-60938-470-8 (pbk) | ISBN 978-1-60938-471-5 (ebk)
Subjects: LCSH: Naval Air Weapons Station (China Lake, Calif.) | Weather control—California. | Climatic changes—Social aspects. | BISAC: NATURE / Weather. | NATURE / General.
Classification: LCC QC928.72.C2 B38 2017 | DDC 551.68/2710979495—dc23
LC record available at https://lccn.loc.gov/2016040706

FOR THE REFUGEES

War is the father of all things.
— Heraclitus, Fragment

Mom's gonna fix it all soon.
— Tool, "Ænema"

CONTENTS

FOREWORD

If you take out the hubbub of academia, there is not much for graduate students to do in Iowa City after working in their apartments on whatever projects they have, other than go out to one of the town's bars to see if there's anyone interesting to talk to or any late-night misadventures to be had. It was during many such nights that Barret and I became friends. I immediately liked his dark, fatalist humor; it was invigorating and often hilarious. He had an insanely keen mind and an insightful and brutal honesty that served to weed out anyone who wasn't up for a real discussion.

At the time, I had finished my first book of poetry and was working on the final edits with my publisher, and Barret was working on this manuscript, which he told me was basically about the weather, the military, and "a lot of other things." Barret and I shared a fascination with cosmic, long-range perspectives on the human species as well as the bizarre, often jarringly juxtaposed realities of our present age. Throughout our conversations, I often thought of the words of the poet Robert Hass, who said in a lecture that if World War II and the Holocaust had been the big historical events that his generation of poets had had to address, then the big historical event that our generation of poets had to deal with was the crisis of our relationship with the planet, an event that is happening now whose big acts are just getting started. I agree with Hass: the catastrophes we've set up for ourselves are such immense, looming presences that anyone interested in making art that is at all concerned with the human condition finds them impossible to ignore.

The vision I was struggling to express in my poetry was one that Barret was actually creating with research and information. To call this work a piece of journalism would be reductive. It is that at times, but it is more a work of art that attempts to handle information poetically, carefully weaving facts in order to carry us through a strange, kaleidoscopic landscape that allows us to see ourselves in the context of millennia.

One of the most valuable aspects of good nonfiction — and of literature in general — is that for the length of time you are immersed in the work, it allows you to hold in your head a much bigger perspective on the world than the one you normally have while carrying out everyday tasks. Such books allow us to think bigger, to hold together a picture that would be hard to imagine or sustain on our own. Often, when we put them down, we find that that picture has transformed our view of the world. This is precisely what Barret Baumgart's book does — with sprawling, frenetic energy. The future is the realm of uncertainty, and in that fact lies the only real hope given us by *China Lake*. It is to the future's uncertainty that the author leads us, but he leaves us equipped with a better comprehension of where we stand.

Jesús Castillo
Santa Fe, New Mexico

CHINA LAKE

YESTERDAY

July, Mojave Desert . . . midday, with strings of tortured air rising, hypnotic and toxic, off the asphalt in rippling jets of transparent flame, a hooded figure draped head to toe in white rounds the bend beneath a wall of volcanic rimrock and continues dragging himself across the distance, his heavy rhythmic breaths scraping through the silent desert stone, each exhalation like a blind woman's broom brushing a cathedral transept, and as the rasping wanders closer, in the distance another figure begins bobbing in a mirage pooled up over the bend, drifting slowly until he seems to rise and wade out from the light, onto the shore of black asphalt, where he continues plodding through the boiling heat just as a third figure rises in the mangled pyrite, followed by a fourth and a fifth, some forgotten fanatical sect of medieval self-flagellants, the deranged and roving victims of mass famine, megadroughts, and black plagues, these gasping white-clad penitents just keep climbing out of the desert, dripping blood and sweat, their outlines flickering in and out through the horizon's heat haze, and as they pass, their white neck capes bouncing, deep breaths blowing, it's hard to tell if they're coming or going, winning or losing, or what that might even mean in all this gigantic pitiless distance.

There's nothing here but heat and dust, dust and light, time and space — no great upheaval beyond the mute accumulation of aeons, no setback beyond the routine catastrophe of morning sunrise. Daylight sears and returns every speck of rock and sand, every pore and follicle of human pride and daily grime, every miserable stick of charred inedible plant life back to the perfect sterility of lunar space. What passion could be conceived here, what sin, what germ? One wonders what these pilgrims could possibly have found to flee from or toward—how they sustain their faith in this landscape that seems to preserve a single celestial truth, to radiate but one overwhelming fact: indifference, the indifference of a dying star that insists on spraying, across this last fossilized infarct of California, the fire, light, and silence of 100 billion hydrogen bombs bursting every second.

In the shade it's 119°F. On the asphalt it's 180°F. In such weather, the body can lose a gallon of water in just a few hours. That's over eight pounds of liquid. As the brain begins to coagulate, it envisions water everywhere. Across the road, the dead lattice of the dwarf trees twists, blurs, and pulses like seaweed inhaling the crests of coastal waves. The undulating layers of fossilized strata stain the cliffs with the leak and drip of virgin springs. The highway mirage ripples cold with alpine refreshment. The pale granite domes high above the scrub pines scream of melting snow. The coyote rotting along the roadside smells of healing sulfur hot springs. Water—the last thing you'll find and the only thing you need. Most people would turn to carrion if they stood on the blacktop over an hour. But somehow these bastards are running on it . . .

Every July, they return to erase themselves in the Mojave, and most summers, as I pass the desert en route to the mountains, I see them suffering. People always ask them the same question— why?—and their answers seldom vary.

"I run because I learn so much about God when I run."

"I'm always searching for a feeling of freedom and flight . . ."

"To reach a point of nirvana."

"It's about the journey, not the destination."

"There's these people chasing me and I have to get away."

The first time I saw them, I was standing at the end of Centennial Road, a bumpy dirt track that runs across a broad wash, away from the rim of Death Valley, to the mouth of a narrow lava canyon. My friend Kyle and I had carried in water and whiskey and camped beside the ruins of an old ranch in the upper flats. We'd had a couple of days off, and neither of us gave much thought to the heat or to the fact that we'd be sleeping another night on hard ground. We were working for the US Forest Service that summer, breaking rocks and shoveling scree, repairing old trails above the tree line, and the hard work had made us trail-tough, or so we thought until the next morning when we drove down from the canyon and stopped the car to watch the runners come over the ridge. One by one. Dressed in white. Their faces beamed as they stared past us, beyond the Coso Range, toward the granite peaks of the Sierra Nevada.

We didn't know it then, but they'd already been at it for twenty-seven hours. During that time they'd crossed over two mountain ranges. When they finally collapsed sometime the next night, they'd put 150 miles on their sneakers, summited Mount Whitney—the highest peak in yet a third range of mountains—and endured an overall combined vertical ascent of 19,000 feet. All this without sleep.

"God, we're pussies," Kyle said.

We climbed out of the car, stood in the dirt, and stared east along CA 190, shading our eyes and inhaling the idling engine fumes until we both suddenly shrieked, crouched down, and covered our ears. A bullet-shaped F-16 fighter jet ripped out from the south, exploding the sky behind us before it tore north for another mile in the span of two breaths. We watched as the runners stopped in the middle of the road and started jumping and cheering, waving good-bye to the warplane as it dipped a wing, cut east, and disappeared over Death Valley. When all was quiet, the runners continued plodding west.

"Yet another special treat out here in the desert," recalls Arthur Webb, a Badwater veteran. "It must have cost the race director a bundle to put this display on."

The Badwater Ultramarathon calls itself the world's toughest footrace. It is very likely "the most physically taxing competitive event in the world." Beyond such trite and true taglines, the extreme endurance race is also known for its extraordinary hallucinations, not the least of which being the fact that an obscure and brutal contest offering no prize money beyond a belt buckle can afford to pay the military to cheer on its suicidal contenders* or that such frequent flybys should constitute anything beyond the routine rehearsal of foreign war over the world's largest and most isolated naval base. Nonetheless, as we stood below Centennial Canyon that day, the runners' enthusiasm felt contagious, convincing. The power, speed, and levity of that plane, for all its violent cacophony and dormant murder, seemed to fly in the face of that mute and inhuman desert — a cheerful sovereign noise, no matter how long it lasted.

"Kill 'em all!" Kyle yelled after the runners.

Badwater finisher Dave Bursler's official race report captures how much competitors depend on those military planes. "As we walked, I told Dori how disappointed I was that I hadn't seen the F-16 fighter jets that David Bliss told me we might see." But then suddenly, "As if God above was answering my prayers an F-16 came out of nowhere and did a fly by. A few seconds later a second F-16 flew by us. It was an unbelievable experience that gave me an emotional rush. Seems I was going to experience everything Badwater had to offer."

Bursler says that it's at Badwater where he found the strength to open up his heart. "This is where I learned that things don't have to be seen to be true."

Kyle and I had both been disappointed the night before when we didn't see anything at the perimeter of the base. Walking the upper flats, headlamps lit, we'd half-expected some contingent of military guards armed with machine guns climbing out of camo Humvees to scan our licenses, credit cards, and cell phones; inspect our packs, notebooks, and pupils; and confine us in some underground detention center for past sexual treasons, future unpaid parking tickets, or at least our present public drunkenness. But there was nothing out there. Not even a single obscure flashing light to entertain our fear or encourage a guess about what exactly they might be studying, building, or testing in the dark. Nothing but ink-black night, a dusty deserted road, and a long sagging rope of rusted barbed wire insufficient to keep out even the least curious passing burro. Several shotgunned signs reflected the spray of our headlamps: Warning — Restricted Area. No Trespassing.

"Pretty lame."

"Yeah," Kyle agreed.

I watched him walk around to the back of the car, lift the tailgate, and grab a water bottle from his pack. He tossed me one and started coughing, then smiled as he closed his eyes, covered his mouth with a fist, and tried to point a finger over my shoulder.

This time I didn't flinch.

"We should give them a ride. They look like they're waving for help," I said.

The runners stopped in the road as a second plane roared past us. Kyle took a deep breath and shut the trunk.

"They're just happy," he said.

If the road of excess still leads to the palace of wisdom, then for those runners crossing the earth's hottest desert in the world's hardest footrace, the amazing superfluity of those planes must have seemed a near-providential sign, the most auspicious omen; it was as though Gaia herself had screamed "Eureka!" and sent not one but two eagles, a certainty twice spoken: these brave runners would conquer the titanic forces working against them. The promised land lay near, they seemed to say. Anything can be accomplished, as long as the will remains strong.

Yet if it's true, as Dave Bursler's memoir suggests, that things don't have to be seen to be believed, then shouldn't the opposite adage also hold true? Don't believe everything you see.

I never ran the Badwater Ultramarathon and I don't ever intend to, but I suppose I've always been drawn — for better or worse — to the human extreme, that border between light and dark, terror and ecstasy, faith and absurdity. Albert Camus called it a "waterless desert where thought reaches its confines." The point he believed was to stay there, "insofar as that is possible, and to examine closely the odd vegetation of those distant regions." But you can't stay there for long. The things you see will either destroy you, rouse you from a dream, or send you running as fast and as far as your feet will carry you. "To say that that climate is deadly," Camus wrote, "scarcely amounts to playing on words." It took me years to realize what I had actually seen in those upper flats besides piled scabrock, junipers, and Joshua trees — a disturbing vision hidden in the cliffs just beyond the dry wash of Centennial Spring and its threshold of rusted barbed wire.

The runners of the Badwater Ultramarathon speak openly of their visions, the trance-like hallucinations that occur often during the second night of their journey. They see ghosts and demons, decaying corpses on the roadside, mutant mice monsters crawling in the darkness, and extraterrestrials in the distance. One runner, Jack Denness, reports that he saw a spaceship that had smashed into a mountainside: "Smoke was still rising from the crash. Around the spaceship were these tiny aliens. I saw this from a distance of seven miles." Runners have been stalked by women rollerblading in silver bikinis, low-flying passenger planes, and Satan himself. "He was all red, had horns, fork-tail, and carried a three-pronged tripod. . . . Every time I turned around to look for him, he would dodge behind a tree or rock, just showing his face." Others in their altered states have calmly jogged across a transplanted Golden Gate Bridge, over the improbable excrescence of computer microchips, and into dreams of drifting ocean vessels, covered-wagon trains, and lost gold miners. "It was still 114 degrees at 2 AM . . . I started to hallucinate, seeing this grizzled old 49er holding his gold pan. I thought it was filled with water. I went to get some. I woke up when I heard the water from my own bottle sizzling on the pavement."

Sheep may be the ultramarathon runners' most common hallucination. They fly among the stars, wander the highway in thin herds, and scale the basalt outcrops above the highway guardrails. Ian Parker, a veteran of nine Badwaters and a neurobiologist at the University of California, Irvine, recalls once accepting the spirit guidance of a desert bighorn. "I noticed a figure walking slowly up the trail a few hundred yards ahead of me which, looking more closely, resolved into a bighorn sheep. This was exciting, because bighorn sheep are normally very timid . . . suddenly it stopped and turned to look at me. Fixing me with a baleful stare ('Come on slowcoach!'), it waited until I had caught up. At that point I wondered if I ought to be worried — bighorn sheep weigh more than 200 pounds, the males charge each other at speeds over 25 mph, and the narrow trail ran above a high cliff — but this one looked to be a juvenile female who was just curious about this intruder into her rocky lair. She let me approach within a few feet, then started upward again at a pace that looked languid but still left me trailing behind. Again, though, she paused to let me catch up, all the while fixing me with her intent stare, and again set off upwards when I was almost close enough to touch. This little game carried on for around 10 minutes before she tired of it and bounded effortlessly away up a steep talus slope. The memory of our brief encounter stayed with me throughout the cold, hard slog through the darkness up to the rim and, like all good pacers, my bighorn sheep provided a psychological boost at the toughest time during a run."

Ian Parker apparently did not understand the point of the game. He should have killed that sheep.

"Bump, bump," she says.

She sets her elbows down on the dark wood table and smiles. A candle glows beside the napkin holder and the light catches her eyes as they search mine. I glance away, staring down at the dogs sleeping beneath the table. It's late and we have to wake up early.

"Bump, bump?" I ask.

A lonesome Native American flute drifts across the kitchen from the plasma flatscreen. At night she keeps the TV tuned to channel 943, Soundscapes. I've always called it her magic cave music. She'll say she likes these songs. "They're relaxing." They help her escape.

"Come on. You know what 'bump, bump' means," she says.

She mounted a rainbow-colored map of the world behind the television recently. Alongside it, on the top shelf of a bookcase crammed with travel guides, stand dozens of handmade miniature wood-carved animals from Oaxaca. She lifts them each day and dusts them, careful never to crack their fragile toothpick limbs. She's never traveled outside the country except to Mexico once. I want to help her.

"Let's go to sleep," I say.

I hear one of the dogs beneath the table wake. Velvet hound ears flapping. Collar jangling like chiseled car keys. If I cup the glowing tip of my e-cig in my palm, rest my elbow on the table, and hold my fist to my lips, I can smoke without her noticing. I inhale, staring down at the candle flame flickering between us. The sticker says April Rain, but I don't smell it. It's late October and San Diego hasn't had a drop in six months.

"You really don't remember?" she says. "If I get sick, drop me behind the car, put it in reverse, and back over me."

Bump, bump.

This dark image contradicts the color on her walls. She keeps her morbidity at bay throughout the day, but at night, when she drinks, she lets it escape. Or maybe it's just because I'm here. I tell myself she inherited it from her father. "I yam what I yam," he used to say, quoting Popeye, when she'd beg him to quit smoking—that's what she told me. Lately, unlike him, she's tried to change. She's managed to eliminate most of her bad habits, everything except alcohol.

She raises her champagne glass and taps the crystal. "Refill, please," she says.

I walk past the hundred multicolored indigenous craft art crucifixes that cover the wall beside the table. All authentic, she'll say. Next to the kitchen sink, a small electric fountain gurgles between the toes of the enlightened Buddha she bought at Marshalls. I open the refrigerator and squint.

She told me she paid a lot of money to hear some guru speak downtown at a hotel last week. After his speech, he stared in her eyes and said he saw a vast reservoir of light, but she had to learn to love herself first if she ever wanted to heal. She interpreted this to mean that she could still enjoy a couple of drinks each night.

"You know I'd cut my right arm off for you," she says while I pour.

I've never doubted her love. We slept together in the same bed for eleven years. When I was eight, she told me she'd had two abortions before me. But she chose me. "I wanted to have you," she said. My grandmother worried; she thought our prolonged attachment would soften me, turn me into some kind of queer. Say "I yam what I yam," my mom used to tell me when I'd try to stop the bad kids from catching and killing the lizards in the rocks after school. They only danced around me, singing: "Popeye the sailor man, he lives in a garbage can. He turned on the heater and burned off his wiener. He's Popeye the sailor man."

"Alcohol is really an excellent painkiller," she says. "Sometimes I think it helps my back more than the Percocet. Your hair looks horrible, sweetie."

When I was fourteen, I started listening to metal and stopped showering. My mother married for the first time and started menopause. We no longer touched except when she smacked me. My stepfather never saw our fights because he was always at the office. It's still the same today. I worry about how much he works, how much time my mother spends alone, and she worries the same for me.

A small Yorkshire terrier bursts through the doggy door.

"Moby, come here, baby," she says.

My mom has three lapdogs: Moby, Maddie, and Mogwai. Alliteration is a hereditary disease. So are degenerative disk disease and generalized anxiety disorder. She pats her knee and Moby, the smallest and most bashful of the bunch, jumps and climbs over her chest to lick her face. She turns him around to face me.

"Moby, you remember your brother, don't you?"

The dog shivers and stares at the TV.

Last Christmas, after Moby ran away, she started giving him her antidepressants, cramming little doses inside hot dogs. There was nothing wrong with this — dogs are often prescribed the same antidepressants as their owners — but after a week the vet told her to stop. "See if Moby's symptoms haven't improved." Apparently they had. Now, as some form of holistic canine stress reduction therapy, she keeps the Disney Channel on all day. She thinks the cartoon voices comfort the dog. At night, however, the television belongs to her.

"Go see your brother," she says, handing me the dog as she lifts the remote and turns up the magic cave music. "You don't have any pot, do you?" she asks.

Earlier during dinner, when I told her the real reason I wanted to come home, she set down her fork and switched the TV to mute. She tried to explain what she often found so frustrating about my presence. "You're so . . . esoteric," she said, settling on a nice word. "Why poison?"

Usually she can tolerate me for a week or so, but already now, while she continues drinking and her filter keeps coming down, I can feel that I'm no longer necessary. She says that she saw it years ago, that when I went away to college I started to change; something must have happened, something to make you lose compassion. Moby tilts his head back and yawns, a little squeak escaping before his jaws clap closed.

"Who's a pretty boy?" She leans toward him, smiling. "Yes, you is," she says. "You's a pretty boy. Yes, you is."

While she wonders how I can possibly endure the alienation I create for myself by reading all day, I wonder how to prove to a woman whose most meaningful connections are shared with canines that I love her without licking her hand.

She sighs and seems to stare out the window, beyond the sliding glass door, into the blackness of the backyard, but really she's just staring at her own reflection.

"Honestly, honey, don't you enjoy anything? Can't you just relax a little?"

In Iowa, when I showed up at the Health and Wellness Clinic, they told me nothing was wrong—"your heartbeat is normal"—and tried to give me Xanax. I didn't take it and I'm still not on any pills and I don't have a TV either. Sometimes I wish I did. More and more, as I grow older, I've come to appreciate the value of such machines, a reliable way to turn off your brain. I don't know exactly what happened in Iowa. Maybe it was the midwestern flatness, an alien geography devoid of pinnacles and canyons, a pervasive monotony that seeped into my mind and made me so restless some nights that I wondered if I didn't really want to dive into that town's toxic river and simply float away. Instead, for one winter, I went running—five, six, seven miles. Every other day. Endorphins drove away the panicked feeling but only for a time. Stepping off the treadmill, I'd watch the snow piling up outside beneath the streetlamps and see that I hadn't gone anywhere. There was nowhere to go.

I watched a morning broadcast of the Colorado floods on a TV at a bar down the street from my house in Iowa City. Reports claimed the quantity of rain falling probably happened only once every thousand years. "Biblical rainfall amounts reported in/near the foothills," the National Weather Service said on September 12 at 10:00 a.m. An offscreen reporter shouted through the rain while the station cut between helicopters and cameras on the ground. Every shot showed another angle from another vantage of the same image—angry brown torrents gushing down the Rocky foothills and washing out everything in their path, including roads, homes, and people. The montage continued on a loop while the reporter kept calling through the hiss of relentless rain.

I don't know why I went to the bar that morning. I really just wanted to drink coffee and read James Agee, but instead I ordered another beer. I couldn't take my eyes off the screen. The images of the brown cataracts ripping through sheer canyons, the waters rising and coalescing in a river of mud a mile wide, felt strangely, somehow, soothing to me. It was real and it mattered. I wanted to go there. I wanted to wade into that mess of water. But I had no idea what I was really getting into. During a commercial break, I opened my laptop.

My mother only texted me two days later. She told me "to pray for those poor souls."

The massive six-day deluge caused $2 billion in damages and killed eight people.

While the media portrayed the floods as a freak act of God, the Internet was abuzz with conspiracy theorists who blamed the catastrophe on government cloud seeding, a weather modification technology developed by General Electric's Schenectady, New York, labs in the 1940s that allows airplanes to spray clouds with chemicals like silver iodide to increase rainfall. "Is it a coincidence," one blogger wrote, "that Boulder happens to be the epicenter for cloud seeding with silver iodide, calcium chloride and other toxic chemicals, including using CO_2 to supercool the atmosphere before seeding?" The blogger went on to say that he and his wife had seen massive chemtrails the day before the floods started. "We live in the South Western part of Colorado, and I watched the weather patterns carry the chemtrails right into the Boulder/Ft Collins area."

Corporate media outlets were quick to debunk these theories with testaments from local experts who claimed that cloud seeding could never produce such substantial rainfall. "You would have to be seeding over massive areas continuously for this to happen,"

Andrew Heymsfield, senior research scientist at the National Center for Atmospheric Research in Boulder, said in one NBC article. "You cannot create the precipitation we had by cloud seeding. There is no way that man can do that." By the time Heymsfield was quoted on September 17, his lab's parking lot still lay under several feet of water. In two days, Boulder had received more than its annual average precipitation, and seventeen Colorado counties were in a state of national emergency.

After the NBC article, chemtrail bloggers began to concur that the September 17 shooting in a Washington, D.C., navy yard, in which nine people were killed, had been staged by the government to distract the nation from the storms chemically engineered over Colorado.

"You don't believe in any of this conspiracy shit, do you?" my mom asks, draining the last of her champagne.

I rub Moby's head and take another drag off my e-cig.

"No, but a lot of people do."

After my mother's subarachnoid hemorrhage two Aprils ago, I find it matters less and less what either of us believes, as long as we can be kind. While her sloppy New Age mysticism annoys me most of the time, if it helps her I can't complain. But I'm not sure it does. I got upset earlier when she wouldn't go to my grandma's house with me. "That's our family," I said, "the last of it. It's only you, me, her, and Uncle Mark." But she was adamant. "I don't like going over there," she said. She can joke about her own premature health problems by saying "bump, bump," but she can't bear to watch her own mother's totally natural decline. Grandma's eighty-six and she's going senile. Sometimes she doesn't recognize my mother, but she always seems to remember me.

"Oh hell!" she shouted when I pulled into the driveway. "The lawn man's due any minute." She sat on the porch in her plastic rocking chair drinking a Natty Light through a bright yellow elbow straw and eating peanuts. The sky was clear, still another hour of light left, but soon, my grandmother said, we'd have to go inside.

"Where's Uncle Mark?" I asked. My Uncle Mark and I always got along. He'd been writing an epic sci-fi novel over the past several years, something about corporations colonizing space and an alien cover-up, but he put it on hold after moving in with my grandmother. "He's at the Food Basket," she said.

And sure enough, just as I sat down, the lawn man rolled up.

"He's a sweet soul," my grandmother said.

A large man in his late forties dressed in dark navy blue overalls stomped around to the back of the van, unfolded a wooden ramp, and started tugging on the handle of the heavy gasoline mower.

"Every time he comes, he gives me a big wet kiss on my cheek," Grandma said. "Just watch."

Rob battled the mower while blue jays dive-bombed the last peanuts strewed around Grandma's grass.

"Here, jay," she called. "Don't be afraid."

She sucked the dregs from the bottom of the beer can and turned to stare at me. She wanted me to get her another.

"I feel bad for him," she said.

"The blue jay or Rob?" I asked, starting toward the refrigerator in the garage. I assumed it had something to do with the precarious state of the lawn care business in San Diego. Grandma's grass looks green this year, but it's no thanks to the lawn man. Southern California, like most of the West, is rotting without rain. On the US Drought Monitor map, the western half of the country looks gangrenous, its "severe" yellow sores pocked by raw spots of burning red. *Scientific American* says the West remains locked in "the worst drought since the Dust Bowl of the 1930s."

"Why do you feel bad for him?" I asked, opening her another can.

Rob disentangled the mower and rolled it down the ramp.

"He's a little slow," Grandma said.

The wheels buckled and the mower ground over the concrete. Rob pushed it out into the grass, then came around the side of the porch and gave my grandmother a hug.

"Hi, Mom," he said.

"Get away from me, you booger," she joked.

A khaki bucket hat covered Rob's sweating pink face. He smiled and she offered him a beer.

"I got to get home soon," he said. "I can't visit tonight."

It's Friday. My grandmother asked him if he finally found a date.

"No," he said.

Removing his hat, Rob grabbed a handkerchief and dabbed his eyes. Drops of white sweat dripped down his temples like vanilla ice cream tears tangling stickily in red cheek stubble. He packed the handkerchief back in the breast pocket of his overalls and pointed upward. Miles above the trees, twin jet engines pulled a white trail across the sky.

"They're spraying us again," he said.

The condensation drifted east over the telephone wires, a weightless ribbon fraying into easy corrugated cirrus clouds.

"Spraying what?" I asked.

Rob wiped his forehead with the handkerchief again.

"Poison."

Rob said you could recognize a chemtrail by how long it lingered in the stratosphere.

"Chemtrails last a long time," he said.

By this I took it to mean that they last longer than normal contrails, the ubiquitous condensation clouds any jet plane will eject in cold, humid skies.

"It's really bad when they start checkerboarding."

The long white line continued to blur behind Grandma's crisscrossed telephone wires.

"Probably aluminum strontium," Rob guessed.

He pulled the chain and the lawnmower started to chug as I grabbed another beer and followed Grandma inside.

Earlier that morning, things were calm inside the Denver International Airport. The crystal-flecked marble floors reflected red neon pizza lights as I carried my coffee alongside the flat peoplemover escalators that hissed toward the United Terminal. I found an empty seat near the gate and stared out the windows. Beyond the tarmac, the grass stretched a brown no-man's-land out to the faraway barbed wire fences while the sun lifted over the Rocky Mountains.

The night before, I'd spoken with Joe Busto, program coordinator for Colorado's Weather Modification Board. Busto said he receives a lot of concerned calls about cloud seeding's effects, but "it's only in the past five years that folks have begun to link the government chemtrail conspiracy theory to cloud seeding." Busto pointed out that among the ten western states that seed clouds, the link between chemtrails and cloud seeding is nowhere weaker than in Colorado. The state seeds not from airplanes but from "exclusively ground-based ice nuclei generators." On top of this, even if Colorado did seed from the skies, the silver iodide particles would remain invisible from the ground—they'd leave no trail. Furthermore, Colorado cloud seeding does not begin until November 1. "No programs were in operation."

Busto echoed Andrew Heymsfield. "Cloud seeding," he said, "cannot generate large amounts of precipitation. Not like what we saw in September."

The message is clear: the chemtrail theory, as far as it relates to cloud seeding, is bunk.

Sitting in the empty terminal, I opened my laptop. There was an e-mail, an anonymous reply from one of the chemtrail websites, Aircrap.org. I'd e-mailed them to ask a few questions about the origins of the chemtrail theory. The link in my in-box took me to a website where someone claimed to have tracked down a top secret government document proving that the government is poisoning people. The document, it turns out, was the 1991 manual for the Air Force Academy's Chemistry 131 class, entitled "Chemtrails." The old childhood fear flits through me as I scroll through the syllabus— too many abstract numbers standing beside abbreviated elements for my associative brain to handle. "The goals of this course are to train you to think like a scientist (develop curiosity), teach you basic chemical principles, and develop your ability to communicate." A modest agenda, given the purported grand scheme of global geoengineering. Under the heading "Classroom Materials," I read that "you must bring your textbook, 3-ring binder, paper for taking notes, pencil or pen, and a calculator." It's just another tedious math-heavy undergrad chem course, something I could never have survived. The homework policy, however, seems fair. "In general, homework will not be collected or graded."

A link takes me to Dennis Kucinich's proposed House Resolution 2977, the flouted Space Preservation Act of 2001. Under the heading of supposed exotic weapons that Kucinich wanted banned, the bill lists "chemtrails" as well as "extraterrestrial weapons" and "environmental, climate, or tectonic weapons." Nobody knows what these titles refer to exactly. But chemtrail hopefuls, exploiting the vagueness, find full proof of a worldwide toxic conspiracy. Reading through the websites, I find it difficult to pinpoint exactly what the chemtrail programs are accomplishing. One site claims the government is injecting the ionosphere with electricity-conducting particles to trigger earthquakes via the High Frequency Active Auroral Research Program. Another says they're spraying sulfuric acid to block the sun and cool the planet. Another says they're pumping CO_2 to continue heating the planet. Another says they're seeding the sky with heavy metals, aluminum, barium, and strontium, to reduce the world population. "Everything is connected." Despite the contradicting claims, everyone seems to agree on one thing: the government is doing something to alter the earth's atmosphere. All the websites show the same eerie photos of multiple contrails crisscrossed in checkerboard patterns.

A link takes me to Alex Jones' Infowars.com, where a September 2013 article, "Chemtrail Poisons Are Ruining Your Health from Above, and You May Not Know It," claims that aluminum levels in the snow on Mount Shasta, California, have reached 4,610 times their normal level. When I click the reference link, it's dead. Searching the claim turns up a jpeg of a flier stapled to a telephone pole, "illegal weather modification programs . . . Here are the facts, You Decide." I click to another site that demonstrates how spraying vinegar in your backyard can dissolve chemtrails at altitudes up to 30,000 feet. Another site insists, "We have witnessed deaths of entire ladybug colonies after 3 extremely heavy days of spraying." The website summarizes the primary symptoms associated with chemtrails, the "Big 4": aneurysm, stroke, heart attack, and cancer. Other listed symptoms include "Fatigue, Headaches, Sinus pain, Muscle pain, Joint pain, Depression, Diabetes, Insomnia, Anxiety, Anger issues, Inability to concentrate, Looping thoughts or songs, Salty-metallic taste to the air, Chemical taste to the air, Swelling or inflammation, Elevated blood pressure, Upper respiratory infections, Loss of balance, Stomach pain, Frequent illness, Vivid or restless dreams, Frequently cracking joints, and Morgellons."

I click on a picture of a pretty girl, Laura Eisenhower, great-granddaughter of the president who warned us about the military-industrial complex. Laura explains, "The nerve toxins of chemtrails keep us in a state of permanent nervous system disorder . . . infected emotionally and psychically. The lower alien races and their technologies chose Earth allies to create programs with." According to Laura's Cosmic Gaia website, "Laura is powerfully creating global transformation on the Venus path. Taking on the darkest forces on Earth, Laura reveals the influence of the false matrix and conquers the hidden agendas that are affecting our personal freedom."

When I asked Joe Busto about the NBC article, the one that sought to debunk the Colorado cloud seeding/chemtrail connection, he said that the conspiracy theorists were right to a degree. "The article was a bit inaccurate." In the media's brief discussion of the history of cloud seeding following the September floods, they referred only to the Colorado ski resorts that, endangered by climate change, pay to seed clouds over the Rocky Mountains. Busto told me that "there are about forty entities that pay for cloud seeding in Colorado and only eight of them are ski areas." In other words, most of the cloud-seeding operations are paid for by local water districts, that is, with public funds. The same is true for most states throughout the West but nobody, neither the state nor the media, seems anxious to advertise the fact.

"The conspiracy theory people are in the back of our minds always," Busto said. "We are making snowflakes and they think we are making checkerboard patterns in the sky to poison the planet or whatever. You can't win some folks over. I have a woman who lives in the mountains. She's always picking on seeding programs, reading letters to senators, and showing up at conferences. For eleven years I have tried to put the science in front of her, but there is little I can do to change her mind."

Joe Busto and other cloud-seeding authorities seem caught in a classic bind, what psychologists call confirmation bias. People tend to prefer information that supports their existing beliefs. And often, when confronted with contradicting evidence, people become emboldened. Psychologists Lee Ross and Craig Anderson described the phenomenon in a seminal 1982 paper, stating that "beliefs can survive potent logical or empirical challenges. They can survive and even be bolstered by evidence that most uncommitted observers would agree logically demands some weakening of such beliefs. They can even survive the total destruction of their original evidential bases." If the national media runs a report, if respected university atmospheric scientists chuckle, if the EPA, NASA, FAA, and NOAA release a joint "Aircraft Contrails Factsheet," as they did in 2000, or if Joe Busto shows up at meeting after meeting outlining Colorado's strict cloud-seeding protocol, explaining that at most cloud seeding can increase annual precipitation only partially, and if he explains that, as an added safety precaution, cloud-seeding operations cease once snowpack levels reach a defined limit, it only proves that Busto, like everyone else — the media, the universities, and the federal government — is lying.

"People just have their minds made up," Busto said. The paradox seems clear: the more you refute, the more you affirm. Perhaps in such a situation, it's better simply to keep quiet.

"People know little about cloud seeding because they know little about the natural world," Busto said. "America makes music and movies. It's not a country invested in science. Climatology, meteorology, hydrology, and resource management — they're all topics that are largely boring outside of the scientist geek world." While I agree with Busto, I can't help but wonder if there isn't a deeper reason for the public's skepticism.

As I click through the labyrinthine world of chemtrail websites, it's clear that these people are not stupid. They know how to read. They know how to write HTML script. Real people devote inordinate amounts of time to updating these sites daily, linking new articles, compiling evidence in the form of syllabi, unlinked lab reports, and dead House bills. And the more informed and enterprising among them probably manage to make a few extra dollars every month peddling their homemade DVDs and red donate buttons. The more optimistic — and cynical — explanation is that we're dealing with a few entrepreneurial charlatans. While this certainly seems true for a few glossier websites, like Alex Jones' Infowars and Laura Eisenhower's Cosmic Gaia, I get the impression that most of these pages belong to lonely individuals who, genuinely concerned, feel driven to document some emerging global crisis both for themselves and for whoever may be listening. The trouble is that nobody can decide what they're actually afraid of—besides death. Across the globe, 1.75 people die each second, and 105 die each minute. Are these numbers high? In the time it took me to fly from Iowa to Denver, more than 12,000 people perished, a sum greater than the total number of humans living during the population bottleneck of the Late Pleistocene epoch.

Over the airport intercom, I hear a flight attendant call "boarding group 3" and close my laptop.

"Enjoy your flight," he says, scanning my boarding pass.

As we lift off from Denver, I study the downtown streets, looking for some evidence of catastrophic floods, but in the early-morning light the blocks glitter as pristine and polished as the marble floors inside the airport terminal. When it's safe to turn on FDA-approved personal electronic devices, I slip on my headphones, switch on blasting metal, and shut my eyes. The dissonant guitar lines crisscross, collide, and jam as I picture the white contrail unfurling beneath us, miles over the mountains, a thin white ghost carrying me clean across the desert.

I'm flying back to California because I've been granted a rare tour of Naval Ordnance Test Station China Lake, a 1.1-million-acre bombing range larger than the state of Rhode Island that abuts Death Valley in eastern California. The base's newspaper, the *Rocketeer*, neatly summarizes China Lake's weather modification history: "Between 1949 and 1978, China Lake developed concepts, techniques, and hardware that were successfully used in hurricane abatement, fog control, and drought relief." The man behind China Lake's cloud-seeding research, Pierre St.-Amand, summarized it more succinctly: "We regard the weather as a weapon. Anything one can use to get his way is a weapon and the weather is as good a one as any."

The weapon St.-Amand speaks of—cloud seeding—was deployed across Vietnam for nearly a decade beginning in 1963, when CIA planes began seeding clouds over Saigon to break up Buddhist protests. Following St.-Amand's directions, in 1967 the air force launched the top secret Project Popeye, which began routinely seeding North Vietnamese clouds in an attempt to extend the length of the monsoon season and flood Vietcong movements along the Ho Chi Minh trail. The $22-million program, uncovered in 1971 by Jack Anderson in an article for the *Washington Times,* continued for several more months until the Pentagon Papers and the *New York Times* confirmed the story and the military suspended all operations. Bump, bump.

When I open my eyes again, the flight attendant informs the several other sleeping passengers and myself that the captain has turned on the Fasten Seatbelt sign. Staring out the airplane window, I see the Colorado Aqueduct, 30,000 feet below, slithering along the barren Mojave floor — a long emerald snake following me home.

————

As a child I did rain dances in the dead grass for hours, only to throw my dried yucca stick against the fence and lose faith in God. The sun tore down in relentless monotony for eighteen years. After my rain stick finally shattered, I found not the promised cactus needles but thousands of little opaque shards, curled and white like broken hangnails. "Probably plastic," my mom said. I used to say that paradise repulses me, but I don't feel that today. Not after coming from Iowa.

Inside my grandmother's kitchen, as Rob's lawn mower rips over the grass, she tells me about the day she and my grandfather pulled into the driveway.

"It seemed like a desert," she says. "Your grandfather forgot how dry San Diego actually was since being stationed at Coronado," the island naval base in San Diego Harbor.

My family landed in southern California, like most, after World War II. Perhaps it was in the spirit of Allied victory that the suburbs fifteen miles from the coast were called Allied Gardens. It was men like my grandfather who settled the place. Each bringing barbecues and sprinklers to install his own stable oasis. Wives to water roses and cut oranges, telephones to call catalog trucks for color televisions, shiny cars to drive to work and send well-dressed sons and daughters to kindergarten — each man seeking the control, peace, and nuance of his own fenced-in single-family Eden.

"Your grandfather thought it would take years to make it green," my grandma says. Scanning the yard, he supposedly spit. All along the length of their white stucco bungalow, there was no grass. Dirt banks studded with boulders rose up from the street, lining the property, a corner plot. Inside, internalizing the outer dryness, the house had brown carpet, walls painted the color of sand, and three small bedrooms.

Corky, a grey shih tzu, licks my grandmother's hand. "Tell me what you want," she says.

The dog blinks.

"Quit batting your eyes like a toad in a hailstorm," she says. "Talk to me!"

When Corky groans, she feeds him a piece of bacon. "Good boy." He scuttles away into the living room to devour his dessert.

Grandma's walls are white now, the carpet an emerald pavement of dog-trampled odor, but sixty years ago, she says, "I was thrilled to death." My grandpa, however, simply said the place was sufficient. I've often wondered whether it was an attitude he affected, some German melancholia, a hereditary pessimism he played into, or something real, something he brought back from the war, the ethos of FUBAR, a fatalism he felt, that things were fucked up beyond all recognition.

Standing at the kitchen counter, staring out the window down the block, I imagine the fire hydrants poking out from the sidewalks not yet poured. In the distance, denuded trees destined to become power poles hang black beneath cranes, crisscrossed like marionette handles with the puppets broken off. If my grandfather thought that the neighbors, the realtor, himself, and his wife — just like the actors in the films he never went to see because he knew he'd panic — if he thought that they were all following a poorly written script, he didn't say anything. I picture him standing outside in the bright sunlight, signing the papers: Adam Baumgart, German for "Treegarden." And that was exactly what the place needed: privacy and plenty of trees. A wall of trees to line the grass, shelter the family, and keep out the street.

"You know your grandfather was the first to import the Volkswagen west of the Mississippi?" my grandmother says.

"Is it true?" I ask. Evansville, Indiana, is a hundred miles east of the Mississippi. I don't correct her.

She laughs. "Of course, it is. Up your nose with a rubber hose." She grabs the remote from the kitchen table and turns up a game show.

My grandmother doesn't know the precise cause of the dealership's downfall, but perhaps in the early fifties the citizens of Evansville still needed a few more years to forget the war, to separate the German folk from the glittering VW hood ornament. My grandfather fell into a depression after he lost his car business, and it was suggested by the family doctor that perhaps the California climate might cure him. I picture him crossing the Sierras in his own Beetle, the little motor singing melodiously as it climbed, my grandmother in the front seat, my mother and uncle in the back. It had been years since he'd seen the ocean, tasted the salt-laden air, but often in his dreams he smelled it, revisited horrible nights of blood, smoke, and burning. I always assumed it was some fashionable pretense of propriety that pushed couples into separate beds during the fifties, but, returning to the deck of the *Anderson* in his sleep, he'd wake my grandmother kicking and thrashing, calling through the insane blasts of the ship's alarm to a friend already gone. He spoke of it only once to my grandmother, men running upright with heads missing and tripping overboard. "Like chickens with their heads cut off," he'd said. "Shroud duty," picking up and organizing body parts, sealing them in bags — that's what he called it.

Next to my grandmother's closet in the tiny hall by the bathroom, there hangs a picture frame full of black-and-white photos. As a child, somewhere between the living and the dead, with a sensation of past selves and the prescience of future lives, I'd stare up into my grandfather's eyes, gray and fierce. While I grew taller and began to see more clearly, to face the frame directly, it never seemed to me that the world used to be other than black-and-white, forever a restrained, dry, monochrome experience. Throughout the photos, my grandfather's stare never changes — his eyes meet the camera in all seriousness, the hard aspect of a man still working, a man who won't settle, who'll resist all reckoning and likely never admit that he's made his all or let on that any of his successes have come close to meeting his initial vision. Bare-chested, impassive in a folding chair, Sisyphus on pause, he stares out of the dirt lot, rocks piled at the corner while the trees begin to sprout tiny buds, gray instead of green. Sweat glistens on his arms, not bronze but silver. He stands before the black Volkswagen that was actually blue, watering the ashen grass while my mother, a tiny china doll, cartwheels beneath the transplanted palm tree.

How else could a child account for such a complete record of so many silver iodide people working gray days in a binary world? But the world was never anything like those fossils; the drained and captive ghosts that I believed in and thought I felt in the chipped records of faded photographs did not exist. Everything was more than that. When did I learn that a blood just as rich and deep in red once flowed through my grandfather's lips trapped so sullen and monochrome?

He dug the rocks out of the hills and planted myoporum trees. He worked hard calibrating gyroscopes at the base, and just before his pension kicked in he got displaced by computers. He worked hard at being ordinary and succeeded, dying of cancer when I was five.

"When was the last time you talked to your own father?" my grandma asks when I return to the kitchen. I don't know what she imagines has changed.

"It's still been years," I say. Eight years.

"Your father is a bastard," she says.

When I was a small boy, he used to pick me up from Grandma's late in the evenings after school. Pulling up, he always had the black-and-white weather radio in the front seat. He made me excited about the weather. He seemed to have so little control over his world. The most minimal influence he could manufacture consisted of his ability to predict the next day's weather. I'd tune the bloodred tongue to 162 MHz. In San Diego, this was no special skill. But I always trusted him. He was the weatherman. He knew. El Niño hit in 1996 when I was nine years old. "What does that mean?" I asked. "It means 'the boy,'" he said. At night, more than anything, I longed to feel the granite scrape of stubble when he kissed me good-bye.

My grandmother flicks on the kitchen light. "Leland, get me a beer," she says. Leland is her son, my other uncle. I open the refrigerator door and don't correct her. He killed himself eight years ago.

Backing out of the driveway, I turn on the radio and scan for the weather. I suppose I'm being selfish, but I don't want it to rain. If it rains, the navy will cancel our China Lake tour.

As I drive down Zion Road, the twilight colors temporarily mitigate the visible effects of drought. I brake at a stoplight in front of the Catholic church, and across the street as I flip the turn signal, I see a house with synthetic plastic grass, the same sharp rug made from recycled Nike shoes that's becoming more and more ubiquitous. In the fading light, the lawn looks almost natural. The brittle plastic spears no longer reflect the sun's onslaught but huddle together in a modest black pool, just a shade darker and an inch shorter than the neighbor's dead crabgrass. Although the San Diego County Water Authority insists that no water-use restrictions are planned—"projections show San Diego Region's water resources are sufficient for 2014"—our neighbors in Los Angeles aren't so sure.

Next week marks the hundredth anniversary of the completion of the Los Angeles Aqueduct. On November 5, 1913, the notoriously terse William Mulholland, city engineer of Los Angeles, gave the signal and the engineers opened the floodgates. Speaking through the glinting rainbows of rising water mist, Mulholland began his speech. He spoke six words to five hundred people. "There it is, gentlemen, take it."

Perhaps he was merely exhausted. More likely he feared assassination. Under the guise of procuring farmland, between the years of 1905 and 1908 Mulholland collaborated with former Los Angeles mayor Fred Eaton in the surreptitious purchase of the fertile farmlands alongside the Owens River, beneath the steep eastern edge of the Sierra Nevada, for "ranching purposes." When the aqueduct project was finally uncovered, the citizens of Owens Valley responded in outrage. President Roosevelt, however, sided with the interests of Los Angeles, declaring the future growth of the metropolis paramount compared to the welfare of "a few settlers in Owens Valley." Roosevelt expanded the boundary of the Sierra National Forest to protect the aqueduct, even though the only trees in the region were those the settlers themselves had planted. In the mid-1920s, a fresh round of rainless years, combined with the rapid rise of LA's population, led the city to tap the entire flow of the Owens River. In 1924, settlers responded by dynamiting a forty-foot hole through a span of aqueduct beneath the Alabama Hills. In 1927 alone, saboteurs blew up the aqueduct fourteen times. "The people here have shown that they can protect their homes," boomed the *Owens Valley Herald*, "and they will show it again if it becomes necessary."

Unfortunately, the water wars continue today. The dry dust bowl of Owens Lake—lying just north of Naval Ordnance Test Station China Lake, beyond Centennial Road and the volcanic Coso Range—remains the single largest source of particle pollution in the United States. Already since 2000, Los Angeles has spent $1.3 billion attempting to keep the dust down. But its efforts aren't over. This year, the city was court-ordered to stop draining Owens Lake entirely and also to further extend its air pollution–control measures.

While the desiccated salt bed no longer meets LA's water needs, a recent University of Colorado Boulder study estimates that— taking into account a modest population increase and climate change models—there is a 50 percent chance that the Colorado River reservoirs that today feed Los Angeles and San Diego and provide much of the arid Southwest and northern Mexico with the majority of their water will run dry by 2057. While the settlement of southern California was made possible only after a series of violent and protracted water wars, the land's desertion will likely occur only after another series of bloody battles. Unless we can come up with some kind of magic solution. Los Angeles is today attempting to reinstate its own cloud-seeding program over the local San Gabriel Mountains, just north of LA, one of the oldest programs in the country, but county attorneys keep blocking its efforts. In 1978, when LA cloud-seeded the San Gabriels, catastrophic floods ripped through the city, causing $43 million in damages and killing eleven people.

Arriving back at my mother's house, I park the car. High over the ocean, like a streak of gold leaf brushed against a milk-blue dome, an airplane contrail catches a last flicker of sun glowing as it rolls inland. I unlock the door, cross the living room, and watch my mother drop a spoon, abandon a pot of soup, and seal her lips.

"Shhh . . ." she says.

She turns up the television.

"What?"

"Be quiet!" she snaps.

It's cruel, convenient. It can't be, but it is — on the local evening news a woman reports that earlier today in Ridgecrest, California, the small desert town abutting China Lake, a man went on a psychotic shooting spree that wounded three people, killed one, and ignited a sprawling police chase that closed down Highway 395 north of Kramer Junction and culminated in the man's death.

"Good thing we didn't leave today," my mom says.

On the TV, the woman says, "Police are puzzled."

Staring at the television, I cannot help but wonder if the violence wasn't staged to distract me from continuing my own weather modification research, a spectacle conjured by the government, as the online Colorado conspiracy theorists postulated of the previous Washington navy yard shooting, to keep me from traveling to China Lake in the morning.

As my mother and I sit down to dinner, the weatherman steps on-screen. He goes through the region's daily highs, the overnight lows. He shows the radar. Somewhere over Santa Barbara a cluster of yellow pixels flares, then vanishes. Across the country, they have wet cold weather, but what's in store for San Diego? Surprise: sunny skies and warm temperatures. James Brown suddenly howls. "I Feel Good" plays in the background while the weatherman twirls. I don't know how he survives the boredom. I've never trusted his ebullience. He's been forecasting for this station for more than twenty years, and I have watched him perform the same steady routine ever since I can remember. Sometimes I suspect he's actually part of the computer animation projected onto the newsroom's green screen. He isn't even there.*

"He looks good for his age," my mom says.

The other newscasters get to talk about shootings, but all the weatherman gets to say is that the sky's blue. No mention of drought. No mention that 2013 is shaping up to be the hottest year in history — warmer than all ten preceding years — a decade that was itself the hottest on human record. Such slowly accruing events don't sell well, not like tornadoes, hurricanes, school shootings, and police chases, and they're hard to film. Blood spills much faster than it evaporates and nobody has the time or the attention to watch.

My mother turns off the news. She refills her champagne glass and switches to magic cave music. "How was your grandmother?" she asks. "Did that Jehovah's Witness finally come clean up her yard?"

Southern California is obviously not the only region in America facing a bleak water future. Things also look bad for San Francisco, Phoenix, Florida, and much of Texas. While the world continues to warm, almost 2 billion people live without access to fresh drinking water. The United Nations estimates that as of 2010, 50 million people have already been displaced from their homes by the effects of climate change. It is difficult to imagine how humanity, already half-starved, its numbers increasing, will reorganize itself to survive the coming scarcity and, if we should fail, the chaos, violence, and suffering that may ensue. Although it seems unlikely, perhaps bloodshed will furnish the solution.

The link between weather and warfare is an ancient one. Plutarch, writing in the first century, observed that "extraordinary rains pretty generally fall after great battles." He wondered whether Mother Nature felt the need to cleanse the "polluted earth with showers" or whether the "moist and heavy evaporations, steaming forth from the blood and corruption . . . thicken the air" in some way that generates rain. Apparently Napoleon observed the same phenomenon but couldn't explain it. Walt Whitman watched it happen during the American Civil War. "After every great battle, a great storm," he wrote, asking in the title of a brief war memorandum, "The Weather — Does It Sympathize with These Times?"

The first scientific account came in 1871 when a man named Edward Powers, seconding Whitman, published the book *War and the Weather*, in which he advanced his theory of concussionism.

Powers claimed that superloud explosions, the concussions detonated in military battles, were capable of artificially producing rain. Over the next twenty years, renowned concussionists received thousands of dollars from the US Congress to test their theories. The most famous case occurred in West Texas in 1891. Beginning on August 9, General H. G. Dyrenforth subjected the drought-ridden Texas skies to a two-week-long full-scale military attack, detonating dynamite, launching homemade rockets, and releasing balloons strapped with bombs, all in the hope of summoning rain.

"A beautiful imitation of battle," one observer said.

Dyrenforth, as it turned out, was neither a general nor a scientist, but nobody bothered to look into his background, nor did anyone —government or media—bother much to confirm his exuberant reports. On August 11, Dyrenforth's telegraphs began flooding Washington. "Fired some explosives yesterday. Raining hard today." On August 18 he reported that rain fell "in torrents for two and a half hours." August 26: "Several inches of rainfall following explosions." National media outlets were quick to capitalize on Dyrenforth's sensational experiment. "They Made Rain!" erupted Denver's *Rocky Mountain* headlines. The program is "elaborate, the material abundant, and the science involved exhaustive," confirmed the *Washington Times*. Victorian readers were aroused by the image of a retired maverick general embattled against Mother Nature over the West Texas plains, gradually pecking away at her frigidity, forcing her to surrender her life-giving tears. The *New York Sun* waxed poetic: "I am Cloud-compelling Dyrenforth, a mighty able weight. / I can call the clouds together with a load of dynamite."

In reality, the only independent measurement tallied Dyrenforth's prowess to two hundredths of an inch.

His fame lasted another year. For the site of his next glorious battle, General Dyrenforth chose a hill in full public view, four miles north of downtown San Antonio behind the Argyle Hotel. In October 1892, Dyrenforth arrived dragging forty tons of dynamite, his pockets $10,000 thick with taxpayer cash. The opening parlay commenced as Dyrenforth's men packed a mesquite tree full of explosives and lit a fifty-foot fuse. After the smoke cleared, the tree had disappeared and so had every window in the Argyle Hotel. Against the mounting boos of the assembled townsfolk, the bombardment continued for eight days, but it never rained. *Scientific American* criticized Congress for yet another "expensive farce," calling Dyrenforth's experiments nothing but "foolish fireworks," and federal funding ceased. Newspapers dubbed him General Dryhenceforth, and he died an obscure patent lawyer in Washington, D.C.

Perhaps an even more fantastic case of weather modification failure occurred in my hometown in 1915, when the San Diego City Council, confronted with a booming population and sinking water reserves, agreed in a 4-to-1 vote to pay renowned local rainmaker Charles Hatfield the going rate of $10,000 if he could fill the newly built Morena Dam. It was no small task. According to *Harper's Weekly*, the dam was "the biggest in America . . . the largest in the world." The magazine described it as the ninth wonder. But Hatfield wasn't worried. He'd long given up on the theory of concussionism. "I do not fight Nature," he told the *Los Angeles Examiner*, "I woo her by means of this subtle attraction." Hatfield had established a solid reputation among southern California farmers by releasing a secret twenty-three-chemical cocktail from a special tower that his brother had nailed to the top of Mount Lowe outside Pasadena. But in San Diego he outdid himself. In early January, standing upon a new twenty-foot platform built beside the Morena Dam, Hatfield perfumed the atmosphere with his secret potion and within hours the rain began to fall. And it kept falling. When the storms finally cleared two weeks later, all the city's dams had flooded, two had ruptured entirely, and fourteen people were dead. The city council held Hatfield responsible for $3.5 million in damages, while Hatfield countersued, claiming he'd done his job and demanding his money. The courts ruled against both parties, calling the rain "an act of God."

After the disaster, charlatan rainmaking appears to have died out until the Depression, when it experienced a short-lived resurgence throughout the Midwest. Unfortunately, the only storms delivered consisted of black dust clouds.

The history of real rainmaking began in General Electric's

Schenectady labs. In 1946, Vincent Schaefer sprinkled dry ice inside a freezer chest he'd converted into a cloud chamber. Incredibly, when Schaefer leaned over the freezer, he saw the moisture from his breath instantly transform into millions of glowing crystals. Schaefer had unwittingly produced an ice cloud from supercooled water droplets. As he later wrote in his notebook, "It was a serendipitous event, and I was smart enough to figure out just what happened. . . . I knew I had something pretty important." Schaefer's technique was further refined by another GE researcher, Bernard Vonnegut of MIT — brother of the novelist — who discovered that silver iodide worked as a better nucleating agent than dry ice. Silver iodide's crystal molecular structure more closely resembled ice, allowing it to bind more water molecules around itself and produce more snow.

Four months after the discovery, Schaefer rented a plane and seeded a four-mile stretch of cloud outside the Schenectady Airport. He wrote that the cloud "almost exploded, the effect was so widespread and rapid." As the snow began to fall, Schaefer's boss, Irving Langmuir, watching from an airport control deck, picked up the phone. "Opening Vista of Moisture Control by Man" ran the next day's *New York Times* headline. "A single pellet of dry ice, about the size of a pea," the article said, "might produce enough ice nuclei to develop several tons of snow." Langmuir, a Nobel Laureate whose own weather modification research began while he worked for the navy during World War II, was adept at manipulating the media. Over the next several years he expanded his reports, predicting that cloud seeding might soon guide hurricanes away from the Atlantic and Gulf Coasts, eliminate airport fog, and eventually transform the deserts of the American Southwest into a vast emerald oasis.

He imagined other applications as well.

In December 1950, after appearing on the cover of *Time* above the tagline "Can man learn to control the atmosphere he lives in?" Langmuir urged the federal government to capitalize on cloud seeding's potential as a new Cold War weapon. "In the amount of energy liberated," he said, "the effect of 30 milligrams of silver iodide" used to seed clouds "under optimum conditions equals that of one atomic bomb." The Pentagon responded by organizing a committee to research the development of a large-scale weather weapon. Military planners hoped that cloud seeding might soon be used tactically to bury enemy lines in snow, drown their tanks in mud, and ground airfields in fog.

In 1954 Captain Howard T. Orville, the new chairman of President Eisenhower's Advisory Committee on Weather Control, outlined some of the possible large-scale advantages such a weather weapon could afford US armed forces. "We may deluge an enemy with rain," says Orville, "or strike at his foodsupplies by withholding needed rain from his crops. Countless other benefits may accrue." An illustration accompanying Orville's influential *Collier's* article depicts a woman massaging the shoulders of a masculine engineer as he grips a thick lever, gazing away from her, the veins in his forearms bulging as he pulls back slowly, unlocking not the floodgates of an aqueduct but the atomic power of pregnant white cumulus clouds. There it is, gentlemen, take it.

"In this age of the H-bomb and supersonic flight," Orville writes, "if investigation of weather control receives public support and funds for research which its importance merits, we may be able eventually to make weather almost to order." In the article, he optimistically asserts that "Russia would be at a disadvantage" during any future weather war because "weather characteristically moves from west to east."

In 1958 the father of the H-bomb, Edward Teller, sounded much less sure. Addressing the Senate Military Preparedness Subcommittee about the potential of a large-scale Russian weather weapon, Teller said, "I would not be surprised if they accomplished it in five years . . ." Later that same year, the *American Weekly* seconded Teller: it remained to be seen "whether Russia or the United States rules the world's thermometers." *Newsweek* hopped on the bandwagon, proclaiming "a weather race with the Russians." In 1961, renowned aviator engineer Rear Admiral Luis de Florez upped the stakes: we needed to "start now to make control of the weather equal in scope to the Manhattan Project which produced the first A-bomb."

Propelled by the chorus of voices, the following year the federal government launched Project Stormfury, which began researching the effects of cloud seeding on hurricanes. Unfortunately, the words of the *Nation* lampooning General Dyrenforth's West Texas cloud-busting balloon bombs might just as well summarize Project Stormfury. Overall, a few silver iodide flares sprayed on a hurricane eyewall amounted to less than "the effect of the jump of one vigorous flea upon a thousand-ton steamship running at a speed of twenty knots." All experiments proved inconclusive, and the effects of Schaefer's and Vonnegut's seeding methods came under question.

In the words of a 1964 paper titled "Scientific Problems of Weather Modification" published by the US National Research Council, "the decision where to seed and when to seed and how much to seed is an extremely complicated one that cannot be forecast by present methods." The results of current research, its authors state, "are not sufficient to warrant any operational seeding project which simply puts freezing nuclei in the air. We conclude that the initiation of large-scale operational weather modification programs would be premature. Many fundamental problems must be answered first."

Ostensibly, after a decade of hopeful and highly speculative projections, the possibility of any immediate large-scale weather weapon appeared to have burst. In reality, across the country at NOTS China Lake, research was progressing wonderfully. When the National Research Council report was published, the United States had already been cloud seeding the skies over Vietnam for a year. The program's success led to Project Popeye in 1967. In 1969, under a Pentagon project called Nile Blue, the CIA began seeding clouds outside Cuba, hoping to suck out rain and starve Castro's sugar crop.

Sitting in the spare bedroom at my mother's house, I pack my army surplus bag for tomorrow's trip while tinny metal music plays on my laptop speakers. The album is called *Enemy of the Sun.* I found it when I was fourteen in a box of tapes and VHS cassettes abandoned beside a grocery store dumpster. There was a picture of a man burning alive on the cover of the album, so I took it home and listened to it constantly. Throughout the distorted guitars and screaming, there are very few moments of calm and very few intelligible words. I haven't listened to the album in a long time, not for these reasons but because the songs belong to a different chapter of my life, and they too easily summon a nostalgia I'd rather not waste. Yet it's strange the way things you used to love have a way of returning to haunt you anew. One of the few quiet moments on this particular Neurosis album occurs on the third track. It's a sampled newsreel that describes the most famous of Vietnam's Buddhist protests, the same protests that the CIA began using cloud seeding to break up in 1963. Apparently, that day, June 11, 1963, their efforts failed.

The most dramatic was one day in Saigon, when a Buddhist parade started off with a sort of hypnotic chant, the yellow robed priests marching along, and then there stepped forward a very frail old man in his seventies who turned out to be this priest Quang Duc. And he assumed the lotus posture. And another priest stepped forward and poured gasoline on him. And then suddenly a towering flame. The priests and the nuns moaned and prostrated themselves toward this burning figure. And he sat there unflinching, the smell of gasoline and burning flesh in the air for ten minutes — people thought they saw the face of Buddha in the clouds that night.

The man speaking in the recording I know now is David Halberstam, who was then filing reports for the *New York Times*. A black-and-white photo of Quang Duc's self-immolation taken by Halberstam's American colleague, Malcolm Browne, later won the Pulitzer Prize. I turn down the volume and click away as grinding bass and beating toms come welling through a blur of newsreel sirens. In the adjacent bedroom, I hear my mother snore. My stepfather still isn't home from the office. Online the website Weatherunderground.com, named after the 1960s American antiwar guerrilla cult, proclaims a 10 percent chance of weekend rain in Ridgecrest.

I lie back in bed, lean over, set the alarm for six, and stare at a dream catcher on the nightstand. The spare bedroom is vaguely Indian-themed, mostly woven baskets, decorative bowls, and animal sculptures, though some of it looks more African than Native American. There's also a painting that doesn't really belong here.

When I was a kid, my mom had a client who sometimes couldn't afford to pay her properly. The man owned an art gallery in Palm Springs, and occasionally he'd give her original artwork. Along with a few paintings of Native American women clutching babies and a depiction of Juan Bautista de Anza's arrival in Riverside, he also sent a couple of prints. One of them my mother insisted on hanging in my bedroom because there was no more wall space anywhere else and besides, she said, it was colorful and supposedly educational.

The original artwork, a mural, I learned later in eighth grade, measured twenty by thirty feet, was named *Westward the Course of Empire Takes Its Way*, and was painted by a German-born artist named Emanuel Leutze in 1861 for $10,000. It covers the wall above the western staircase in the US House of Representatives. My mom's print hung above the little retro TV in my bedroom and wasn't much larger.

I roll out from the mattress now and lean against the wall, studying the painting in yet the fourth bedroom since my boyhood. It's supposed to be a happy scene, a depiction of a wagon train gaining the final pass over the Sierra Nevada, the pilgrims gazing at their Promised Land, El Dorado — California. But I never got that growing up. I could never decide if the woman sitting at the center of the painting was offering a prayer or clucking like a hen. She always looked cross-eyed to me. She sits perched precariously on a rocky ledge, her palms pressed over her breast, elbows flung out, while some version of Daniel Boone, as if to draw back an invisible curtain, sweeps his giant's arm above her. The woman won't look. Anger and exhaustion mix on the husband's face as he fails to lift the fog. Their son stands below, staring, worried, toward the sunset. As a child, after school in the evenings before my mom came home, I'd often wonder what that boy saw there and whether his bayonet might help him.

Below him at the far left, a trapper waits expressionless with his heavy arm held out, buckskin fringe drooping from his jacket like strips of torn web. And the throng of pilgrims piles up behind him, their eyes stretched wide with astonishment, and it's still hard to tell, of some of them, whether they're coming or going, winning or

losing—fleeing from disaster or heading right for it. The trapper stares straight through them. He doesn't seem to care either way. Detached from those in his charge, not so much guide as orderly, death's indifferent chauffeur, he opens the invisible doors, asks no one's name, and simply escorts the ruined flock onward to slaughter —down toward dim redwoods lit with flashing ax blades.

I always asked my mom to take the painting down. It gave me bad dreams. I thought it looked like some sort of zombie scene, a snapshot from some late-night horror film I'd click through quickly while she snored, but she just told me to grow up.

Flicking open the late-afternoon blinds, leaning closer toward the painting, I used to stare at the lower center where a pilgrim limps alongside his father, struggling to the summit to glimpse the Golden Gate just once. His brother, gripping a bundle of arrows, some of which have been snapped from his sibling's ribs, carries a squirrel carcass. I used to imagine that boy had determined from the trip's outset, no matter what misfortune should befall his family, not to participate in such a sin as cannibalism. How many weeks had he carried the rotting rodent? And standing there, I'd start to wonder which boy was the lucky one. At eight or nine years old, I'd only met my own half-brother once, and I'd often worry whether something innate bound us. If we found ourselves in similar adverse circumstances, would he carry the squirrel for me, would I hold it for him, or would we act as strangers, as animals, as monsters?

I lift the frame from the nail now, stash it in the closet, and zip up my rucksack. Flicking off the light, I crawl back in bed. It's strange. Over the years, whenever I've attempted to summon *Westward* to memory, very few characters come to mind. Rather, it's always the empty spaces that appear, the blue water and the brown sky, two solids gradually blended that, like a dye, bleed into my mind's fabric and with their combined stain supply a subtle acrid flavor to my dreams. It's not the birds, strangely outgrown, flying like griffins to devour the tiny men at the summit's platform that I remember but the sky's metallic quality — scattered clouds lending the texture and patina of pyrite, a scarred quality, to something that should be so soft and yet seems ready to topple. Peculiar as well is the bay's panorama at the bottom of the work. Once blue, it rests silent except for a single ship cut loose from anchor, drifting out to sea in a blur. Above it, the barren brown hills of Berkeley rise misted in the background — my college dormitory still fifty years away from being built.

Before closing my eyes, I check my university account a last time. There's an e-mail from Darin Langerud, one of the directors at the North American Weather Modification Council. It's amazing how willing scientists are to talk to you if you simply tell them you're a graduate student doing research. I'd written Langerud to ask if he and other cloud-seeding authorities had trouble at times defending a technology with a dubious scientific background that was largely developed as a military weapon at China Lake.

Langerud responded during normal office hours.

"One of the biggest problems, and an issue we still battle today, is that cloud seeding was initially over-sold as a cure-all for weather-related problems. The initial exuberance in the early stages of scientific discovery was overplayed without complete knowledge of the complexities of how precipitation forms in and falls from clouds. We have come a long way in the last 60 years and now understand that cloud seeding, when properly designed and applied, can have meaningful results, but that not every cloud is suitable for seeding — far from it. Cloud seeding is not a drought-buster, as during a drought there is a general lack of clouds available to produce rain or snow, thus there are few opportunities to have an effect through seeding. Cloud seeding requires clouds — the right types of clouds — for it to have the chance of being successful. Lacking that basic ingredient, a seeding project cannot succeed."

Regarding my suggestion that cloud seeding was developed largely as a military weapon: "I strongly disagree," Langerud said. "The vast majority of research and development in weather modification has taken place at universities, national labs and in the private sector. The initial discovery that clouds could be seeded with silver iodide and dry ice to enhance ice formation occurred in the private sector, at the General Electric Lab in Schenectady, New York, in 1946."

Recently I spoke with Ed Holroyd, "the oldest living student of the founding fathers of cloud seeding," as Joe Busto introduced him to me. Holroyd worked closely with Vincent Schaefer as a high school student, as a graduate student at SUNY, and in dozens of research projects throughout the country. "Dr. Bernie Vonnegut was one of my professors," Holroyd told me. When we talked, he said that most of the weather modification research that happened during the fifties and sixties after Schaefer's discovery went toward improving the effects of silver iodide on cumulus clouds.

"In the 1950s there were numerous experiments to see what could be done. In the 1960s there was randomization of experiments and the appeal to statistics. One of the problems may have been that not all clouds were suitable for experimentation. Supercooled water needed to exist in the clouds and not enough snow crystal concentration to naturally consume that water. So unsuitable cloud conditions diluted the experiments." When I asked whether the US military played a part in solving these problems, Holroyd wasn't sure. "The China Lake program was sometimes addressed in the proceedings of weather modification conferences I attended." Holroyd said that "Dr. St.-Amand was often there," but they never spoke. "I visited China Lake in August 1974 when my work in Australia had ended and I was searching for my next job." Holroyd doesn't really know much about the China Lake work. "Being a military study, parts of the research may be classified."

Many of the details of the program remain classified, no doubt. The only information I could track down concerning St.-Amand and the overall importance of China Lake's role in the development of cloud seeding came from a 1974 US Senate hearing. After Jack Anderson's *Washington Times* article exposed Project Popeye, public outrage spread to the point that it spurred a US Senate resolution calling for a global treaty "prohibiting the use of any environmental or geophysical modification activity as a weapon of war." Pierre St.-Amand of NOTS China Lake was called to testify in a "top secret hearing" before the Senate Subcommittee on Oceans and International Environment.

St.-Amand, addressing Senator Claiborne Pell of Rhode Island, makes clear the extent and importance of China Lake's weather modification research.

A substantial portion of the critical scientific theory was developed at NWC* [Naval Weapons Center, China Lake]. Our contributions include clarification of nucleation theory for the formation of ice in clouds, solution of Smoluchowski's equation in general form. Methods for calculation of the time required for a solid of a given size to dissolve in a solvent were developed. . . . A number of new nucleating compounds were developed for use at temperatures warmer than that at which silver iodide functions, and were tested. Improved acetone burners for ground based and for airborne use were developed.

This last development appears to be the most crucial. St.-Amand says that previously "cloud seeders had been using a substance similar to, and derived from, silver iodide but which was not silver iodide. . . . In those days, clouds were seeded by use of an acetone burner that produced, instead of silver iodide, a complex of silver iodide and one of several alkali iodides . . . another compound quite different in physical properties."

St.-Amand politely acknowledges the early days of GE's research, *à la* Schaefer and Vonnegut, and bids them adieu. According to St.-Amand, the problem "had been elucidated in 1949 by Dr. Bernard Vonnegut, the inventor of the acetone burner, but had been ignored. . . . This meant that people who were seeding clouds with the older system did not do what they thought they were doing. Indeed in many elaborate experiments based on the premise that clouds were being seeded with silver iodide, the clouds were not being seeded at all, or were being seeded in a manner different from that postulated." He goes on: "This single fact led to most of the confusion that has developed as to the effectiveness of cloud seeding."

St.-Amand credits himself and his team with the crucial refinements that have led to the practice of modern cloud seeding. "The seeding techniques that we have in large part developed are now in use in almost every country in the world," he says. "We have made such information freely available to people here and abroad who chose to carry on development on their own."

Senator Pell asks point-blank: "Along this line, then, you share freely with other countries. Did your laboratory have any relationship with the weather modification in Southeast Asia that was reported in the press?"

St.-Amand parries: "I am appearing here as a private citizen. I am not authorized to express any opinions whatsoever one way or the other on the subject, gentlemen. I must decline to answer."

Avoiding the question of Vietnam, St.-Amand is quick to point out the "humanitarian uses of the things we have done in a naval laboratory." He lists the numerous states and locales to which he and his team lent their expertise throughout the late sixties and early seventies, including the Philippines, Okinawa, the Azores, the Bihar and Uttar Pradesh Provinces in India, and Texas.

"In 1971, Air Force crews that had been trained in the Philippines were called upon for a short time to relieve a drought in Texas. Once again, NWC furnished seeding materials and equipment and aided in training."

In each intervention, the technology was "remarkably successful," St.-Amand says. "It was estimated by the Philippine government that at least $60 million in additional foreign exchange was developed by agricultural use of the rain resulting from the cloud seeding. In addition, another $25 million was saved because it was not necessary to import corn or rice."

Toward the end of the hearing, St.-Amand mentions that he and his team are currently working on "a technique for slowing down portions of winter storms and changing their trajectory so that the rain along the Pacific coast of California might be spread out a little more equally, thus reducing the perennial drought in southern California."

What exactly this technique consists of St.-Amand does not specify. The word "chemtrails" appears nowhere in the report.

He does say, however, that in each experiment he and his team were careful to avoid creating catastrophic floods — the type of artificial precipitation Joe Busto, Andrew Heymsfield, and the City of Los Angeles all say is impossible. "No untoward incidents have occurred and none are expected because of the care with which we have set up the experiments to preclude excessive precipitation as a result of our efforts."

St.-Amand credits his team's success to "a concatenation of circumstances and abilities to be found at no other single place in the country." That single remarkable location St.-Amand speaks of is China Lake.

––––––

China Lake is indeed a remarkable location. According to the navy's website, the base remains "one of the preeminent research, development, test and evaluation institutions in the world." Occupying 1.1 million acres in California's upper Mojave Desert, the base covers an area larger than Senator Pell's home state and represents 38 percent of the navy's landholdings worldwide and 85 percent of its research, development, and testing grounds. As of March 2008, China Lake had received more than $625 billion in defense contracts. Altogether the complex employs roughly 4,000 civilians, 800 military personnel, and almost 2,000 contractors. The base was founded in the summer of 1943 during the height of WWII. While US soldiers stormed Sicily and my grandfather was fighting in the Solomons, the United States Navy and the physics brains of LA's Caltech began scouting the Mojave Desert for a place to test their bombs. When they chose the China Lake site at the southern end of Indian Wells

Valley, the lake had been gone for some time, and so had the Chinese borax miners from whom it had received its name.

The land lay empty, the days stood soundless.

But that didn't last. Testing began immediately and so did construction. The sudden pouring of men and materials into the remote Mojave region earned the base the moniker Secret City. Today, however, while research, development, and testing have never really ceased, only 5 percent of China Lake's lands are developed, and the location isn't so unknown. Ridgecrest, the town supporting China Lake, has 28,000 residents, a median household income of $60,000, and 360 sunny days per year. Not everyone who lives there, though, is happy.

The day after the Ridgecrest shootings, my mom and I packed the car and took I-15 north over the avocado orchards of Fallbrook, past Riverside's deracinated orange groves, and up toward Cajon Pass at the threshold of the Mojave Desert. I exited the interstate near Victorville, before the world's tallest thermometer in Barstow, and pulled toward the drive-through at In-N-Out. Despite my mother's incipient diabetes, she ordered a double-double and a Dr. Pepper.

"I'm excited," she said.

I managed to talk her into coming on the trip after I upsold her on one of the base's more remarkable and lesser-known features. Although my mother is superstitious and believes in American Indian cures, she does not accept chemtrail theory. Thankfully her mind still functions. After suffering a stroke two years ago — one of the chemtrail Big 4 — she blamed it on smoking. That the hemorrhage left no long-term damage, only headaches, she attributed to God. Her doctor at UCSD did not disagree.

"It's a miracle," he said.

He and I, however, shared an awkward glance over the summer when my mother told him that her headaches vanished after sitting inside one of the famed Native American vortex sites outside of Sedona, Arizona.

Determined to get her active again, I phoned her from Iowa a month before the trip and told her that inside the bounds of China

Lake resided a handful of narrow lava canyons in which lay the largest concentration of Native American rock art in the Western Hemisphere. I told her that the images were a National Historic Landmark, a sacred site to the Paiute-Shoshone Indians, and the best-preserved rock art in the country.

"The navy's mapped over 100,000 images by satellite,"* I said. "Somehow they avoid bombing them."

She called me back the next day and said she'd applied for a spot on the tour.

My mother maintains the single largest collection of Native American craft art I've ever seen inside a single-family southern California home. She'll always be happy to imbibe a further dose of ancient Indian elixir.

"Great," I said.

At present, only two ways exist whereby a member of the American public may enter China Lake legally. One is by visiting the US Naval Museum of Armament and Technology; the other is by taking a navy-guided tour of the petroglyphs in the Coso Range. The museum lies a few hundred feet behind the main gate in Ridgecrest. The petroglyph tour takes you back fifty miles inside the base. You have to sign and mail back a contract that says if the navy bombs you, it's your fault. While the rock art sounded exciting, my concern was getting inside the base, talking to those who worked there, and finding out what if anything the military was doing to alter the atmosphere.

Of all the places that might have been chosen to study rainmaking, China Lake seems an unlikely location. The base stands today at the center of one of the most brutal and unforgiving landscapes on Earth, midway between Mount Whitney and Death Valley's Badwater Basin, the highest and lowest points in the contiguous United States. In 2012, the World Meteorological Association officially recognized Death Valley as the hottest place on Earth. China Lake, lying one valley west, is only slightly cooler. Summertime temperatures often wander upward of 110°F, while annual precipitation totals hover near three inches. It's these weather extremes and the site's extreme isolation that attracted the military. Walled to the west by the 14,000-foot Sierra Nevada batholith, to the east by the Panamint Mountains, and the north by the volcanically active Coso Range, the Sierra rain shadow provides pilots with perfect visibility, while the rugged mountains ringing Death Valley ensure a vast empty bombing range, and the geothermal energy of the volcanic Coso Range powers the labs around the dry lake bed. It's this concatenation of circumstances I find most interesting. The base, like the desert itself, is an elegant, self-sustaining system. A place where state of the art meets the staid indifference of the desert. Where the tinted towers of black-budget research speak only as much as the landscape reflected in their glass.

Gripping the steering wheel, I stare out the window beyond the last stoplight in Victorville. Across the desert nothing stirs save the occasional gray grocery bag trolling like a lost puffer fish over the scorched and mottled seafloor.

"Have you seen this?" my mother says.

Printed on the bottom of her palm tree–themed In-N-Out cup are the words "Revelations 3:20."

"Yeah, I've seen that," I say.

"Weird," she says.

Outside, brown cigarette butts huddle in the gutters like something seasonally shed in the land of no leaves. The only trees around aren't really trees but yucca palms. Starved Mormon settlers crossing the Mojave in the 1850s saw their twisted branches as pairs of praying arms and named them after the prophet Joshua, who in similar posture commanded the sun and the moon to stand still over Gibeon — and "the Lord hurled large hailstones down" and "the more of them died from the hail than were killed by the swords of the Israelites." In the rearview mirror, the trees stand like lone and wild sentries guarding empty space. Behind them, the stucco walls wrapped around southern California's final subdivision burn white and reflective against the desert sand. Another grocery bag comes bouncing across the intersection and wraps around the roadside barbed wire. I watch it turn over with each touch of wind, lifting up and inspecting itself like something wounded before it falls back again, deflating with a hiss.

"Yo," my mom says.

She's pointing straight ahead. The light is green.

We follow giant anthropomorphic power poles as they stretch out from the city limits. The furthest advanced flicker in and out through the horizon's heat haze like a line of pilgrims pursuing some otherworld. Along the roadside, spray-painted plywood signs advertise dirt for sale without a phone number.

"There goes your Christmas present," my mom says.

She taps the glass screen of her new smartphone, then sets it on the dashboard.

"I hate this thing," she says.

Ahead on the right, a line of signs celebrates impending world government, the imminent rapture: Support the UN. Jesus Is Coming.

My mother sips the last of her soda. "Look busy."

I switch on the radio as we sweep past another painted sign advertising a high-frequency FM station.

"Do we have to listen to this?" my mom says.

Through the static, I hear callers putting questions to some celebrity pastor. People want to know when they'll get their new bodies and what they'll look like. "We'd all love to know the answers," the man says. "My opinion rests with what's printed in scripture. Everything will be perfect." A burst of praise splutters through the dashboard tweeters. My mom flicks the volume and reclines her seat.

"Let's have quiet."

She says she took a Percocet. She's worried about her back going out.

I ask if I can play a CD.

"No," she says. "All your music sounds like screaming."

As we pass through Kramer Junction, the helicopters are gone, as are the yellow tape and the two people the cops found shot and locked in the trunk the day before. I grip the wheel tight and keep right of the semitrucks passing beyond the two-lane highway's double yellow line. It seems to stretch forever, bending like a bow through the wide desert basin. Stacks of red hills ripple away into brown mountains sawing against the blue skyline. Clumps of blackened sage and burrobush look like coral bones, the withered reefs of some long-dead sea as they crust over the incandescing sands.

When humans first arrived in the Mojave, they discovered a verdant savanna grazed by mammoths. It must have taken thousands of years to track their migrations south through the maze of ice-free corridors in Canada's Cordilleran Ice Sheet. Speeding north over the broad sunbaked benchland, I try to envision that long-gone labyrinth, the screaming razor scrape of towering shifting ice, walls a continent wide driven by snow piling at the poles, chewing, swallowing, and dissolving rocks the size of stadiums, their cold radiation freezing the hairs of a hunter's nose as he knelt sniffing reindeer dung beneath a godless gray sky shedding eternal snow, pristine blankets clothing the crevasses into which mammoth, mother, and world routinely vanished. Thirty thousand years ago, mile-high ice mountains covered Iowa. Then toward the end of the Pleistocene, the earth began to warm. Glaciers retreated. The frostbitten skin clamped over California's Sierra Nevada started to melt. A massive inland sea bled down from Mount Whitney, filling the Mojave lowlands high, streaming hundreds of miles over the red dirt. But the earth continued to warm. It continues today. Extinctions followed and the sea evaporated, its last surviving puddle siphoned off by Los Angeles in 1926.

After a long winding rise, the road steadies as I turn on the air-conditioning and read a road sign. Red Mountain, Population 19. A century-old forsaken mining outpost. Yards covered over with the rusted organs of extinct automobiles. Wind chimes tangled over rotten porches, bumping against bolted doors. Glinting tongues of orange Playskool slides disgorged onto piles of broken glass. A café eternally shuttered with sun-stained urine curtains. Refrigerators waiting in fields, their freezers full of bodies, memories, boys — children who went for a drive and never came home for dinner or ever.

Speeding past the town's sole economy — a billboard advertising the McDonald's drive-through in Ridgecrest — I hear a choking sound and see that my mother is snoring. Slowing down, no cars behind me, I imagine taking a tour of a Red Mountain residence. The old man is hard to picture, he won't look at me — the three dozen times I've driven through this town I've never seen a single human soul — but he takes my hand, guiding me up from the road, leading me beneath a flapping blue tarpaulin, along the narrow side yard, and out to a field of dirt where he points out every car part, every sun-cracked appliance, coffee makers, vacuums, and various infomercial gyms, the rusted rails he ripped from the mines, livestock trailers missing feet and tipping forward for the cattle ground to dust, a decaying rowboat camouflaged among the burrobush, a thousand hubcaps piled in a pyramid of coins alongside the front porch. The gold is gone but nothing can be thrown away. Each object has significance and may yet prove its worth. If not, just as well — mess gives meaning. The disorder and chaos of life itself can be managed if you confine your dreams to your own junkpile. The mobile home's plywood door claps closed behind me. Towers of printed white paper fill the living room like columns upholding the sagging fabric roof liner.

"The bathroom's outside but the microwave still works," the man says.

Black flies take turns sculling down a narrow hall lined with golf clubs and gold-plated trophies. A few Native American arrowheads adorn the ashtray on the coffee table. The shriveled wires of telephone, Internet, and cable systems intertwine across the couch in abandon. Everything's connected. Nothing can be thrown away. Time's noblest offspring is the last. Idling past the last littered yard, staring through the car's glass, I feel guilty, a useless voyeur gawking at lonely ghosts. At one time there was probably a rational theory: better safe than sorry, better to save and not need than to need and not have. But at a certain point the hoarding impulse transforms. One keeps collecting to conceal the fact that nothing's really there.

The old man walks me back to the road. He releases my hand and points at the sky.

"You seen them checkerboards yesterday?" he asks.

"I saw them," I say, gripping the wheel and pressing down on the gas pedal.

Thirty miles north of Red Mountain, we pass the Ridgecrest McDonald's and continue straight along China Lake Boulevard to the visitors' center at the gates of the base. I wait outside while the woman checks our IDs and car insurance. Scraps of plastic bags flap silently among the chain links and razor wire. The oldest resemble Indian prayer ties — multicolored shreds of soft cotton knotted in rusty brambles. According to the local Paiute-Shoshone, mankind was birthed in flames from the mountains above China Lake. Coso, in Southern Paiute, means "fire." Today at the foot of the Coso Range, mankind continues to perfect his essence.

Inside the US Naval Museum of Armament and Technology, I read a quote on the Quick Facts Sheet from Donald Rumsfeld speaking in 2003 of the newly remodeled Hellfire missile. He sounds proud of China Lake. That thing "can take out the first floor of a building without damaging the floors above, and is capable of reaching around corners, into niches and behind walls to strike enemy forces hiding in caves, bunkers and hardened multi-room complexes. It went from development to deployment in less than a year."

A placard says that China Lake has played a "significant role in every U.S. military crisis since WWII." Another says the base was responsible for the "integration and development of more than 80% of the weapons used in theater during Operation Iraqi Freedom." There's a picture of Obama on the wall but no mention of drones. A painting appears to depict the complex landing gear that China Lake built for the last Mars rover.

Across the room, I read a quote from Paul Wolfowitz, who in 2003, celebrating the "victory" of the Iraq War, thanked "China Lake where we have, perhaps, one of the best civilian work forces any country could ever have — private sector or government. It's produced some of the most remarkable technological breakthroughs. I think that flexibility in management has improved the capability of the civilian work force — and has allowed us to keep the very best people around."

China Lake's renowned productivity extends directly from its original operating ethos, known as the China Lake Way, which put Caltech scientists and corporate investment on an equal command level with the military. This less hierarchical approach allowed China Lake to innovate new weapons faster. Some of the most sophisticated and destructive weapons on the earth were developed here, including the Phoenix, Sparrow, Maverick, Hellfire, and Harpoon and the heat-seeking AIM-9 Sidewinder, the world's "first truly effective air-to-air missile, widely imitated and copied." The

Sidewinder exhibit wraps around the corner of the room, working through each of the nine expanding prototypes. Their empty, bisected, and growing cases remind me of a freeze-dried fetus installation I once saw in Portland at the Oregon Museum of Science and Industry.

Throughout the museum's narrow chambers, black-and-white pictures abound. Pictures of the good old days when the base was just a cluster of bungalows, a bunch of sweaty men working full time for the good war, scientists developing fuses for Fat Man and Little Boy during so many silver-sunned days of yore, when the world was still black-and-white, when evil wore a Hindu cross and the Japs looked like monkeys.

"Trust me," I hear an elderly man say, pointing a ringed forefinger toward a missile for his granddaughter. "You'll never know what it was like to press that button."

Total war. The good war. The lo-fi typewritten 3x5 cards pierced with long pins and stuck to padded felt walls smack of kindergarten classroom decor and contrast sharply with the long glinting carapaces of $1.4-million bombs. Other applications of China Lake research have resulted in prenatal ultrasounds, NFL slow-motion replays, global positioning satellite navigation systems, neon glowsticks, automobile airbags, and . . .

I don't quite understand why Darin Langerud or any cloud-seeding authority should express discomfort at the suggestion that their particular industry directly extends from millions of military black-budget defense dollars. Hasn't it always been this way? Isn't this the heart of the American military-industrial complex, what we patriots prefer to pour our dollars into rather than health care, education, or the arts, a tacit compact that our ongoing quality of life and global stability itself depend upon an enduring and uncontested Pax Romana American rule? If modern cloud seeding is the product of a military weapon, who cares? The computer I type this sentence on is the distillation of the Defense Advanced Research Projects Agency — DARPA — and the Pentagon's Cold War fantasy of rapid information processing. Every tool in our repertoire of present-at-hand technical fluency is the product of war. Yet circling the museum, I find no reference to Project Popeye, drought relief, hurricane abatement, or fog control.

At a second top secret Senate subcommittee hearing in March 1974, Lieutenant Colonel Ed Soyster of the Joint Chiefs of Staff was able to speak more openly than Pierre St.-Amand about Project Popeye. "The purpose of this operation was to make difficult the North Vietnamese infiltration through the Laotian panhandle. . . . The results of the project cannot be precisely quantified," Soyster says. "However, the Defense Intelligence Agency . . . estimated that rainfall was increased in limited areas up to 30 percent above that predicted for the existing conditions."

Following Soyster's testimony, Senator Pell, like many others, wonders why, out of all the military's operations, Popeye received such strict top secret status.

"I'm reminded of the old saying," Pell says, "an elephant labored and brought forth a mouse."

The rainfall figures do not appear to be very substantial.

"What was the reason for this great secrecy?" Senator Pell asks.

It seems a fair question. What's worse, melting millions of acres of rain forest with Agent Orange, dousing children and babies with burning napalm, or making a little extra mud along the Ho Chi Minh trail?

Earlier in the hearing, Thomas Malone, director of the Holcomb Research Institute, proposed a theory: "The sordid secrecy that shrouded the alleged weather-modification operations in Southeast Asia [leaves] the thoughtful reader wondering whether national security was really involved or whether the veil of classification was drawn over these activities to shield shoddy science and extravagant claims from the scrutiny of peer review by which the soundness, integrity, and effectiveness of scientific programs are maintained."

Several weeks ago, I spoke with Brian Heckman, one of a handful of pilots who flew for Project Popeye. After Vietnam, Heckman received a PhD in meteorology and served four years as a National Weather Association councilor. He said the secrecy wasn't an attempt to cover up shoddy science, nor was it an issue of national security. Rather, the United States was attempting to preserve the worth of its international word.

Heckman described the day he arrived as a twenty-four-year-old air force pilot in Udorn, Thailand, to report for his new "special" mission.

"I was totally unprepared to attend the first briefing in this small office where a navy guy said our project was cloud seeding over the Ho Chi Minh trail. Holy cow . . . we were doing what?"

Heckman said that he and the several other pilots were told that this was a top secret mission that very few people knew about, "very few to the point that the project was being concealed because President Kennedy gave a speech at the UN in 1961 promising that the USA would never participate in weather warfare."

The navy guy informed Heckman that only President Johnson and a few other people knew about the operation.

"I thought it was all scripted at the time," Heckman said, "typical DoD bullshit. They said if you crash-land your C-130, get away as fast as you can because a fighter strike would destroy the plane and us if we were in it. I didn't believe them, but after Jack Anderson's article came out, I realized it was true. They wanted to keep it top secret."

Heckman said that a China Lake navy meteorologist — it wasn't St.-Amand — flew in the back of the plane during each sortie, directing them toward the right clouds to seed. Often they wandered illegally over Laos. Only a couple of times did they see any immediate results, yet after they'd landed, the precipitation reports always came back overwhelmingly positive. I asked whether, if sordid science wasn't involved, then did the government exaggerate the success?

"Yeah, they probably did," Heckman said. "There was already so much moisture in the air that whatever we did had little effect. Somebody just made up their mind to do it."

According to Heckman, Project Popeye represents just another feckless strategy in a long terrible war. "It was like everything else. The whole thing was a waste of time and money." But Popeye differed in one crucial respect: the operation probably didn't kill anybody. In that regard, Heckman has no regrets. "I'm grateful I didn't have to drop any bombs."

In sum, he says, "The science was sound, but the project was useless."

I ask him about chemtrails.

"People don't trust the government because the government often lies. It's good to stay on your toes. Be skeptical. But personally I think those people are wackos. They're not listening to science — only YouTube. It's a shame that cloud seeding has entered into that fray."

Across the museum, beyond the rows of bombs, a bell rings. I watch my mother pat the interface of her new cell phone.

"Your stepdad says hi," she says.

"Hey, Craig," I call.

A woman steps beside my mother and waits for her to send the text.

"The museum will close in fifteen minutes," she whispers.

We're the last ones left.

"You ready, sweetie?" my mom says, turning.

At the exit, the woman consoles me.

"We'll reopen Monday," she says.

Her voice is a blend of maternal sympathy and administrative impatience. I arrived too late and the candy store is closing.

"Monday through Saturday, eight to four," she says.

Outside, it's nearly twilight. Dark lilac shadows pool beneath the mountains, gathering up the valley's silence.

"Are you hungry?" my mom asks as we cross the parking lot.

"Not really," I say.

A semitruck rumbles up the road.

Starlings twist out from the dirt, fading west like a puff of smoke.

Over the mountains, the sky throbs like an open wound.

"Where do you want to go?"

We watch the glow drain away, the wan flesh rising from the glistening red. The frozen granite peaks ringed about the valley seem to soften as the last light rubs along their flanks, licking closer toward the tips, and as the climbing light drags the shadows higher, the peaks appear to tremble, like blue-black petals, a flower curling in the last inch of light, folding just before the shadows fill it, and we're left standing there cupped inside the humming autumn night.

"Anywhere."

We park up the road. A strip mall full of alternating bright corporate signs and abandoned storefronts. It's Saturday night, and the restaurant is crowded with large families and lots of kids. My mother says the museum sucked, but she's excited about the petroglyph tour tomorrow. She tells me about the Sedona vortex, how she hiked with a friend up into the red rocks last year and sat and watched the sunset.

"I can't explain it," she says. "I simply sat down and experienced this remarkable calm."

The waiter hands us menus and we both order alcohol.

"After I walked away," she says, "the headache from my stroke was gone. I swear to God, Barret. Don't laugh."

But the headaches didn't stay gone. Nor have her backaches. Nor her depression. She says the geothermal energy of the Coso Range is supposed to contain remarkable healing power.

"Is there any actual science to any of this energy vortex stuff?"

She rips the paper seal and mashes wasabi down in the soy sauce with her chopsticks.

"The scientists can't explain it," she says. "But it's well documented. The Indians used the vortexes for healing for hundreds of years."

Apparently Sedona became a spiritual mecca around August 1987, a few months after I was born, when the earth was supposedly in danger of sliding out of its time beam and disappearing into the nethervoid of space. In order to prevent this catastrophe, spiritual leaders called for a worldwide synchronized meditation at several of the earth's key vortex sites. Sedona was among the several towns boostered by the global Harmonic Convergence. Although no UFO spaceship materialized out of Bell Rock's soaring red turrets, apparently the planners' prayers succeeded. The earth continues its orbit, and Sedona is today the center of the New Age movement in America. In Sedona you can buy sacred medicinal energy stones, have your aura read, mapped, and painted by a Caucasian shaman, and for a modest $10,000 you might unlock your spirit warrior at any number of luxurious weekend sweat lodge retreats.

China Lake, however, despite the authentic antiquity and well-known abundance of its petroglyphs, remains a much less popular pilgrimage point. It's hard to mold a viable tourist option around the navy's largest worldwide landholding, a rugged missile range in which state-of-the-art bombs are researched, developed, manufactured, and tested on site. Your personal enlightenment and holistic health constitute the last agenda of the American global defensive strategy, and regardless of cloud cover, wind, or rain, base commanders reserve the right to cancel your tour without warning, explanation, or a refund of your $40 fee.

It wasn't always this way. A July 1860 interview published in the *Daily Alta California* with miner M. H. Farley provides the first written account of the volcanic Coso Hot Springs. Farley had just returned to San Francisco from a four-month sojourn in the Coso Range, where he found "cheering evidence of an exceedingly rich as well as an accessible mineral country." Besides the existence of gold, Farley's report describes "boiling hot springs to the south" of Silver Peak, just east of China Lake, and coincidentally also provides the first written reference to the surrounding petroglyphs. "These were evidently the work of a former race, for the intelligence necessary to produce them does not exist among the squalid creatures now inhabiting that country," Farley says. "A few scattered Indians live on herbs, roots and worms. They run swiftly upon seeing the whites."

In 1895 a man named William T. Grant acquired the land rights to the boiling hot springs south of Silver Peak.

In 1909 he established a resort.

His magazine advertisements championed the Coso Hot Springs as the "Greatest Natural Radiant Hot Spring in America."

Native Americans had known as much for many centuries. Numerous ethnographic accounts describe the Coso Hot Springs as "the most powerful of many healing springs in the west." Records exist of Indians traveling from as far away as Nevada and Utah to bathe in the sacred thermal pools. After 1910, however, their visits grew less frequent. A new railroad connecting Los Angeles to nearby Rose Valley began transporting southern California's invalid population to the remote hot springs that "cure everything from VD to constipation." Soon, with the invention of the horseless carriage, vacationers started arriving from as far off as San Francisco, and the resort reduced Indian bathing hours to before nine and after five.

For those ailing white invalids who couldn't handle several days of travel, one-quart glass bottles of Coso Sour Water—"America's Wonder"—were available in local drugstores. "Fortified with Magnesium Sulfate. Non Genuine without Red Sediment. SHAKE WELL." The water, sediment, and mud from the Coso Hot Springs formed "a vitalizing blood builder which aids digestion, destroys invading bacteria . . . thus eliminating toxic water, the neglect of which often causes nervousness, high blood pressure and rheumatism. Recommended four doses daily."

Native American informants described the condition of the Coso Hot Springs during the meager tourist boom: we all "feel sorry for the water because it looks so sad."

In 1917, Owl Drug Company began selling jars of mud from the Coso Hot Springs for three dollars, roughly fifty-five dollars today—"Volcanic Health and Beauty from Nature's Great Laboratory." The arrival of tourists and shipments of mud continued until 1943, when the federal government declared eminent domain and canceled everything. Nature's Great Laboratory, however, keeps on running. Since 1987, the boiling water beneath the Coso Range has fed the Navy 1 Geothermal Power Plant, the United States' second-largest producer of geothermal energy. In subsequent years China Lake has begun to allow Native Americans back into the hot springs, but the power plant's relentless hiss and chug distract them from their prayers—and the water's too hot to touch.*

Despite the austerity of the base's management and the success of its research, depending on whom you ask, China Lake's silver iodide cloud-seeding crystals may amount to little more than fortified sour water. Much like the skeptical 1964 US National Research Council paper, a more recent NRC report, this one from 2003 entitled "Critical Issues in Weather Modification Research," states that "although there is physical evidence that seeding affects cloud processes, effective methods for significantly modifying the weather generally have not been demonstrated. . . . The science underlying weather modification is replete with uncertainties and knowledge gaps. These include . . . the effectiveness of seeding methodologies." The report concludes: "There still is no convincing scientific evidence of the efficacy of intentional weather modification efforts."

When I asked Joe Busto about the National Research Council report, he sounded impatient. "I don't really want to talk about 'Critical Issues.' All it proves to me is that the NRC can publish a bunch of junk and they are fine with it so long as it's on glossy paper. They didn't review any of the fifty years of science and research."

Brian Heckman said he had not read the report but he'd heard of it.

Online, Colorado and California state weather modification programs both claim that the NRC report largely ignores winter orographic seeding, which both states employ. Both prefer to reference reports from the American Meteorological Society and World Meteorological Organization. Colorado claims that "between 5–20% more snow is produced in a target watershed," while California estimates that "seeding can produce seasonal precipitation increases of about 10%." Besides Colorado and California, eight other US states currently cloud-seed. These include Nevada, Idaho, Utah, Wyoming, Texas, Oklahoma, Kansas, and North Dakota. Today governments all over the world seed clouds. China, the United Arab Emirates, Israel, and Russia all have national weather modification budgets. In 2011 alone, the China Meteorological Administration spent $150 million on a single regional cloud-seeding operation. It's unclear how much the CMA spends annually nationwide. By contrast, the ten US states that seed clouds spend only $15 million each year. There is currently no federal weather modification budget in the United States.

Perhaps after the scandal of Project Popeye, the United States remains reluctant to be seen scientifically endorsing and economically funding any intentional weather modification efforts. Two years following St.-Amand's testimony, during the height of the Watergate scandal, the Soviet Union saddled the Ford administration with yet another embarrassment when it brought the question of large-scale weather weapons to the attention of the United Nations. The Convention on the Prohibition of Military or Any Other Hostile Use of Environmental Modification Techniques (ENMOD) was ratified by seventy nations, including the United States, and went into effect in 1978. The treaty forbids the use of any weather modification technique capable of producing "widespread, long-lasting or severe effects as the means of destruction, damage or injury to any other State Party" and defines environmental modification as "any technique for changing—through the deliberate manipulation of natural processes—the dynamics, composition or structure of the Earth, including its biota, lithosphere, hydrosphere and atmosphere, or of outer space."

Cloud seeding, however, hardly fits into this category. St.-Amand himself ultimately acknowledges as much during the 1974 Senate hearings. "It has been suggested the control of the environment would constitute a truly horrible weapon of war. If one could do all the things that the proponents of restricting the use of geophysical weapons imagine could be done, this might be true. As it stands one can only make rain, clear fog, and reduce hail at the present time."

Given this fact, St.-Amand recommended to the Senate subcommittee that they preserve the use of weather modification in wartime "for the benefit and protection of our fighting forces." And what great advantage does St.-Amand imagine? He cites US supply lines mired in fog during the Battle of the Bulge.

"Available techniques" could have cleared the fog "in a matter of 30 or 40 minutes," allowed troops to advance against the Nazis, and "shortened WWII by several weeks if the technology had then been available." Many of the world's airports today depend on the same fog-clearing technology to escape the complaints of delayed tourists, itinerant business travelers, and bickering holiday families.

Rather than some continued dreaded association between cloud seeding and Cold War weaponry, a more likely explanation for the lack of US federal funding lies in the fact that nobody really needs it. All state programs are currently operating at full capacity and, depending on whom you believe, they're either accomplishing nothing or marginally augmenting annual precipitation. More money won't do much.

Among the many weapons developed at China Lake, cloud seeding must rank as one of the worst failures. This conclusion is bittersweet. Sweet in the context of a rapid Cold War arms race where we never innovated a new weapon to erase ourselves. Bitter in the context of the emergent Hot War of global climate change. If drought remains the long-range forecast for half the world in the coming centuries, cloud seeding hardly constitutes a reliable weapon in humanity's battle to restore the health and equilibrium of the planet. As Darin Langerud told me, "Cloud seeding is not a drought buster, as during a drought there is a general lack of clouds available to produce rain or snow; thus there are few opportunities to have an effect through seeding." All the published scientific articles appear to say the same.

Given this fact, St.-Amand's drought-busting claims in the Philippines, Okinawa, the Azores, India, and Texas appear to constitute only another chapter in a long history of exuberant and apocryphal rainmaking reports that extends back to the days of General Dryhenceforth.

In the past, while the United States sought to gain control of the weather for strategic purposes to drown enemy lines in snow or deprive crops of much-needed rain, today our primary adversary may be just that thing that we've never learned to master — the atmosphere we live in — yet that, paradoxically, we've exerted a profound and inadvertent influence upon.

"Come on," my mom says, "you're smarter than that. The climate's been changing forever. There's no proof that humans are to blame."

At a stoplight in front of the sushi restaurant, a kid on a BMX bike forms a gun from his pointer finger, thumb, and fist, firing an imaginary bullet at my head. His knees row beneath a shaved chin as he glides out over the crosswalk and disappears behind a liquor store.

The city streets are quiet. I cup my e-cig and inhale carefully.

"We have to wake up early," I say. "Let's not argue."

Up the road, we turn into the driveway of the Heritage Inn and Suites and park beside a lifted red pickup with a Lockheed sticker stamped at the corner of the tinted rear window.

"Have you heard of Miley Cyrus?" my mom asks once we're situated in the room. She says the girl seems talented. My mother reads me bits from her *People* magazine while I watch the Infowarrior Alex Jones interview a supposed Project Popeye pilot online. The pilot sits at his desk, a photo album full of blurry Polaroids open before him.

"Show me one of her music videos," my mom says.

The pages of her magazine flap in the empty room like flimsy cymbals while I stare at the screen, listening through a single earbud.

"There was a bridge," the old man says, glancing up at Jones. Staring down, eyes black, jaw clenched, Jones looks like a gangster who just barged in, some sinister stiff-arm come to collect the mob's monthly racket. It's night and the room is poorly lit, poorly furnished. Military service has not made the man wealthy. "Bombs could not get rid of it," the old man says.

Jones clears his throat. There is no sympathy or understanding anywhere on his face, only the grim, set expression of get-to-the-point. A pale liver-spotted hand quakes as it points toward another picture. No bridge. Just a blur of trees.

"This heavy rain," the old man says, "took that bridge out."

Jones waits too long to respond. He's frowning. "So you guys finally got it done," he says. You get the sense he isn't really listening. He wants to see more pictures. The old man points to a photo of some seeding mechanism built into a wing. As he begins to explain the system's innovative aerodynamic design, Jones runs out of patience. He asks if Popeye was the only time the US government engaged in top secret weather modification.

"Yes. This was the only time," the old man says.

Jones crushes his lips together in an attempt to control his rage. There is something heroic and heartbreaking in the old man's inadvertent senile honesty. He's forgotten his lines. It's late. He stares blankly, jowls flapping, until Jones' expression softens. Rather than forcing the old man to say the magic poison word — chemtrails — Jones congratulates him on having been one of the few proud American men granted top secret clearance during such an important military operation. "You're the father of something," Jones says.

"What are you watching?" my mom asks.

"Porn," I say.

I click over to a picture of a dozen tangerine chemtrails crisscrossing and dueling over a dusk-laden sky. The commentary below the image claims that Miley Cyrus is a robot designed by the US government to distract us from the fact that we're being poisoned to death. A triangle YouTube play button hovers below the chemtrail photo, awaiting my mother's click.

"You're not still falling for this shit, too, are you?" she asks.

"No," I say. "I wish I could."

Cyrus stares. She blinks. A tear falls out from between her tarantula lashes. She licks a sledgehammer. She's naked. Riding a wrecking ball, she says she put something in the sky and it won't come down. The earth turned while she burned. Now we're just dust on the ground.

There must be something comforting in staring up and seeing those ephemeral drifting strings of clouds crisscrossed in checkerboard patterns. The enemy is clear. The government is playing a game and you're the pawn. Pessimistic as such a perspective may appear, it's still preferable to the alternative: that there's nobody pulling the strings. Sewed together across the sky, the chemtrails form a tapestry that both dramatizes our fear and blocks a window into something deeper. A force perhaps even more vast, impersonal, and frightening than our own imagination.

The earth is currently warming at a rate faster than it has during any time in the past 65 million years. This rate apparently exceeds by 200 to 300 times the rate that occurred during any previous major extinction event. The greatest-known planetary extinction occurred 250 million years ago and killed off 95 percent of all existing species. During the Great Dying, as scientists refer informally to the Permian-Triassic extinction event, the earth warmed 6°C over a period of 80,000 years. Today, although we've warmed only .87°C since the days of industrial England's textile mills, we have already entered into what scientists consider the sixth mass extinction in our planetary history. Almost 200 species vanish daily. This pace exceeds the normal background extinction rate by 1,000. What we're experiencing may match or even exceed the rapidity and force of the Great Dying.

In 2007, the International Panel on Climate Change published its *Fourth Assessment Report*, which said that the earth would likely see a temperature rise of 1°C by 2100.

Two weeks after Colorado's September 2013 floods, the international panel published a third of its *Fifth Assessment Report*, which predicted that the planet will likely surpass preindustrial temperatures by 1.5 to 2°C at or before the year 2100. This estimate may be generous.

In September 2009, the UN Environment Programme predicted an increase of 3.5°C by 2100.

Three months later, the Copenhagen Diagnosis predicted an increase of 7°C by 2100.

In December 2010, the UN Environment Programme upped its estimate to an increase of 5°C by 2050.

Even the World Bank warned in a 2012 report that "indeed, present emissions trends put the world plausibly on a path toward 4°C warming within the century." The report states that there is "no certainty that adaptation to a 4°C world is possible. . . . The projected 4°C warming simply must not be allowed to occur."

Such a range of numbers reflects less any real uncertainty about the science and more a disagreement as to how soon, and how seriously, human beings will attempt to reduce greenhouse gas emissions.

In November 2013, the International Energy Agency predicted a 3.5°C global average temperature rise by 2035. The list goes on. Whatever warming occurs will last at least a century and possibly a millennium.

Three million years ago, trees were growing in Antarctica.

A hundred million years prior, the continent was a lush tropical rain forest that supported dinosaurs with big-pupiled eyeballs adapted to six months of polar darkness.

Following the way of the dinosaurs, the last of these trees vanished at the start of the Pleistocene epoch when 2.5 million years ago, for reasons still unclear, the earth began to cool. Today, just a few years into the Anthropocene epoch, grass is growing in Antarctica again.

At the other end of the world, the permanent ice floes of the Arctic Ocean are shrinking.

This month, of all people, US Navy researchers released a report claiming that the Arctic Ocean may see ice-free summers within three years. Very few scientists profit from advertising what may happen after the loss of the Arctic ice. Nor do they offer to interpret the results of a study released in April by the North Carolina firm Public Policy Polling, which found that 12 million Americans believe the US government is run by "shape-shifting lizard people." The same poll found that 37 percent of Americans believe global warming is a hoax — and 8 percent think chemtrails are real.

When I was in first grade, my mom took me out of school to see *Jurassic Park*. I remember being most afraid during the scene when the acid spitters devoured a laughing Wayne Knight during a power outage. Whispering in the gray robe–draped cinema darkness, Mom told me to imagine the movie being filmed, Spielberg behind the camera directing, everyone pointing lights, microphones, and gaffs, the engineers swapping batteries in the dinosaur butts between scenes, while the stunt doubles stood bored eating chips and salsa, zipping up their leather jackets, and smoking: it was all staged, made up, a fiction.

She used to tell me the same thing at night when I was eight and we'd watch *The X-Files*, *Millennium*, and *Unsolved Mysteries*, tacky shows about aliens and apocalypse, ghosts and serial killers. The fear of vast extraterrestrial spaceships docking beyond the canyon in our backyard often kept me from sleeping at night. My mother, in her strange way, used to rub my back before sending me to bed. She said if the aliens ever came we'd just climb up on the roof, lay out a beach towel, and drink champagne. She said we'd smoke pot.

"We'll get high and kiss our asses good-bye."

This picture of painless euthanasia was supposed to comfort me, but it only succeeded in scaring me more. I don't know when I stopped fearing aliens. It was probably around the time I stopped praying to God. Lately, when I contemplate the future, when I wonder if I should have kids myself, I find the opposite of my childhood fear almost as frightening: the possibility that perhaps we are in fact alone, that there's nothing out there. Often at such times, when I feel anxious, I do as James Agee did and drink a lot of beer. At other times, I follow his written advice and listen to music extremely loud. Put on Beethoven, he says, "Turn it on as loud as you can get it. Then get down on the floor and jam your ear as close into the loudspeaker as you can get it, and stay there, breathing as lightly as possible."

Tonight, though, back at the motel in Ridgecrest, my mother's sleeping and I didn't bring any Beethoven. I keep buying beers at Tommy T's Bar, but nobody knows anything about weather modification or the murders the day before and no one seems too inclined to talk to me. They all want to swipe their credit cards at the online jukebox and dance to drunken country. I can't blame them. Somehow even Merle Haggard sounds happy tonight, even knowing there'll be no more you and me, only misery. I catch the eye of the bartender as she glances down the long arm of the wooden bar, staring at me like some scab she'd love to flick off. I look up at the TV and watch NFL slow-motion replays. Someone taps my shoulder and asks if my name is Jared. I check my phone for texts, but the in-box is empty. Behind the taps, my reflection floats inside a neon Budweiser frog hanging over a golden mirror. I drop a bill and the bartender pours me another IPA. She leaves the money, hoping I'll disappear.

Starting the car, I turn up the road and take the highway toward Death Valley. As the streetlights fade behind me, I roll up the windows, put in a fat lip of tobacco, and feed the dashboard a disk, Krallice's *Diotima*. Distortion drones as the drummer counts four and the speakers explode.

"Concentrate everything you can into your hearing and into your body," Agee says. "You won't hear it nicely. If it hurts you, be glad of it. As near as you will ever get, you are inside the music."

The double yellow line unfurls on empty space, guiding me up over the darkened tableland as the tremolo chords weave around each other, their notes racing like ribbons of desperate light while an avalanche of drums and nicotine buries my chest.

"Is what you hear pretty? or beautiful? or legal? or acceptable in polite society or any other society? It is beyond any calculation savage and dangerous and murderous to all equilibrium in human life as human life is; and nothing can equal the rape it does on all that death."

I grind the gas pedal down, turn the volume up, and consume the straightaway. I like this music. Most people just hear cacophony — distorted guitars and screaming — but to me it's peaceful, a bludgeon so far pursued that it subverts its own dissonance, becomes something fluid, frictionless, the sound of dust and light expanding infinitely into space. Somewhere off in the distance, I imagine Beethoven frozen on a dune of white ossicle bones, his wild hair blowing, arms and fingers open and flexed like Joshua tree fronds as he conducts another deaf prayer on darkness.

Braking at the curve, I row the wheel in tandem with bursting cymbals and the veering fulgurous guitars, trusting my life to the narrow yellow line as it wanders naked through the night. The screaming lyrics quote the later enlightened insanity of Hölderlin.

"You, favorite of the heavenly muse. You, who once reconciled the elements, come and comfort me against the chaos of our time, order the raging battle with the peaceful music of heaven."

At the top of the ridge, I release the gas and let gravity guide me down. The automobile gathers inertia as I shift into neutral. My eyes flicker between the crystal road line, the blackness bordering and the chandeliers pulsing above in countless distant star candles.

Scientists previously thought there were only two or three habitable planets in the Milky Way. But astronomers at Berkeley announced this month that they'd found 20 billion Earth-like planets orbiting sun-like stars in our galaxy. All in the habitable zone. All potentially capable of supporting life. And yet . . . how to account for the overwhelming silence of space? Why hasn't a single satellite dish ever caught some distant dazzling dispatch of alien electronica? Why are there no super Crab Nebula shoegaze metal riffs traveling among heaven's radio waves, no six-armed musicians sending us some truly artful contemporary jazz?

I let go of the wheel and spit in the old In-N-Out cup. Below in the distance, if I don't stare directly, the alkaline flats of China Lake glow like virgin snow reflecting the littered starlight. The Italian physicist Enrico Fermi, regarded alongside J. Robert Oppenheimer as the father of the atom bomb, was the first to notice the contradiction between high estimates for the probability of extraterrestrial civilizations and the total absence of any evidence concerning their existence. Fermi contemplated a disturbing solution to the paradox. Perhaps it is the nature of intelligent life to destroy itself. Throughout the universe, innumerable civilizations may have reached a stage of technological development sufficient to record their music, but they killed themselves before they could ever share it. Enrico Fermi, a nonsmoker, died of the cancer caused by his research.

Spitting in my cup, I stare up through the windshield while Krallice feigns astral chaos via Hölderlin and both fall infinitely short. "For not everything is in the power of the Gods, and Mortals would sooner turn into the abyss. Each day I shall give my cinders to your flame, and rise up another man." Beyond the black wall of mountains, the stars appear to breathe in purple-emerald light. I pull into a turnout, switch off the car before the song's crescendo, and step outside. The air smells of sulfur and sagebrush. I listen for coyotes, the sucking sound of distant killing car tires. Nothing but the abiding press of space. A quiet punctured only by the clock of blood beating in my inner ear. Five miles across the valley, the taillights on 395 don't move but float through the refracting cold, blinking like the wild eyes of a cartoon demon dream. I pull out the lip of tobacco, toss it, and scrape my hands across my jeans. Something rattles in the bushes along the roadside. I turn and stare, concentrating on the sound, breathing slowly, but it's gone. There's nothing really there. Far away, a star slips its perch and pitches down from some balcony behind the Coso Range.

Earlier, inside the Museum of Armament and Technology, I found a brass placard describing the navy's remarkable desert stewardship. It mentioned the Coso Range petroglyphs. It said the engravings constitute a priceless cultural resource that the navy is committed to protecting. Only American citizens are allowed on rare military-guided tours. With access so restricted, the navy considers the risk of vandalism low and the preservation of the rock art likely. The navy, however, said little about the ultimate preservation of its own operations at China Lake aside from a neat little quote from Air Force Spokeswoman Stephanie Powell that I read beside the AIM-9 Sidewinder exhibit: it is actually "very possible that the Sidewinder will remain in Air Force inventories through the late 21st century."

Tonight, while the military continues to perfect ever-new systems of defense, drones that drop bombs accurate to a tee of a safety-pinned burka, lasers powerful enough to suck white lightning from black thunderheads, and Hellfire missiles so smart they can swim through caves in Afghanistan without ever brushing a wall, I find myself pissing in the roadside weeds along the Coso Range, staring out over the trembling grid of Ridgecrest's sodium streetlamps, picturing the missiles as they glide through the distant canyons, float over mountain arroyos, and plumb the pregnant black caves, never scraping a single mountain sheep horn, never knocking the bow from the hunter's hands, never touching or injuring a soul, and gazing at the white lights wrapped around the China Lake labs, I wonder what will last longer, us or those carvings, who are we today who protect the traces of past man while, in the same breath, in the same cratered desert, we perfect the art of erasing him from the present? Some of the petroglyphs depict peculiar anthropomorphic creatures, neither human nor animal. Are these nameless beings the last image of our progress, the extraterrestrials we must become in order to escape from ourselves?

The odds are we'll be fine. Every generation has its war. Every epoch its apocalypse. The CIA is currently funding a twenty-one-month study conducted by the National Academy of Sciences, among others, into the various technological means by which we might lower the temperature of the planet. According to the NAS website, the study will investigate "both solar radiation management (SRM) and carbon dioxide removal (CDR) techniques."

Of the two techniques, solar radiation management is generally seen as the more efficient and cost-effective approach.

In 2010, David Keith, a professor of applied physics and public policy at Harvard, warned a congressional committee that because of the immensity of atmospheric CO_2 concentrations, CDR techniques, things like planting trees and building CO_2 scrubbing towers, "will always be relatively slow and expensive."

On the other hand, as Stanford climatologist Ken Caldeira told the US House of Representatives in 2009, "The most promising solar radiation management proposals appear to be inexpensive, can be deployed rapidly, and can cause the Earth to cool quickly."

The most promising SRM proposals involve dumping millions of tons of opaque white sulfur aerosol dust into the stratosphere to reflect the sun's light back out into space.

Physicist Lowell Wood has suggested that a convoy of B-747 crop dusters might deliver the reflective particles by conducting round-the-clock spraying over the Arctic Circle.

Wood, a student of Edward Teller, the father of the hydrogen bomb, who worked for forty years in the Lawrence Livermore National Laboratory, now clocks hours at Stanford's Hoover Institution. He argues that his global climate stabilization plan would provide "instant climatic gratification" by establishing a "planetary thermostat" at a fraction of the cost of "the bureaucratic suppression of CO_2."

Similarly, Nobel Laureate Paul Crutzen has argued for injecting 5 million tons of sulfur per year into the tropical stratosphere by cannon or balloon. This planetary shade, as Crutzen calls it, would mimic the effects of the 1991 Mount Pinatubo eruption, which cooled the planet .5°C over a period of two years, and could be achieved at a cost of less than $150 billion annually.

A 2012 study conducted by Harvard's David Keith, funded in part by Bill Gates, found that the fastest way to deliver 5 million tons of sulfur 100,000 feet into the stratosphere annually would be by firing them from sixteen-inch-wide naval cannons 70 million times per year over a period of two decades. This approach, estimated to cool the earth 1 to 2°C, would unfortunately cost $700 billion per annum — roughly four times the rate of spending during the recent Iraq War.

David Keith's study concludes that a more lo-fi, cost-effective sulfur delivery strategy lies in a fleet of fourteen B-747s spraying the skies twenty-four hours a day out of a series of bases stationed on or around the equator. This method, Keith estimates, may cost as little as $8 billion annually. "SRM," he says, "could offset this century's global-average temperature rise a few hundred times more cheaply than achieving the same cooling by emissions cuts."

"Solar radiation management has three essential characteristics," Keith told Congress in 2010, "it is cheap, fast and imperfect." It's these imperfections that the CIA-funded study aims to investigate.

Among the many imperfections associated with solar radiation management, one is poison. David Keith calmly acknowledges that spraying the stratosphere annually with 5 million tons of sulfur from a fleet of fourteen Boeing 747s would likely "contribute to thousands of air pollution deaths a year."

Another problem is that all this spraying would likely turn the sky white. Nobody really knows how the human psyche would respond to the loss of our blue terrestrial dome, our sparkling night sky. Another problem is that this loss would, for all intents and purposes, be final. Once the spraying starts, it will have to continue indefinitely, that is, for hundreds of years if not a thousand. The reasons for this are complicated. Another problem is that such a solution appears to support the delusions of one of the most paranoid sectors of the American population: the chemtrail conspiracists.

TOMORROW

"Look!" the redhead says. "An alien wearing a space helmet!"

She halts in the creek bed, her boot heels spraying a rattle of dry sand across the granite rocks at her ankles. She lifts the camera and presses her finger down. Click. She smiles. I catch my mother's eyes as she stands behind the redhead, staring at the back of her skull, and mouths the words "shut up." The redhead is apparently either some kind of failed archaeologist or an aspiring comedian. Nobody laughs. There are ten of us left. The other fifteen on the tour turned back for the shaded picnic bench beside the gravel parking lot.

"Look, an alien with a cell phone!" she shouts, pointing across the canyon at yet another one of the strange round-headed humanoids chiseled into the rock wall.

A small box floats at the end of his stick-figure arm.

"Take a picture of it," she says, gesturing at Tom.

Tom's long mustache jerks in the breeze as he stares at her with bright blue eyes, the sun reflecting off his shaved scalp. But for the redhead and an amateur photographer from Utah named Dan, most people have stopped taking pictures. There's really no point anymore. We've been hiking through the rugged canyon over boulders the size of Volkswagens, squelching over the deep sands of the dry creek bed, and staring up at thousands upon thousands of stick-figure sheep engravings, innumerable abstract carved zigzags

and spirals and checkerboards, and hundreds of creepy anthropomorphs, and our camera memory cards have begun to wane along with, it seems, any enthusiasm for the petroglyphs. Everyone seems pretty much intent now on just reaching the cliff at the end of the canyon and eating lunch, everyone except the ebullient redhead.

"Which petroglyph?" Tom asks. He's a Vietnam vet turned private military contractor who works on the base and has been guiding petroglyph tours for more than a decade. He describes his job as information technology.

The redhead points again at the wall.

"That one," she says.

A palimpsest of several hundred scratched images covers the entire rock surface from base to summit. Tom lifts his camera and fires randomly.

"There you go," she says.

She turns and looks at the group, smiling, then dances down behind the other guide, Randy. Earlier in the tour, Tom tried to correct the redhead. "Archaeologists call those patterned body anthropomorphs," he said. But the redhead would hear none of it. "No, I think those are aliens." Tom told me afterward that he doesn't like telling people how to interpret the petroglyphs, but the whole alien thing really annoys him. Apparently the idea became popular in the sixties after a man named Erich von Däniken published a book called *Chariots of the Gods*, in which he argued that all ancient technological and artistic achievements—pyramids, sacred texts, and Paleolithic cave paintings—were made possible only after the tutelage of extraterrestrials who visited Earth and fathered humanity.

Speaking of the rock art in Inyo County, the county of the Coso Range, von Däniken writes, "I should like to be generous and am willing to postulate that the primitive artists were unskilled and portrayed the figures in this rather crude way because it was the best they could do. But in that case, why could the same primitive cave dwellers [in Europe] depict animals and normal human beings to perfection? So it seems more credible to me to assume that the artists were perfectly capable of drawing what they actually saw."

And what did the artists of the Coso Range actually see? According to von Däniken: aliens.

"That writing as careless as von Däniken's," Carl Sagan wrote in 1976, "whose principal thesis is that our ancestors were dummies, should be so popular is a sober commentary on the credulousness and despair of our times."

After nearly fifty years, von Däniken's book is still in print and remains a major source of inspiration for New Age mystics, Beverly Hills psychics, and the plastic shamans of Sedona's weekend sweat lodge retreats.

Tom said the Coso Range petroglyphs are a sacred site for the Paiute-Shoshone. "It's incredibly disrespectful to infantilize their ancestors in such a way." Local Native Americans, unlike the average US citizen, are allowed to visit the petroglyphs year round, provided they give the navy thirty days' advance notice.

Somewhere off in the distance there is a deep rumbling sound.

"Is that thunder?" the redhead asks.

No one seems inclined to respond. Zero clouds, birds, planes. A pale sickle moon floats like a feather curled on pond water.

"You're on a military base, sweetie," Randy says.

"But I don't see any planes," she says.

"How much farther?" the man from Utah asks.

"Oh, not far," Tom says. "Half a mile."

Randy says that it's worth it, that the best images are in the lower canyon.

Earlier, when I tried to slip off to take a piss, I found the man from Utah crouched behind a rock, lighting a spliff. Squinting through the smoke, he reached out a hand and asked if I wanted a hit, but I told him no. It didn't seem like a good idea out here. And not because of the navy.

"Look! A bighorn!" the redhead cries suddenly.

"All right, bitch," my mother whispers behind me. "Last one."

She's formed a friendship with a woman several years her senior who, apparently, went to the same high school as she did though they were in different classes and never met. The woman's straight silver hair dangles over her shoulders in some kind of long-frozen hippie waterfall.

"I think I've seen enough bighorn sheep to last me the rest of my life," the woman whispers. "But I love these fall colors." She stands at the shaded base of a black basalt wall crusted over with bright lichens. "Orange and chartreuse . . ."

"Wonderful," my mom says. I listen to her tell the lady how she managed to attach redwood moss to the top of her computer monitor with hot wax.

"Wow, I never thought of that," the woman says. She seems genuinely impressed. The petroglyph tour appears to have devolved into some kind of walking New Age networking tool. The man from Utah told me he wanted to come here because his spirit animal is the bighorn sheep. I told him I haven't found my spirit animal, but my first name means "bear-strength" in Old German.

"Right on," he said.

Ever since I was young, I've always sort of assumed that my mom was on acid when she named me. My middle name, Donatuis, she claims, is a family name. The records, however, indicate otherwise, that is, that she hallucinated.

"Here, take my picture in front of this one."

"All right," Randy says, continuing to humor the redhead's asinine insouciance.

It's hard to tell if her joy is genuine, if the rock-carved pictures that she regards as whimsical kid scribbles have actually revived some childish wonder, or if it's all feigned, the swan song of an ailing coquette. While she flutters away over the rocks, I watch Randy's gaze slide slowly up from her leather hiking boots, past her woolen socks, and up over her glinting shaved calf muscles. His eyes lock somewhere along the rear seam of her faded cutoff jeans. She jumps between two boulders and perches up beneath the canyon wall.

"Nancy, be careful!" her taciturn friend suddenly calls. She adjusts the black solar shield of an enormous pair of bug-eyed Gucci sunglasses. A silver-sequined peace sign floats at the center of her maroon tank top.

Randy smiles and lifts the camera. "Ready?"

I puff my e-cig and stare.

Whatever the redhead's intentions, she does seem younger, especially as she continues to point out and name every petroglyph — she's like a toddler stuck in the reference stage. To name and point is to pretend to know, to imagine control. I'd managed to avoid her earlier at the gates of the base while she went around asking everyone where they were from and what they were grateful for. She handed her card to those who drove from Los Angeles: Elizabeth Rainmoon — Spiritual Healer. As she made the rounds, men with machine guns filed between the rows of SUVs, station wagons, and sedans, while stragglers unzipped suitcases and slipped on extra sweaters. Pale blue streaks of light wormed along the steel doors as they slid open and closed. The sun hadn't yet cracked over the mountains.

"It's going to be a beautiful day," Tom said.

I stared at the myriad hatchbacks, doors, and hoods propped and glinting like the broken wings of chloroformed beetles while house sparrows chittered softly in the bushes behind me. The sergeant's voice boomed out from the mouth of his plywood guard box: "If you have any guns, knives, or explosives, any homegrown pharmaceuticals, any pills outside their prescription bottles, anything sharp in your bags — insulin syringes or whatever — let us know now. I don't want my guys getting stuck by anything when they search your bags." Twenty-five people stood silent on the curb at the gates of the base before a decrepit bungalow bathroom.

"Yeah, it's looking pretty good," I said, staring at my mother's car.

A white van protested the stab of an ignition key still switched on. The dull mechanical bell blended strangely with the bleating birds as they continued to tune for the dawn chorus. The night before, I swallowed half of one of my mother's Percocets to help me sleep. The other half now sat inside the pocket of my sweatshirt, which I left lying on the passenger seat cushion. During the night I dreamed that navy guards escorted me away from the gates of the base to a padded cubicle where they injected me with an experimental drug that made me feel like all my bones were breaking simultaneously.

"There are no drugs or weapons allowed on the base," the sergeant continued calling, "and we don't want to find any. In addition, we don't want to find any Al-Qaeda fighters, illegal immigrants, or exotic pets stowed in your trunk, glove compartment, or gas tank. If you have anything you wish to declare, do it now. If my men find anything they shouldn't, the entire tour's canceled."

Pairs of latex gloves popped quietly in the gathering dawn. The sergeant finally gave the signal, and my mother walked off toward the bathroom as the men started unzipping bags and lifting seats.

"If you need to use the restroom, feel free," the sergeant called. "But avoid your morning jumping jacks — that floor is as old as I am."

He looked to be about sixty. I stared past him west at the granite peaks of the Sierra Nevada. It's always been a game for me to see if I can single out Mount Whitney, but the angle wasn't right. We were too far south. An arsenal of crows came sculling across the neon sky, cawing up their morning phlegm. They looked like fresh-ground black pepper twirling in beaten-egg batter. I sipped my Styrofoam gas station coffee and waited several minutes until the sunlight struck the eastern wall of the Sierra Nevada and started dripping down.

"This your first time out here?" Tom asked.

I turned to face him, a massive bald man with a gray tombstone mustache. A fat black camera sat perched on his belly while the glittering sky appeared to pass perfectly through two round windows bored in his skull.

"Yeah, yours?"

"Oh, no. I'm a guide. I work on the base — Tom."

He stretched out a hand, smiling. While his blue eyes fixed on me, I found it nearly impossible to look away. I could feel him downloading some data, peering into me, sifting through probabilities, already extracting a sharp hypothesis — besides a nine-year-old boy in a red Led Zeppelin shirt, I'm by far the youngest out here. Everyone else is an aging baby boomer — white skin, thinning hair, graying hair — with one exception, the middle-aged redhead who stood cackling near the guard box.

"What brings you out here?" Tom asked.

He smiled softly while his eyes clicked back and forth, weighing my words.

I felt unable to lie.

His face lit up as I mumbled something about the chemtrail conspiracy, weather modification, and the history of cloud seeding.

"Ah, yes. Dr. St.-Amand was one of our best," Tom said. "We lost him several years ago."

"You knew him?" I asked.

Tom nodded and his gaze dropped for the first time.

"I knew him well," he said.

The sadness in his voice sounded genuine and checked my desire to probe.

"Well, maybe not well. But we were acquainted. He was a very dynamic individual."

My mother tapped my shoulder then. "Sweetie, go pee," she said. "You should go before the drive."

I told her that I didn't have to go and she said that was good.

"Those bathrooms are atrocious."

She stared at Tom, and he smiled. Then he stared at me.

"You don't believe in chemtrails, do you?" he asked.

"No," I said. "That shit's garbage."

"Which ones are the chemtrails?" my mom said.

"Okay, people, listen up," the sergeant called. He explained how we were to conduct ourselves once inside the base. "All cameras will remain stowed in locked glove compartments. Binoculars will remain packed away and out of reach. In addition, cell phones will remain powered off for the entirety of the drive out to Renegade Canyon."

All along the sidewalk, everyone started digging through their jeans, clawing frantically.

"If anyone turns on their cell phone, I'll get a call from the laboratory over the hill telling me someone is transmitting an illegal signal and interrupting their tests. You don't want that, and I don't want that."

The sergeant waited for the parade of goodnight glissandos to pass.

"I don't want to have to drive fifty miles back into the base to confiscate all your phones and cancel the tour."

"In addition . . ." the sergeant continued, but the redhead raised her hand.

"Sir?" she called.

He cast a patronizing sidelong glance at her and continued talking. "If you planned to take pictures on your cell phone you may, provided you only power your phone on once you reach the floor of Renegade Canyon."

He assured us we'd have no reception. He told us to be careful. "No broken bones or rattlesnake bites, please."

"You will drive single file," he said. "No one will exceed the base speed limit of fifty-five miles per hour. Each vehicle will follow the other in front of it at a distance of one hundred feet. If any car stops for anything other than a stop sign, the entire tour will be canceled. You will not share any information written or spoken with friends, family, colleagues, or any other foreign party, national, corporate, or otherwise, concerning anything you see inside the base outside of Renegade Canyon. You are all appearing here today as guests of the United States Navy and these rules will be strictly enforced."

Given these official orders, I cannot disclose anything I saw on the drive, especially not the fleet of Boeing 747s that stood in the shadows of towering green hangars, or the crews beneath the planes screwing hoses into some kind of chemical reservoir with sprinkler-looking pipes jutting out the back, or the pair of titanium saucers we saw grounded outside a palm tree oasis at the north end of the lake, or the clouds of reflective nanoparticles that wrapped around Telescope Peak, glittering like a golden halo, or later the partially collapsed Twin Towers replica we saw still smoking at the end of a white dust bowl. In reality, it was Sunday and the base was empty. Outside our ten-car caravan, we encountered neither another living soul nor a single source of movement, with one exception. At the top of a narrow winding canyon, the road opened onto a plateau crammed with Joshua trees, and through the flitting trunks, several hundred feet off the road, a white horse stood alone, swishing its tail and staring at the horizon. The only wild equine I've ever seen.

"Look!" I said, pointing, but my mother didn't see. "You're lying," she said.

The caravan parked in a drifting plume of dirt. Everyone waded outside, stretching, tightening boots and the straps of backpacks, blowing noses, and drinking bottled water. Tom took a head count while the boy in the red Led Zeppelin shirt wrote "Wash Me" on a dusty truck tailgate. In the distance, Renegade Canyon stretched west across the wide desert terrace, like a black gash split across a tilting marble table, its exit at the lower ridge too far off to see.

The first thing my mom did was turn on her cell.

"How do you make it do the panorama thing?" she asked.

I thought we'd at least make it to the floor of the canyon before the guards came to confiscate our phones, at least I'd see a couple of petroglyphs, at least I'd get a minute to talk to Tom about China Lake's current climate modification research, but the guards never came. It was all scripted. DoD bullshit.

A floor of white plastic interconnected erosion-control hexagons wound through the burrobush, sage, and creosote out from the edge of the parking lot to the rim of the canyon. My mother held my arm as the trail turned to dirt and sloped down thirty feet through a side wash. Below, the tall and blackened walls tried to shine as they faced each other across the barren creek bed, like some hallway full of warped and burned-out mirrors.

"Do you hear how quiet it is?" my mother asked.

Sunlight burned against our backs, painting our blue outlines as we filed forward, voices hushed. Long gray swaths of granite, polished from millennial floods, peered out from the floor in places, shining like the bodies of breaching whales.

"Be careful," Tom said. "They're slick."

I listened as his steps continued crunching through the deep sand behind me. No one was allowed to move beyond Randy, stationed at the front of the group, or Tom, staked at the rear. Three other guides inside the main column made sure no one slipped out of sight. The walls looked like oxidized iron, jet-black boulders rubbed with green-yellow chalk, stained with sorrel watercolors. Along the eastern horizon, a pair of perfectly formed volcanic domes lay like soft breasts tanning in the morning sun. Forty thousand years ago, one of them exploded, releasing a river of basaltic lava that milked off for a mile, cooled, hardened, and eventually got eaten out by melting glaciers, giving birth to Renegade Canyon.

I ask Tom if basalt and obsidian are the same thing.

"No," he says. "There is excellent obsidian in the Cosos, but not in Renegade Canyon."

My mother grabs the hand of another guide, scooting down a boulder carefully as the canyon narrows. Everyone keeps scanning for the first petroglyph, trading excited guilty glances, like some band of eager apostates tiptoeing toward pretend communion. After several minutes, we find them. Digital camera shutters click in the distance, reproducing the wisdom of white Wikipedia articles, a soft sound like brittle sticks snapping, a yearling inching through dry underbrush.

"Aw, look at the little guy," the redhead says.

A dozen people stand right elbow out, aiming at the dark basalt, while others crouch and kneel, jostling for position. Five shoe-size stick-figure sheep engravings cover the cracked wall. Vague geometric designs wrap around the periphery. A man moves in for a close-up and Randy tells him that he's near enough.

"Everyone, please keep back at least two feet from the walls."

He tugs on the brim of a white baseball cap, clears his throat, and offers an interpretation of the petroglyphs.

"Archaeologists call it sympathetic hunting magic," Randy says. "The shamans thought that if they carved bighorn sheep, they'd help the hunters kill game. The bighorns were a major food source, and it was the shamans' job to ensure the herd's return and the success of the kill."

Sympathetic hunting magic was first hypothesized in the 1940s by the French archaeologist-priest Henri Breuil to explain the miraculous and recently discovered Paleolithic cave paintings in Lascaux, France. The theory spread to the Coso Range via a 1958 article published in *Science*. The authors, a pair of archaeologists named Robert Heizer and Martin Baumhoff, write: "The petroglyph designs are therefore to be understood as evidence of the practice of compulsive magic by hunters, aimed at ensuring the success of the chase." The Cosos' narrow canyons, they write, "served as migration trails, and petroglyphs are found at certain points where the deer had no alternative but to pass through a bottle-neck." As to whether the hunter or the shaman inscribed the petroglyphs, "the designs were inscribed by the shaman."

Since the article's publication, dozens of archaeologists working in the Coso Range have revised and extended Heizer and Baumhoff's shamanic hunting magic hypothesis.

"On the whole," the two authors write, "it appears probable that the ambush hunt for deer or antelope during the seasonal migrations of these animals was in earlier times in the western Great Basin a special type of hunt carried out at traditional spots by a group which was aided by the local shaman."

Beyond the purported healing power of the surrounding volcanic geothermal energy field, beyond the beauty of the canyon and the antiquity of its petroglyphs and their alien appeal, the primary attraction for amateurs of China Lake's Coso Range remains its association with Native American shamanism.

In broad cross-cultural terms, shamanism refers to a system of beliefs and practices involving personal interaction with the supernatural world and spirits through trance-induced altered states of consciousness. The means of achieving a trance varies across indigenous cultures—some use hallucinogenic drugs while others rely on ritual fasting, sensory deprivation, drumming, singing and dancing, or, in California, a strain of Native tobacco with a nicotine content eight times more potent than contemporary cigarettes—

but shamanism itself remains consistent worldwide in its overall goal: the acquisition of supernatural power.

After 1924, when Berkeley anthropologist Alfred Kroeber first published his *Handbook of the Indians of California*, general consensus spread among anthropologists that the majority if not all of California's Native rock art portrayed the mental imagery of shamanic trance. In Native California, the shaman obtained *poha*, "supernatural power," through vision quests conducted at rock art sites, which were known as *pohakanhi*, "houses of power." For the shaman, walls of impenetrable rock formed a porous boundary between the sacred and the mundane, a portal through which the shaman passed, as if through a veil, to hunt the spirits hidden in the rocks. These spirits usually took the form of animals, spirit helpers who granted specific *poha*. After the trance ended, the shaman recorded the image of the animal he'd encountered, testifying to his contact with the supernatural and the *poha* he'd attained. Shamans who healed snakebites saw and carved sidewinder rattlesnakes, those who cured horses saw and carved horses, while those who treated battle wounds carved arrows. Shamans who assisted the hunt saw and carved bighorns, as seen in the Coso Range, where possibly as many as 250,000 images depict bighorn sheep. No one has counted or discovered them all.

These sheep engravings, together with the geometric abstractions, patterned body anthropomorphs, and other images, constitute the oldest and single greatest concentration of indigenous rock art in the Americas. In simple terms, the narrow lava canyons of the Coso Range remained perhaps the central source of spiritual power throughout the North American West for 15,000 years.

Records exist of shamans traveling from as far away as Fort Duchesne in northern Utah — a 600-mile walk — to conduct their vision quests at the Coso Range. Most who visit the Cosos today arrive largely unaware of just how sacred and significant the site is both for Native Americans and for archaeologists. While the Paiute-Shoshone people still believe the volcanic Coso Range formed the site of humankind's primordial birth, archaeologists no longer accept that the so-called Clovis people first crossed the Bering Strait sometime around 11,200 years ago. Since the 1990s, the dating of the

Coso petroglyphs has largely debunked the Clovis Chronology, one of American archaeology's most deeply rooted dogmas. The Coso Range's 15,000-year-old mountain sheep petroglyphs prove that human beings must have followed mammoth migrations across the strait around 20,000 years ago.

Additionally, thanks to dedicated preservation by the United States Navy, the Coso Range remains perhaps one of the best places in the world to study the origins of human belief. In 1952, the Franco-Romanian religious scholar Mircea Eliade, drawing on the works of Alfred Kroeber and numerous other anthropologists, published *Shamanism: Archaic Techniques of Ecstasy*, an exhaustive worldwide survey of indigenous shamanic practices. Eliade argues that shamanic trance, cross-culturally, produces a state of transcendental ecstasy, a profound mental and emotional experience of joy, reverence, and interconnectedness that formerly, in prehistoric times, provided humanity's initial religious practice.

The shaman, Eliade writes, is the dominating figure across tribal cultures, "for throughout this whole region in which ecstatic experience is considered the religious experience par excellence, the shaman, and he alone, is the great master of ecstasy." According to Eliade, the shaman, in a state of hallucinogenic trance, discovers the possibility of "returning to the origin of time, of recovering the mythical and paradisal moment before the 'fall,' that is, before the break in communication between heaven and earth." In this sense, the shaman's supernatural unifying power makes him "the antidemonic champion," the only person capable of defending "life, healthy fertility, and the world of 'light,' against death, disease, sterility, disaster, and the world of 'darkness.'"

And yet, despite the shaman's grave responsibility, he "undertakes ecstatic journeys to the sky, to the land of the dead, '*for joy alone.*'"

Today, most anthropologists and religious historians agree with Eliade's view of shamanism as the birth not only of religion but also of the modern human brain — the first time the radical power of our minds turned inward, systematically, toward something metaphysical, something higher than the hope of brute daily survival.

In the 1960s the countercultural writings and hallucinogenic experiments of Aldous Huxley, Timothy Leary, Ken Kesey, and Carlos Casteneda helped further codify the connection among hallucinogenic drugs, shamanic trance, and ecstatic religious experience. Our current hallucinogenic vocabulary—for example, taking a trip, getting stoned, and trancing out—continues to reflect the imagination of the shaman's inner journey, the mystical flight that took him through the rock walls into the bowels of the earth and out to the fringes of space, a vast visionary voyage that often resolved itself in artworks carved in stone, like those in the Coso Range, or painted inside the Chauvet and Lascaux Caves: permanent testaments to the shaman's spiritual conquest.

Today, throughout the West, shamanism's association with indigenous culture, personal healing, and religious transcendence makes it an alluring spiritual alternative for people disillusioned with organized religion yet still searching for authenticity and enlightenment. But donning a headdress, dropping acid, and beating a drum won't make you a shaman. The most embarrassing case of non-Native shamanic appropriation occurred in Sedona, Arizona, in 2010, when James Arthur Ray, a former AT&T sales manager turned self-help guru—based out of my hometown, San Diego—led forty-eight of his clients into a 200°F sweat lodge. The ceremony was the culmination of a six-day, $10,000 "Spiritual-Warrior" retreat designed to "accelerate the releasing of your limitations and push [you] past your self-imposed and conditioned borders." Participants had spent thirty-six hours fasting before enjoying a large breakfast buffet and attending financial workshops. When they entered the sweat lodge around 3:00 p.m., Ray informed them, "You are not going to die. You might think you are, but you're not going to die." Ray had previously appeared on *Oprah*, *Larry King Live*, and the *Today Show* and claimed without evidence to have spent two years studying with a Peruvian shaman. "Buddy, you need to pull it together," Ray told a man inside the sweat lodge when he started to complain that he couldn't breathe. When emergency crews arrived two hours later, many people had indeed pushed themselves far beyond their self-imposed and conditioned borders: four were life-flighted to a Flagstaff hospital and two arrived dead. A third died a week later. Fourteen others required serious medical treatment.

Since the eruption of the New Age movement in the 1980s, Native Americans have continually voiced their disgust over non-Native "charlatans selling spiritual snake oil." Autumn Two Bulls, a Lakota Sioux, summarized her feelings for reporters after the James Arthur Ray disaster: "It's a fad to be Indian today. In America, you are an individual. You can be whatever you want to be. When you're Lakota, we belong to each other. So when you take our way of life and put a price tag on it, you're asking for death, you're asking for something to happen to you."

The Paiute-Shoshone shamans of California practiced their vision quests alone in isolated sacred locations. They were not weekend dilettantes but lifetime practitioners who received their calling early in life and passed their knowledge down long hereditary lines. In the remote Coso Range, shamans carved bighorn sheep continuously from the end of the Pleistocene epoch to around 600 years ago.

"Some of the images show stick-figure men with atlatls or spears," Randy says, removing his hat and pointing at the petroglyphs. "In others they carry bows and arrows. The weapons have helped archaeologists date the petroglyphs. We now know today that the bow and arrow did not arrive in California until around A.D. 500. So shamans must have carved any picture with a bow and arrow within the past 1,500 years."

People keep vying for position while Randy talks, standing on their toes with cameras raised, as though the tiny darting sheep were actually alive, actually running away, fleeing the hungry tourist photographs. It's always impressive the way some adults will behave once they are sure that they paid for something and find themselves before it. It doesn't matter if you tell them there's enough to go around — 100,000 more sheep engravings farther down the canyon — they still act like children, shoving in line, scared they might miss out on free ice cream. Terrified of missing my own opportunity, I climb up among the rest, raise my cell phone, and shoot, thinking, this is how we certify our contact with the sacred.

"He's a big sheep," the redheaded woman says.

"They are cute," my mother says.

I ask her how she's feeling.

"My back's a little tender, but I feel fine. What about you?"

"Fine."

Tom stands beside my mother, smiling. I watch his blue eyes flicker in their sockets, studying my expression, until his gaze cuts toward my mother and he offers to take our picture.

"Smile," he says.

I'd wanted to feel some kind of ecstasy. I'd had a vision in my mind of something more grand, the unconfined joy of the human mind testing its power within a virgin world born anew each day from darkness, something like Herzog's *Cave of Forgotten Dreams* — ecstatic, vast, and flowing images of horses, rhinos, and mammoths, panels of gods and spirits revered, feared, and feasted upon nightly—but the Coso petroglyphs are of an entirely different order. They do not rank among humanity's supreme aesthetic achievements, nor do they inspire awe. Erich von Däniken is right: these mostly crudely pecked stick-figure engravings can hardly compare with the vivid lifelike paintings of Chauvet and Lascaux's Paleolithic caves. I hadn't intended to consciously compare them, but as people kept saying how simple and childlike the drawings looked, I felt disappointed.

A woman wearing a heavy turquoise ring unzips her windbreaker and says she taught elementary school before retirement. The drawings remind her fondly of her old kindergartners.

"They're probably older than you now," she says, turning to me and smiling.

A man looks up from his digital camera display and points at the boy in the red Led Zeppelin shirt.

"We have some drawings like these on our fridge at home, don't we, bud?"

"No," the kid says.

An older man rises from his knee, peering through the elongated nose of a zoomed camera. He takes a step back, slips off a polished boulder, and hits the ground with a dull lung-crushing thud. Several people rush to his side.

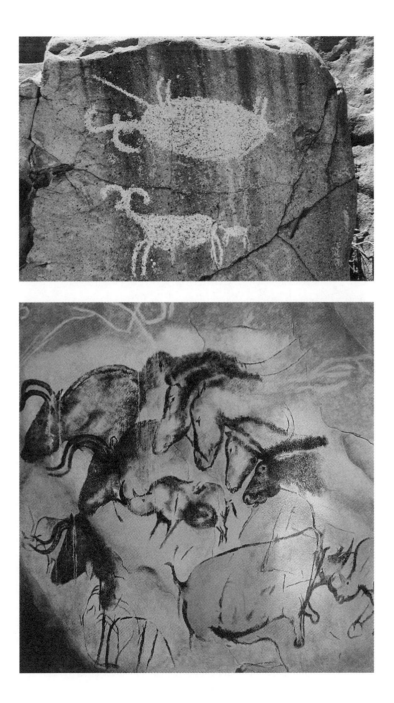

"Are you okay?" Tom asks.

Back on his feet, the man appears puzzled. He turns the camera over in his palms like a broken Rubik's Cube.

"It's fine," he says, crouching before the wall.

For a moment, while people sat among the rocks continuing to talk, I thought that in the disparity between the two arts, you could read the disparity between two worlds, and it occurred to me that it was as a consequence of this inequality that I stood facing the petroglyphs now, a guest on an American military base, the descendant of pale European peoples destined to sweep west across the globe and conquer the natives, *la gente sin razón*, people without reason, written language, or true religion, a race of passive pagans who worshipped nature and could either assimilate or bow before progress and await extinction. Considering my lack of awe for anything other than their misfortune, I felt ashamed.

But the feeling that the petroglyphs are something puerile, benign, or alien fades away the farther you walk down the canyon, supplanted by another impression, which is that there are far too many, which in turn gives rise to a sensation of mild dread when you realize that they all mostly depict the same image, and as you continue to wander down the length of the narrow lava canyon, despite the open sky, the clean desert light, and the quiet conversation of the people around you, a feeling of claustrophobia begins to assert itself, and the farther you venture, the more the canyon narrows, and the more pictures you pass, the deeper your paranoia extends, until you start to feel you've entered a place that is not your home, gawked at pictures not made for your enjoyment, photographed images no one ever intended as art, panels of bighorn sheep never made for pleasure but rather in pain, ripped out from the walls by desperate men with bloody fingers over so many lonely millennia, and once you reach the end of the canyon and see how many times that single intentional image occurred, a final conclusion presents itself: something went wrong here.

Very few ethnographic accounts of shamanic trance have anything to do with transcendental states of religious ecstasy. On the whole, they describe the shaman's entry into the supernatural as a terrifying and emotionally violent event. In Native California, the most common metaphoric referents for the shaman's entrance into the supernatural revolve around dying or killing. The same is true for shamanism worldwide.

"In my dreams I had been taken to the ancestor shaman; cut into pieces on a black table. They chopped me up and threw me in the kettle and I was boiled alive."

"Your heart stops. You're dead. Your thoughts are nothing. You breathe with difficulty. You see things, num things"—supernaturally potent things—"you see spirits killing people. You smell burning rotten flesh."

"It was a frightening experience. . . . I was physically ill, psychically terrified, close to death, no control, no direction. It was hell, an endless chaotic battle with no real point."

To this extent, the art of the Coso Range records the mental imagery of a particularly death-obsessed cult. During the shaman's trance, he did not merely contact bighorn sheep—rather, he killed them. Further, the shaman and his spirit helper were semantically and linguistically indistinguishable. They were the same being. In other words, the shaman's supernatural journey required that he kill not only bighorn spirits but also himself. His trance constituted not an ecstatic return to any harmonious paradisal moment before the Fall but rather a direct perilous descent into the grief, fear, and anxiety inherent in one's own suicide.

As archaeologist David Whitley told me, "These were not groovy shamans taking drugs and having a good time."

David Whitley is one of the world's foremost rock art experts. He's studied the Coso Range since the 1980s and was the first American allowed inside France's Chauvet Cave following its discovery in 1994.

"Rock art sites were portals," Whitley said, "entrances into disturbing locations and experiences. Eliade's equation of shamanic trance and ecstasy only makes sense if you define ecstasy in a way that inverts its meaning, rendering the term useless." Whitley said the shamans of the Coso Range did not create aesthetic masterpieces because their artwork was never meant for admiration.

"Shamans were not making art per se but rather proclaiming, at some level, their ability to manipulate and control that darkness, the fear and terror inherent in the supernatural."

Erich von Däniken is perhaps correct in another respect. The shamans were perfectly capable of drawing what they actually saw. They did not depict animals and normal human beings to perfection because the animals and human beings that they saw were not normal.

California shamans recorded a spiritual event foreign to most contemporary Americans' conception of religion. The fact that the petroglyphs are not beautiful perhaps betrays the fact that the shamans' spiritual journey was not beautiful. If we can discern no concern for realism in the images, that's because they depict an entirely unreal supernatural vision. The simplicity of the carvings reveals their function not as works of art but as records of killing, a systematic declaration of the shaman's slaughter of the animal he held most sacred, indeed, a being synonymous with himself: the bighorn sheep. And what was the reward for this torture?

"The thing to keep in mind," David Whitley said, "is that supernatural power was seen as something fundamentally neutral or ambivalent. It could be used for good or evil. Shamans were not just healers but also sorcerers responsible for curing *and* creating illness. Supernatural power was like nuclear power. It doesn't care how you use it. You can either blow up the world or light all the houses in France.

"Today," Whitley told me, "Native American shamanism remains almost totally concerned with healing. But this fact reflects the damage that Native tribes have suffered, at every level, since European contact. They need healers. But that wasn't always the case."

In the shaman's worldview, the forces of darkness — evil and death — were equally essential to the benevolent powers of light and life. The shaman's task was not to reconcile these competing forces but rather to move between them, balancing each pole as needed to preserve the order of the world. Evil was never anything to excise but rather a fixed and vital force inherent in the earth's turning. The shaman's cosmology, Whitley said, "implies that the natural order of things, which all of us inherit, is one we should not, maybe cannot, change: unlike Western conceptualizations of the dialectic, one side never dissolves the other, negating it to form a synthesis. There is instead a constant and continuous state of uncertainty held partly in check, hopefully, by the shaman."

As Americans, we tend to seek good without evil, love devoid of hate, and Christ without Lucifer. We avoid pain, pay millions of dollars to watch the same happy Hollywood endings, and spend our lives drifting among various pharmaceutical, spiritual, and self-medicating cures. In some ways, our insistence on personal success and social progress appears terribly simplistic, even childish, juxtaposed with the shaman's acceptance of the impossibility of achieving such a state of rest and resolution. In all truth, though, we probably couldn't survive without our illusions or, if we were able to, we'd go insane. Such was the case for the shamans. Within their own societies, they were referred to as crazy and considered dangerous, and they often committed suicide. Because of the shamans' erratic behavior and indifferent spiritual power, most people avoided any contact with them altogether. They also steered clear of the places where shamanic power was supposed to concentrate, most notably, rock art sites.

In the Coso Range, fortunately or unfortunately, it appears as though the shamans were primarily working for good. Their bighorn petroglyphs record a constant struggle against the hostility and death inherent in the Mojave Desert's vast and unforgiving landscape.

We find ourselves embattled against the same impersonal environmental forces today. And we don't yet have a solution. It's said that China Lake's cloud-seeding research first began in 1949. This date, however, is misleading. Weather modification research actually began at China Lake much earlier. The navy says that China Lake has remained "one of the preeminent research, development, test and evaluation institutions in the world for more than 60 years." Paul Wolfowitz says that China Lake has "produced some of the most remarkable technological breakthroughs" and that the base's flexibility in management "has allowed us to keep the very best people around." But who are the very best people? The navy acknowledges the antiquity of the petroglyphs and protects them as an invaluable cultural resource, but nobody understands their meaning.

The narrow lava canyons of the Coso Range — situated within the bounds of NOTS China Lake — formed not simply a supreme source of spiritual power. Rather, the Coso Range remained the central pilgrimage point for rainmaking shamans throughout the American West for 15,000 years.

"A dream of mountain sheep gives power."

"A mountain sheep singer always dreamed of rain, a bull-roarer and quail tufted cap of mountain sheep hide."

"Wooden bull-roarers were toys, but those of mountain sheep horns were for rainmaking."

"It is said that rain falls when a mountain sheep is killed. For this reason many sheep-dreamers thought they were rain doctors."

After every great battle, a great storm.

Primitive shamanism and speculative science today preserve the same concern. What is perhaps most primitive is to believe that it should be otherwise. We still inhabit the same terrifying world as the ancients. And yet, after all but erasing them, we have only inherited their misfortune, the endless struggle to balance the forces of light and darkness.

Standing below another anthropomorphic petroglyph — a shaman — I lift my camera and click. The body is long and slender, the face obscured by yellow lichen. The words of Emanuel Leutze come to mind, his absurd written description of *Westward the Course of Empire Takes Its Way*, a list of the minor figures he'd deigned to include in the margins of the mural: "a prairie owl and rattlesnake . . . prairie dog . . . Indian covering himself with his robe sneaking away from the light of knowledge."

It wasn't until the 1980s, thirty years after Heizer and Baumhoff's initial article, that archaeologists went back and reread the early ethnography of Alfred Kroeber and his students. As David Whitley told me, "White college-educated archaeologists felt little need to talk to Indians or read their statements. When they occasionally tried and found that Native American informants couldn't prove their theory, they simply assumed that the Indians had no idea what they were talking about."

The absence of evidence for sympathetic hunting magic prompted the theory's defenders to sympathize with M. H. Farley's initial racist assessment of the petroglyphs, that they "were evidently the work of a former race."

Archaeologists remained unwilling to see the images as anything other than literal depictions, unwilling, that is, to imagine that primitive people were concerned with anything more than directly consuming calories. As David Whitley explained to me, "Seeing the petroglyphs as childlike drawings or the works of tripped-out 'ecstatic' shamans is very essentializing and very Western. These are both completely nonnuanced and, I don't think, very informative views. But the same is true of the archaeological-materialist view, which says, oh, it must be about food because that's what all these people are concerned with."

This approach changed in California in the 1980s. Whitley stopped staring at the walls and started reading the ethnography in its entirety. "It's pretty clear," he said, "if you study the literature." Native American informants throughout the Great Basin continually refer to an association between bighorn sheep and stormy weather. "The images should not be read as literal depictions of hunting scenes," Whitley wrote, "but graphic expressions of the visions of rain shamans that themselves were metaphors for the rain shamans' supernatural control over the weather."

David Whitley's most recent book, *Cave Paintings and the Human Spirit*, ends with a quote from Michel Foucault: "If folly leads each man into blindness where he is lost, the madman, on the contrary, reminds each man of his truth."

I asked Whitley if it wasn't possible that his recently accepted rainmaking interpretation represented nothing more than our current cultural episteme, a reflection of our own anxiety as we stand facing our own impermanence — were we not projecting our own climate fears onto the walls?

He laughed. "That's a nice idea," he said, "but I'm fairly certain they were making rain. It's all in the ethnography. The trouble is no one will read it."

"Barr, bring the water," I hear my mom call.

She's found a tarantula behind a rock and she thinks it needs help. She pours the water in the sand. People gather around and watch as the spider creeps over the dark stain and kneels.

A skinny professor-looking man in khaki cargo shorts and a red shirt leans in against a carving and snaps a picture of himself on his phone.

The redhead laughs. "They're selfies!" she says, pointing over his shoulder at another one of the anthropomorphs.

"The aliens were taking selfies!"

This actually gets a laugh out of the group. My mother hands me the bottle, and we continue down the canyon.

"Look," Tom says. "Look at that one."

At first I think he is joking, making fun of the redhead.

"The big one," he says.

I follow his eyes up the rock wall, but I can't see it.

"Just keep looking," he says. "It's in the middle."

The wall rises up thirty vertical feet from the floor of the canyon. The black boulders at its base are covered with dozens of brightly pecked bighorns, but above the wall appears to be a blank canvas. Colors grade along the rock face, umber to red ocher, weld and then whiten as my eyes scale down, searching for a pattern. It's like looking at clouds, the cottage cheese ceiling of your boyhood bedroom, the soft branching fissures of a lover's palm. I try to daydream, to let my eyes blur as I connect the texture, tracing the cracks and scars of time and weather, line by line, shadow through solid. Quietly, as though summoned out of my own imagination, the pallid thin outlines of a large life-size bighorn begin to glow softly, floating up through the rose-colored wall. When I look away, I can't find it again.

"The aliens must have used ladders," the redhead says.

"They weren't aliens," Tom says.

He asks how the petroglyphs are supposed to help my weather modification research.

"I don't know," I say.

I tell him about the horse I saw earlier, and he believes me.

"There are hundreds of horses on the base," he says. "They're left over from the miners and the construction of the LA Aqueduct."

Tom says they're safe because the navy bombs only on certain days on designated ranges. "It's all very controlled."

"Do you see many bighorns out here?"

He stares at me again with that ice-blue gaze that should unnerve me, but his voice is soft and warm and when he hands over words, they seem to have substance, as though he scooped them up from the sand, weighing out each syllable before entrusting it to my care.

"I've never seen a bighorn sheep outside Renegade Canyon."

Tom chuckles as we step down from the rocks, following behind the rest of the group as they fan out before the empty waterfall at the end of the canyon.

Rather than fear, I find the man inspires calm. It's the cooling effect of a good doctor. Someone who can see inside you, who may know exactly what ails you, but before he can take the pain away you must first relax, start from the beginning, and tell him everything you know. Such calm command might also serve a skilled military interrogator.

I ask Tom if the US government is still conducting weather modification research at China Lake.

"They're definitely looking into it." Tom says he doesn't know the exact extent of their research, only that the problems are still much the same as with cloud seeding. "You never really know if the changes you observe in your tests are actually the results of your efforts. It's hard to create a control group when you're working in a laboratory as large and variable as the earth's atmosphere."

He asks me if I've heard the term "geoengineering."

"Yeah," I say. "Solar radiation management."

"Yes. It's not the same as chemtrails."

The scabbed black excrescence of petrified basalt runs out another ten feet, framing a window onto a familiar yet distant world.

It's a hundred-foot fall.

"Is this the end?" the redhead asks.

"Yep," Tom says, "the next part of the trip's pretty quick."

Part of me would like to see the redhead jump down and disappear, but her breast cancer is in remission, and she told me earlier

that she's only just felt happy again for the first time today. She told me she wasn't scared anymore.

"It's a beautiful view," she says.

Below, through the dust-polluted haze, lies the flat brown island corridor that once connected China Lake, Owens Lake, Mono Lake, and all the sinkhole valleys of eastern California in a massive inland sea once grazed by mammoths.

"Barr, take off your backpack and hand me a sandwich, please," my mom says.

I sit down and open the bag.

"Why does she call you Bear?" the redhead asks.

"That's his spirit animal," the man from Utah says.

The redhead's friend pulls out a small cooler and starts mixing Bloody Marys. There are only two glasses. She drops in the celery sticks and everyone drinks.

"This is fun," Randy says.

Tom asks the redhead if she thinks the petroglyphs were actually created by aliens.

"Of course not," she says. "They were shamans."

"That's right," my mom says, "medicine men."

Recently I tried to find out if the CIA's solar radiation management study was going to take place at China Lake. Someone from the National Academy of Sciences wrote back to me: "There are no field tests planned for this study." No Boeing 747s spraying sulfuric acid, not yet. First the scientists, politicians, and shamans must convene. Online, the National Academy of Sciences website reads: "This study is intended to provide a careful, clear scientific foundation that informs ethical, legal, and political discussions surrounding geoengineering." The study will also examine "historical examples of related technologies (e.g., cloud seeding and other weather modification) for lessons that might be learned about societal reactions, examine international agreements"—that is, ENMOD —"that may be relevant to the experimental testing or deployment."

How might humanity respond?

In America, the 8 percent of the population who believe in chemtrails may find their paranoia vindicated. At least 37 percent of the population — 117 million people — will say the study is superfluous. Perhaps they're right. Maybe there's a chance that the planet isn't actually warming. It's possible as well that even if the planet is heating up, humans aren't to blame.

In September 2013, the 3,500 contributing scientists from 130 countries who wrote the first third of the International Panel on Climate Change's (IPCC) *Fifth Assessment Report* said, "It is extremely likely that human influence has been the dominant cause of the observed warming since the mid-20th century." Nonetheless, "extremely likely" is not the same as "absolutely incontrovertible," a phrase that appears in none of the IPCC's reports.

The year 2013 is already one of the hottest years on the human record. Perhaps not without coincidence, California's current drought is already the worst in the state's recorded history, that is, the worst since 1840, but geologic records provide a history of remarkable natural climate fluctuation. Berkeley paleoclimatologist Lynn Ingram recently announced that the last time California approached this level of dryness occurred sometime around the year 1580. According to Ingram, sediment cores in San Francisco Bay demonstrate not only the existence of prior megadroughts but also the fact that such rainless phases "can go on for years if not decades" and that there are "some dry periods that lasted over a century, like during the Medieval period and the middle Holocene."

A 2013 Columbia University study—confirming California geographer Scott Stine's pioneering research in the mid-1990s—compared the existing tree ring record of eastern California's lake beds and found that during the Medieval period, between the years 850 and 1300, severe prolonged drought plagued much of California and the American West. Climatologists refer to this event as the Medieval Climatic Anomaly. During the anomaly, two extreme dry spells lasted roughly a hundred years. The latter, the worse of the two, climaxed around the year 1150. There were no cars, fighter jets, or coal-burning power plants in California during the twelfth century.

In all likelihood, the drought that the state is experiencing today is part of a natural, routine, and devastating climatic oscillation. The question remains whether and to what extent the current dry cycle has been and will be aggravated by the effects of human-induced climate change. Throughout California's known 3,000-year paleo-climate record, the only drought more severe than the Medieval Climactic Anomaly may be the current one. During the anomaly, drought conditions covered roughly 60 percent of the West. Drought conditions cover 100 percent of California today and 80 percent of the western United States. The IPCC states that global temperatures during the Medieval Climatic Anomaly "were probably between 0.1°C and 0.2°C below the 1961 to 1990 mean and significantly below the level shown by instrumental data after 1980."

Scott Stine recently told reporters: "We may be seeing over the last year or so, the very synoptic (atmospheric) circulation setup that we saw during the medieval climatic anomaly."

Edward Cook, director of the Tree Ring Laboratory at Columbia University's Lamont-Doherty Earth Observatory, said of the arid conditions afflicting the entirety of the West: "The current drought could be classified as a megadrought — 13 years running. There's no indication it'll be getting any better in the near term."

Or as Berkeley's Lynn Ingram reiterates: "We are on track for having the worst drought in 500 years."

Yet despite California's history of severe natural climatic variability, if the computer models, instrumental data, and peer-reviewed papers of 3,500 IPCC scientists mean anything, we may not need a natural megadrought to return to the scorched dust bowl conditions of the Medieval period. According to page 1118* of the IPCC's September report: "While previous long-term droughts in southwest North America arose from natural causes, climate models project that this region will undergo progressive aridification as part of a general drying and poleward expansion of the subtropical dry zones driven by rising greenhouse gases. The models project the aridification to intensify steadily as radiative forcing and global warming progress without abrupt changes. Because of the very long lifetime of the anthropogenic atmospheric CO_2 perturbation, such drying induced by global warming would be largely irreversible on a millennium time scale."

Such effects are hardly confined to California. Progressive aridification is also predicted for much of the American South and Midwest. It's possible that the United States will have to invade Canada if it wants to keep growing corn in Iowa for ethanol.

How might humanity respond?

During the Medieval Climatic Anomaly, rain shamans in the Coso Range responded by carving bighorn sheep. Shamans had already been carving bighorns for thousands of years, but their numbers flourished during the epic droughts of the Medieval period.

Few bighorn sheep engravings, however, have been found after the Medieval Climatic Anomaly. It's unclear if the rain doctors' efforts succeeded or if they failed and the shamans abandoned the cult. The most notable petroglyphs that appear after the anomaly depict skinny men wearing wide, pointed hats and straddling the backs of strange animals, the arrival of aliens: Europeans, the white man.

Today, this second, if somehow at the cost of the entire world economy China, the United States, Europe, and the rest of the globe altogether managed to halt any and all future worldwide greenhouse gas emissions, those already trapped in the atmosphere would still be there, and they wouldn't go away, not during this century—as Stanford's Ken Caldeira recently told the US House of Representatives:

> In every emissions scenario considered by the Intergovern-
> mental Panel on Climate Change, temperatures continue to
> increase throughout this century. Because of lags in the climate
> system and the long time scales involved in transforming our
> energy and transportation systems, the Earth is likely to con-
> tinue warming throughout this century, despite our best efforts
> to reduce emissions. Our actions to diminish emissions *can* re-
> duce the rate of warming and reduce the damage from warm-
> ing, but it is probably already too late for us to see the Earth
> start to cool this century unless we engage in solar radiation
> management.

And perhaps not during this millennium. A study conducted by researchers at Princeton found that even if greenhouse gas emissions suddenly and miraculously stopped, carbon dioxide already trapped in the earth's atmosphere could continue to heat the planet for another thousand years.

"That's the key insight," Harvard's David Keith says. "Carbon casts a long shadow onto the future: a thousand years after we stop pumping carbon into the air the warming will still be about half as large as it was on the day we stopped." Hence, if it turns out that in 2030 or 2050 the effects of climate change have made life on Earth unbearable, halting emissions won't do anything. "The only thing that might actually help" reverse the warming "in our lifetime is in fact geoengineering," Keith says.

By wrapping the world in a vast white screen of sulfur aerosols, solar radiation management — more commonly called geoengineering — could mask the effects of this warming by dimming the sky and reflecting a portion of the sun's light back out into space. But solar geoengineering would not remove the root cause of the projected warming: greenhouse gases emitted by fossil fuels burned by human beings.

For this reason, any solar geoengineering program deployed at full scale would have to be maintained indefinitely for hundreds if not thousands of years. Stratosphere-injected aerosols last only about two years; after that, they begin to fall to Earth and stop reflecting sunlight. Given this brief life span, if the geoengineering system shuts down, if continuous spraying ceases for any reason, the mask it created would rip off quickly. In such an event, whatever warming geoengineering may have blocked for 30 years, 100 years, 500 years — be it 2°C, 4°C, 7°C, or more — would be made up within a decade.

According to Jim Haywood, one of the authors of a September 2013 study published in the *Journal of Geophysical Research: Atmospheres*: "Changes like temperature increases are very much accelerated if you stop the geoengineering mechanism." The study states that "the ability of ecosystems to respond can be compromised if the changes are too rapid."

Another study published in the *Proceedings of the National Academy of Sciences* states that "such a scenario could lead to very rapid climate change, with warming rates up to 20 times greater than present-day rates." Such accelerated warming would "pose significant challenges to adaptation by human societies and natural ecosystems."

Or in the words of Raymond Pierrehumbert, a geophysicist at the University of Chicago, "If you stop — or if you *have* to stop — then you're toast."

Solar geoengineering, if adopted at full scale, would have to continue for centuries while we waited for CO_2 levels to come back down. As the 2013 *Atmospheres* study acknowledges, "The expectation that humankind would be able to continuously maintain a geoengineering effort at the required level for this length of time is questionable, to say the least."

Such findings are old hat, according to David Keith.

"If you ramp it up high and stop suddenly you have a disaster," Keith says, "something everyone has known for the last 20 years." Despite the risks, Keith argues that "it would be reckless not to begin serious research" into solar radiation management. "The sooner we find out whether it works or not, the better."

Only in the past decade has geoengineering entered mainstream scientific debate. For a long time, the idea was considered taboo territory, a series of morally fraught speculative musings confined only to the most ardent, reckless, and gung ho scientists, men perhaps like Edward Teller, who espoused "the peaceful use of nuclear weapons" and also, not coincidentally, later in life authored one of the first influential papers on geoengineering, "The Planet Needs a Sunscreen."

"This is not a new concept," Teller wrote in 1997, "and certainly not a complex one."

Indeed, the idea that through a careful technological intervention in the earth's atmosphere, we might one day be able "to make weather virtually to order" is not a new concept. But if the research of Pierre St.-Amand, Irving Langmuir, and Vincent Schaefer as well as the literature and folly of General H. G. Dyrenforth, Captain Howard T. Oroville, and Edward Powers prove anything, it's the complexity and perhaps vanity of such dreams. As the National Research Council wrote in 2003: "There is no scientific proof of the success of intentional weather modification efforts." Such efforts "include the effectiveness of cloud-seeding." But if the preliminary claims of geoengineers hold any weight, this may soon change — with consequences far beyond the effects of local weather. Science historian James Fleming writes:

> The inherent unknowability of what would happen as a result
> of tinkering with the immensely complex planetary climate
> system is one of the reasons why climate engineering has until

recently been spoken of only sotto voce in the scientific community. It has been seen as a bridge too far. And a certain wariness grows out of the recognition that even the most brilliant scientists have a history of blindness to the wider ramifications of their work. Yet in recent years the concept has been taken more seriously.

"Back in 2000," Ken Caldeira says, "we just thought of it as a 'what if' thought experiment. . . . In the last years, the thing that's surprising is the degree to which it's being taken more seriously in the policy world."

Since 2000, dozens of academic papers on geoengineering have been published. The rapid rise in research conducted by some of the world's top climate scientists at many of the best universities has gradually propelled geoengineering out from shadows of sci-fi speculation and into the arena of peer-reviewed science. And while concerned critics, like James Fleming, describe climate engineers as would-be "Titans" who "consider themselves heroic pioneers" when in large part they're "oblivious to the history of charlatans and sincere but deluded scientists and engineers who preceded them," greater nuance may be required to appreciate the full extent of their ambitions.

David Keith himself admits: "Deliberately adding one pollutant to temporarily counter another is a brutally ugly technical fix" and our "intuitive revulsion strikes me as healthy" because, he says, it "suggests we have learned something from past instances of over-eager technological optimism and subsequent failures."

According to Ken Caldeira, "For most, researching 'geoengineering' is an expression of despair at the fact that others are unwilling to do the hard work of reducing emissions."

Indeed, Nobel Laureate Paul Crutzen claims he introduced his planetary shade idea in 2005 only to startle politicians and spur them into taking real action to limit greenhouse gas emissions.

Yet despite Crutzen's good intentions, his proposal likely achieved its opposite end. Crutzen's Nobel status lent geoengineering its first true strike of legitimacy, and today, while scientists such as Ken Caldeira maintain that they don't want to research geoengineering, that they hope humans never deploy such a system, and that their research represents not a climate change solution but an ugly gamble in the event of a sudden global catastrophe, Caldeira, Keith, and others, much to their supposed chagrin, find themselves furnishing policy makers with the attractive vision of a quick and painless climate change cure.

"The politics of it are, for conservatives, extremely attractive," says Clive Hamilton, professor of public ethics at Charles Sturt University in Canberra, Australia. "You don't have to put taxes on gasoline or electricity. You don't have to ask consumers to change their lifestyles. You don't have to take on fossil fuel corporations."

A 2006 study conducted by the British government estimated that it would cost only one trillion dollars, 1 percent of world GDP, to cut emissions by 25 percent, the amount believed necessary to prevent anything more than a 2°C warming by 2050.

In 2006, the billion people living in the world's richest countries accounted for 76 percent of world GDP. In 2006, Americans spent $265 million on gas and motor oil, $13.7 billion on Valentine's Day cards, and $35 billion on prisons. We spent $38.5 billion on pets. In 2006, US military expenditures totaled $556 billion.

In 2006, "the US spent more on the war in Iraq than the whole world spent on investment in renewable energy," Oil Change International reported in 2008.

In 2008, US presidential candidate Barack Obama pledged to spend "$150 billion over 10 years to advance the next generation of green energy technology and infrastructure." America pledged and spent the same sum of money on the Iraq War every ten months.

On November 4, 2013, the last three living diplomats who led talks at the 2009 United Nations Climate Change Conference said of the looming 2015 conference that "there is nothing that can be agreed that would be consistent with the two degrees" goal set in Copenhagen. "The only way that a 2015 agreement* can achieve a two-degree goal is to shut down the whole global economy."

The first official government acknowledgment of climate change occurred in a 1965 report written by the President's Science Advisory Committee entitled "Restoring the Quality of Our Environment." Lyndon B. Johnson, president of the United States, summarized the report's findings for Congress in February of that same year: "This generation has altered the composition of the atmosphere on a global scale through . . . a steady increase in carbon dioxide from the burning of fossil fuels." The report stated that the burning of fossil fuels had increased the level of atmospheric CO_2 to a degree that may potentially endanger the global climate:

> Throughout his worldwide industrial civilization, man is unwittingly conducting a vast geophysical experiment. Within a few generations he is burning the fossil fuels that slowly accumulated in the earth over the past 500 million years. . . . By the year 2000 the increase in atmospheric CO_2 . . . may be sufficient to produce measurable and perhaps marked changes in climate, and will almost certainly cause significant changes in the temperature and other properties of the stratosphere. . . . The climatic changes that may be produced by the increased CO_2 content could be deleterious from the point of view of human beings.

The report's conclusion states: "The possibility of deliberately bringing about countervailing climatic changes therefore needs to be thoroughly explored."

Nowhere does the report acknowledge the possibility of limiting the burning of fossil fuels.

"Kyoto is, in many ways, unrealistic," President George W. Bush said in June 2001, a week before meeting with European leaders to discuss climate change. Speaking from the White House Rose Garden, Bush explained why he would continue to oppose the greenhouse gas mitigation goals of the Kyoto Protocol: "The targets themselves were arbitrary and not based upon science. For America, complying with those mandates would have a negative economic impact, with layoffs of workers and price increases for consumers."

Bush goes on: "Yet, America's unwillingness to embrace a flawed treaty should not be read by our friends and allies as any abdication of responsibility. To the contrary, my administration is committed to a leadership role on the issue of climate change."

Two months later, the Bush White House hosted a US Climate Change Technology Program conference titled "Response Options to Rapid or Severe Climate Change." David Keith, Lowell Wood, and a dozen other climate scientists advised the president. One conference attendee said afterward, "If they had broadcast that meeting live in Europe, there would have been riots."

A Pentagon report, "An Abrupt Climate Change Scenario and Its Implications for United States National Security," came out two years later in 2003. In its concluding remarks, it urged the government to "explore geoengineering options that control climate" and suggested that it "might be possible to add various gases, such as hydrofluorocarbons, to the atmosphere" to heat the planet. The report assumes the rather misleading, extrahypothetical scenario of rapid global cooling.

"Bush really did a great job fucking us," Tom says, kneeling down to photograph an army of red ants swarming around a random hole in the sand.

"Yeah," I agree.

But it's much bigger than Bush. In 1997, the US Senate passed by 95 to 0 the notorious Byrd-Hagel Resolution, which asserted—during Bill Clinton's presidency—that the United States would not ratify any international emissions reduction treaty that "would result in serious harm to the economy of the United States."

"You don't have kids, right?" he asks.

The thousands of antennae, legs, and teeth create an audible pop and sizzle, like soap bubbles on a drying dish sponge.

"No."

"You an only child?"

We've spent half the day together hiking, chewing through slow semiphilosophic conversation, and the question does not seem presumptuous.

"I have a brother."

But it still always embarrasses me. As Tom's camera continues to click, I wonder how much he can really see. I never know how precisely to carry myself around a man my father's age, a man who seems to take me seriously and wonders what forces might have shaped my brain. The question—only child?—always feels like some kind of criticism.

Tom lowers the camera. He coughs, hacks, and spits. Ants take turns licking the brown phlegm dome as he pulls out a handkerchief and I cup my e-cig.

He asks what my father does for a living.

"He sells drapes."

Tom told me earlier that his son was living in New York doing some sort of marketing work. It's fine. We're just going through the family prattle. It's just how people pass the time. It's what you do on your walk back to a parking lot above a canyon littered with the suicidal art of extinct rainmaking shamans. Though I'm disappointed he doesn't know anything more about solar geoengineering at China Lake.

"That sounds exciting."

"What company does your son work for?"

I don't really listen as Tom can't remember and our conversation falters. I don't tell him that I met my brother only once. I don't tell Tom that, unlike himself, my father escaped deployment late in Vietnam through some dubious appeal to religious pacifism. I don't tell him that, in effect, I really am an only child, and that I haven't seen my father in years, or that I don't think he ever went to church much more than when his wife forced him. Throughout his life, probably the one thing he managed to adhere to faithfully was his five-mile morning run. I only saw him wear shorts a couple of times though. It was always a weekend. Shorts meant something special was happening. It was his dream to climb mountains and he wore them the few times we tried, but we never went very far — especially the day my half-brother joined us.

In my father's tales, however, he always managed to make it sound as if he'd been to the ends of the earth and back — and as if he might one day take me. He'd pick me up once a week from my mom's and we'd get burritos and he'd construct crazy scenes of death and survival and extreme weather phenomena. Hurricanes, earthquakes, avalanches, grizzly bears, and gunshots. Everything a struggle, a life-or-death scenario. He told me about his friend who got his leg trapped under a tree skiing and had to saw it off with a Swiss Army knife. The girl who got eaten by a cougar on Mount Cuyamaca. The rifle that sent a bullet through his arm in high school. Steak burritos tasted exceptional during these talks, when my father fascinated me with tales of terror and freed my mind from the future, five minutes away. He felt like a dad then, and I'd forget that soon he'd have to go home to his real family. When the gruesome store of death began to wane, he'd gather his bags and move on to the last stop: Mount Everest. Here he exhausted his energy, and his tone became wistful. Everest was not just another lurid anecdote to stuff down my throat. It meant something to him. He knew he'd never climb it, but still he wasn't ashamed to call it his dream. "Qomolongma," he used to say, "in Tibetan means 'Mother Goddess of the Universe.'"

When he dropped me off at night, his words remained brief. "Red sky at night, sailor's delight — red sky in the morning, sailor's warning," he'd say sometimes when I asked about the weather. He wanted me to figure it out. I'd humor him, staring at the sunset and interpreting colors while he stood in the driveway retucking his shirt and combing his hair, but I already knew that my father was not a military man, not a real meteorologist, not a bad ass or a hard ass, and that one of the toughest things he ever had to do was back out of that driveway, flick on his headlights, and wave good-bye. "See ya, kiddo."

I still often picture that busted white van clattering over the southern California freeways, chugging between jobs and sons, brakes squealing through the canyons of Poway and La Mesa, the engine steaming over Cajon Pass and rolling out to Mojave before the tires circle back and float down the 405 to Van Nuys, then Carson, toward the coastal fog and sunset cliffs and then back out again, up from Balboa Park and past the office and home to a quiet dinner inland at Arby's. Everything circling back. Back into the van. Back on the road. The weather radio murmurs from the mustard-colored cushion, its warm monotone the only voice he can bear to hear after dark, and it predicts sunshine, clear skies, the overall continuation of the world. His knuckles wrap around the wheel, a tasseled loafer presses down on the gas pedal, and the broken white highway lines rip by like stars at light speed. And he's still blind to the incompatibility between his desires and the reality of the world, still the same antihero trapped in some belated second-rate naturalist novel, the one who married young and

started working hard, pursuing the utopia of his parents' generation, same as my grandfather — a wife and house, green grass, good
job, kids — but it didn't add up for him either, and he couldn't make
money fast enough, and his wife hounded him incessantly, and all
the government could do was tax him to hand out paychecks to
welfare slobs or whatever, and while Barbara kept bitching about
cars and vacations and Mary Kay and church, their son went to
private school and day care and he had to borrow heavily from her
father and when I was born it was as his bastard child and he was
another bitter small-business owner, conservative economically
and socially but no longer conjugally — and I didn't care. I only
remember wrestling in the grass at night during those early days.
If I won, he'd throw me high over his head toward the eucalyptus
trees, high enough sometimes that I saw over the fence into the
neighbor's yard before he caught me again.

It makes sense that he sold curtains and blinds for a living,
opaque textile sheets designed to block light, to bring darkness
and privacy to rooms, to absorb and muffle sound. He installed
them in homes, theme parks, schools, and playhouses. He installed
them in himself. A curtain that stretched across the theater of his
mind, allowing him to maintain, for a time, two simultaneous per-
formances. Two sons, two women, two lives. But the wall wasn't
thick enough. Besides the occasional weekend mountain trip, he
had a single safe haven, a third house midway between the two
families: his office. At first, when he wasn't happy with his wife, he
was "working late," and later when he left my mom it wasn't personal but financial. He needed time to foster the business, then he
could afford alimony, then he could come back.

The company name consisted of his own first and last names
plus the words "and Associates" and had a peculiar ghostly appeal
since it consisted only of himself. Journeying to his office space on
several occasions, I used to hunt around the building for the sec-
retaries, draftsmen, and construction workers hiding behind the
doors, a big party, some gag ready to erupt with champagne corks
and cackles, my father a rich and celebrated man, but there was
never anyone there, just dried coffee stains in the khaki carpet like
inkblot animals, the hollow bones of blueprints huddled in waste

bins, a fat faux-redwood desk pressed against the window over the parking lot. The broken van he'd purchased from a catering company still had a yellow logo fading on its sides. There were no seats in the back, just piles of metal rigging, binders full of fabric samples, and boxes packed with sweaty clothes—everywhere the smell of spilled coffee and spicy peanut dust.

If he ever repaired and repainted that van, he might have written Solar Doctor and Associates on the side after the product his company claimed to provide. But he probably didn't.

"The following of such thematic designs through one's life should be, I think, the true purpose of autobiography," Vladimir Nabokov writes, but I don't find such coincidences heartening. The blinds and curtains my dad sold never really worked. They could keep out the light for a little while, but over time their upkeep grew too complicated. The blueprints, lies, and improvisations spread around him, paving a network more puzzling, dense, and expensive than the ever-expanding profusion of southern California freeways, and they all circled back to the same sunbaked parking lot. He named the company after himself, as though those two words might one day remind him of something, as though they referred to anything at all.

"Barret," I hear my mom call from below the canyon. Far ahead, my shadow threads a long needle through the black walls converging in the distance. I turn back as Tom stops to wait. She's walking with the hippie lady from high school and the hippie lady's waving.

"You okay?" I call.

It's strange to hear my full name spoken. Ten years ago it would have triggered flames, rage, and resentment in my face, but not anymore. That shrill sound that I once hated to hear echo up the hallway at night—I wait for it now. I hear it seldom, and it's rarely my mother's voice. My name arrives by accident when I walk past a booth in a dimly lit bar, see a couple crying on a park bench, or flip on public radio at a red light. Whenever people do terrible things to themselves, I hear my name spoken, sotto voce. "He just couldn't *bear it*," they say.

I do wonder how my father's doing. If he's still alive, if his memory's intact.

If he somehow read in January 2007 that "the US government wants the world's scientists to develop technology to block sunlight as a last-ditch way to halt global warming," he probably choked on his coffee, dismissed it as another liberal tax bilk, and went out for a second run just to clear his head.

Last time we met was at Starbucks, and he said he'd call me and we'd go hike Mount Cuyamaca like we used to, but it's been eight years now and the phone still hasn't rung. My father—armchair mountaineer, meteorology just a halfway hobby, family a pebble he turned over in his mind like a philosopher, something transcendental he longed to instantiate—I did not receive his last name, but I have his blood, and I used to love to play any part in his impassioned but feckless attempts at fatherhood.

In fourth grade, he helped me with my science fair project. We used a magnifying glass to focus the sun and burn through all the fabric samples in his books. We wanted to see which were most durable, but they all melted the same and there were no experimental controls and I did not win any medals. We had fun though.

"The US has also attempted to steer the UN report, prepared by the International Panel on Climate Change (IPCC), away from conclusions that would support targets to reduce emissions," the *Guardian* wrote at the start of 2007, a month after I last saw my father. "Instead," the article continues, the United States recommends that the "idea of interfering with sunlight should be included in the summary for policymakers, the prominent chapter at the front of every IPCC report."

In April 2009, President Obama's new science adviser, John Holdren, said the White House was discussing geoengineering as a potential option to combat climate change.

"It's got to be looked at," Holdren said. "We don't have the luxury of taking any approach off the table." Comparing global warming to riding in a van "with bad brakes driving toward a cliff in the fog," he added that we were already approaching several dangerous tipping points, namely, the loss of ice floes in the Arctic Ocean.

Stephen Pacala, director of the Princeton Environmental Institute, agrees with Holdren, but he doesn't like the term "tipping points": "There is a class of almost instantaneous climate change that I call 'monsters behind the door.' I call them 'monsters' because were they to occur today, they would be catastrophic."

Bowing to the pressures of monsters and Washington, two weeks after the September Colorado floods, the first third of the IPCC's *Fifth Assessment Report* acknowledged—for the first time ever—in the final paragraph of its "Summary for Policy Makers" the existence of geoengineering: "Modeling indicates that SRM methods, if realizable, have the potential to substantially offset a global temperature rise." The report, however, also states that "if SRM were terminated for any reason, there is *high confidence* that global surface temperatures would rise very rapidly to values consistent with greenhouse gas forcing."

In 2011, 160 civil, indigenous, and environmental groups signed a letter urging the IPCC not to include any mention of geoengineering in their *Fifth Assessment Report*.

The environmental organization ETC Group released the following statement after the IPCC published its *Fifth Assessment*:

> . . . geoengineering advocates will use the IPCC's reports to press for geoengineering experimentation and, eventually, deployment. The actual sentences about geoengineering in the IPCC report matter less than the fact that they are there at all. They will be repeatedly referenced, lending legitimacy and respectability to a set of suggestions that were previously considered unacceptable and should remain so. . . . This report marks geoengineering's coming of age even though geoengineering does nothing to address the causes of climate change. It is a techno-fix that could be used by the countries most responsible for climate change to avoid their commitments.

An article published in the *Guardian* on September 19, 2013, states that "expert groups writing geoengineering sections of the IPCC report were dominated by US, UK and Canadian geoengineering advocates who have called for public funding of large-scale experiments or who have taken out commercial patents on geoenginering technologies. One scientist who served as a group co-chair, David Keith of Harvard University, runs a private geoengineering company."

Keith, along with Ken Caldeira, runs FICER, the Fund for Innovative Climate and Energy Research. So far the company has received $4.6 million from Bill Gates to conduct its research, all of which has taken place indoors on computer models. Supposedly, no solar radiation management field tests have yet been conducted. One test, the so-called SPICE experiment—Stratospheric Particle Injection for Climate Engineering—was attempted in Britain in 2011, but protesters shut it down. This frustrated Caldeira: "I think it's very dangerous to tell scientists that an experiment with no risk in itself cannot be performed because we don't like what it might lead to."

David Keith told *Harvard Magazine* in July 2013 that he's eager to start conducting field experiments and working "to develop a test that would send a helium balloon bearing small quantities of sulfur and water into the stratosphere, to monitor how they affect ozone." Although the impact of the test, Keith said, "will likely be much less than a single commercial airline flight," he stressed that he and his team will not undertake the experiment "unless we have some formal governmental approval and public funding."

Given the IPCC's recent official acknowledgment of geoengineering in its "Summary for Policy Makers," perhaps Keith and Caldeira will soon be able to stop looking at computer models and start their real research.

Critics of geoengineering field tests don't fear the effects of trace amounts of sulfur on the ozone. What scares people, says Edward Parson, a law professor at the University of California, Los Angeles, "is the political and social consequences of the research going ahead, followed by bigger and bigger experiments—and then you're on the slippery slope all the way to full-scale deployment."

Alan Robock, a climatologist at Rutgers University, perhaps geoengineering's most vocal scientific critic, doubts that anyone would even learn anything from tests. "You can't see a climate response unless an experiment is so large as to actually be geoengineering," Robock says. University of Chicago geophysicist Raymond Pierrehumbert shares the same fear as Robock and Parson: "Field experiments are really a dangerous step on the way to deployment, and I have a lot of doubts what would actually be learned." Pierrehumbert describes the term "solar radiation management" as a dangerous Orwellian euphemism. "It's meant to give you a feeling that we really understand what we would be doing. It's a way to increase comfort levels with this crazy idea. What we're really talking about is hacking the planet in a case where we don't really know what it is going to do."

In February 2013, David Keith told the *MIT Technology Review*, "I'm not saying it will work, and I'm not saying we should do it." However, "it would be reckless not to begin serious research on it." If the findings look promising, says Keith, "then we have the option to begin gradual implementation if the political will — or necessity — is there."

David Keith has so far advised two of the four committee sessions in the CIA-funded geoengineering study. In his book *A Case for Climate Engineering*, he responded to critics: "All my work on this topic is academic with open publication and no patenting." His book makes no mention of the CIA-funded study. Rather, it simply states: "While there is a long history of military interest in weather control, I am reasonably confident that there is no significant effort on geoengineering."

"I could hit you right now, Barret. Why do you always lie?"

I dig the Percocet out from my jeans pocket, blow off the lint, and hand it to her.

"Let's take a drink of water," Tom says.

A palimpsest of several hundred bighorns covers the northern wall of the canyon. The sun has shifted. Cold shadows creep across the sand. I shield my eyes and stare. Far away, high over Owens Valley, an airplane drags a white contrail across the sky. The engines thunder as close and quiet as a seashell pressed against my ear.

"Don't worry. We're getting close," the hippie lady says.

I read on a blog that if you could climb ten stairs, then you could hike through Renegade Canyon. The walk back up the canyon, however, is not so easy.

Tom and I entwine our forearms, supporting my mother's back as she plants her sneaker on a boulder, straightens her leg, and presses farther up the canyon. He says it's just a pulled muscle. Tom was a medic in Vietnam.

"You're going to be fine," I say.

Tom agrees. "We're just a quarter mile from the parking lot."

Besides the fact that solar geoengineering would likely lead to thousands of deaths from air pollution each year, turn the sky white, and cause rapid catastrophic warming if the spraying ever stopped, it would do nothing to reverse the acidification of the earth's oceans. "The ocean continues to acidify at an unprecedented rate in Earth's history," a 2013 International Geosphere-Biosphere Programme report states. "Latest research indicates the rate of change may be faster than at any time in the last 300 million years." Ocean acidification is caused by the water's absorption of atmospheric CO_2, which changes ocean chemistry, kills plankton, shellfish, and coral, and threatens the entire marine food chain. According to the report, the oceans "may be changing too rapidly for many species or populations to adapt through evolution."

An artificial mask of sulfur aerosols would also accelerate the depletion of the ozone layer—the earth's natural solar screen—increasing cancer rates around the globe. It's possible that in order to walk outside we may soon have to drape our bodies much like the sky in a protective layer of white. At night, there may be less light in our living rooms as solar power cells cease to function. There may be less food to eat. Less rain. Less water to drink. A 2013 study published in the *Journal of Geophysical Research: Atmospheres* ran twelve different climate models in which CO_2 concentrations increased four times above their preindustrial averages. As the researchers expected, warmer temperatures resulted in severe drought for certain regions and increased precipitation elsewhere. When the researchers introduced geoengineering into the models and repeated the simulations, they found that global average temperatures returned to preindustrial levels.

The geoengineering simulations, however, did not restore the climate that existed prior to the explosion of atmospheric CO_2 in the later twentieth century. Rather, they found that precipitation dropped by 6 percent in East Asia, 2 percent in India, 5 percent in South Africa, 7 percent in North America, and 6 percent in South America. Such a seemingly insignificant disruption to seasonal monsoon cycles would likely lead to the starvation of millions of people.

One of the study's authors, climate researcher John Fasullo, summarized his group's findings: "Pick your poison."

Yet no scientific model can ultimately account for the enormous complexity of the global climate system or reasonably predict the cumulative effects of pumping 5 million tons of sulfur 100,000 feet into the stratosphere annually. Scientists have a general idea of the global short-term response — cooling — because geoengineering would basically be reproducing the effects of the 1991 Mount Pinatubo eruption, which injected 30 million tons of sulfur into the atmosphere and caused the earth to cool .5°C. But over the long term? The sulfur from volcanic eruptions falls from the sky after two years. Geoengineering, however, would have to continue for at least a century.

What if after two years it stopped snowing in Russia? What if it wouldn't stop raining in Colorado? What if crops started to die in eastern China? What if Europe wanted the world one degree cooler and India wanted it warmer? Who will control the planet's thermostat? Among the many known dangers associated with solar geoengineering, the greatest may be World War III. Edward Teller himself, imagining such a day, once predicted weather as the probable cause of "the last war on earth."

Vast populations adversely affected by geoengineering would likely call for an abrupt suspension of the system. Yet the future possibility of ever turning it off decreases daily as the technology continues to furnish the hope, albeit a dream, of a painless climate change cure. This dream today steers political will away from reducing emissions, thereby aggravating the CO_2 problem and steadily making geoengineering both more inevitable as a reality and more appalling in its risks.

Throughout our worldwide industrial civilization, in our relentless quest to escape the dominating caprice of Mother Nature, our species has been conducting a vast geophysical experiment that, at last, appears to have trapped us in a brutal no-win catch-22. What will be more painful: the poison or the cure? Geoengineering could end in such disaster — for example, global war, the collapse of the SRM system, and the toasting of humanity in ten years — that it may be safer never to try it. Yet doing nothing appears to doom the world to the catastrophic effects of global climate change. As humans, we will probably not accept the pain we created for ourselves passively. We will resist the effects of our failures. However bitter, if geoengineering can potentially cool the planet this century, we will swallow the pill, close the curtain, and block the sun. And when the 747s begin to engrave the first checkerboards across the sky, perhaps we shouldn't see a vast government conspiracy but, rather, a species conspiring against itself, and as the sun starts to dim, when the white sky begins to grant its rain and drought at whim, perhaps we'll have to ask ourselves whether the changes we observe are really the results of our efforts or whether they're part of some natural routine devastating climate oscillation, and perhaps when the wars start and the geoengineering system collapses and the mask it created rips off, it won't be our fault, we will have only fulfilled what was presupposed, the paradox described by Enrico Fermi, father of the atom bomb—perhaps, we'll think, it's only natural.

"I can't wait to get home," my mom says. "I hope your stepfather fed the dogs."

"Don't worry about them right now," Tom says.

He lets go and we start up the path that leads out from the dry wash to the upper flats. The swollen undulating rocks look like water-sculpted couches, the bizarre discarded furniture of some outsize pioneer family abducted by time. They're smooth as glass and harder than steel.

"What should I worry about?"

"Worry about your back," I say.

As we cross the erosion control hexagons, I try to gaze north toward CA 190 and Centennial Canyon, thinking of those insane runners traveling from all over the world to erase themselves in the Mojave every July. Part of me wants to tell my mom about Pam Reed, the mother of five who won the Badwater Ultramarathon, beating the second-place finisher, a man, by five hours. In an interview afterward, Reed tried to explain her success: "Maybe because we"—women—"have more fat on us, or because we're able to have children, mentally we can go through a lot of pain. There's definitely pain involved."

Instead, I ask if she'd like to lie down.

"Bump, bump?"

"Please do not joke right now," she says.

"We could do it here."

Tom pretends to take another head count as I stare once more over the canyon. Eight, nine, ten. . . . A thick wind rolls in from the west, rubbing along the cars, sweeping sand over my ankles. The Paiute-Shoshone called this canyon and others like it *pohakanhi*, "houses of power." But a house is not a home. The smell of gasoline mingles with the heavy, old-book aroma of dry sage mellowing toward dusk. My favorite fragrance after petrichor. I stand, take another deep breath, and wait for Tom to point at me. Thirteen, fourteen, fifteen. . . . The shadow from my torso stretches twenty feet tall. Stored heat keeps radiating out from the sand at my feet. I try to listen for it. Clack, clack. To imagine it. The sound of quartz on basalt. A staccato clangor, like a stone door knocker banging in the night, but somehow bright, polite despite its insistence, as though the knuckles carried good news, as though the house weren't already haunted. But there's only the redhead's voice, "We *have* to come back." The bolts of automatic doors clicking free. Clack, clack. An empty unlidded water bottle crackling like crushed autumn leaves. Sparks of light flashing on passenger windows. The quiet tinkle of brass and plastic key fobs. Beep, beep. The voice of the boy in the red Led Zeppelin shirt : "Dad, wait." The muffled thud of rubber-padded doors sealing shut. Engines firing. Dust rising. My mother pulls a lever. I shift into drive as she reclines her seat. And everyone is gone.

"For years," David Whitley told me, "I couldn't figure out why we were finding all these quartz chips at the base of the canyon walls. There's plenty more convenient rocks around. I thought maybe some New Agers had carried it in and left it as a sort of offering. You'll find occasionally at some sites that people drop feathers, crystals, tobacco pouches, and whatnot. It can really distract your research. But when we started dating the petroglyphs, when we started looking at them microscopically, we found the pecked portions of the rock were covered in quartz."

The shamans were using quartz hammerstones.

"One tool for thousands of years," Whitley said. "And they had to import sizable pecking stones from quite a distance. But we wondered why, why not use basalt on basalt? Any hard rock would work. The resolve, the insistence on this one stone—it was bewildering. Why quartz? It really drove me crazy. I couldn't figure it out."

Two hours from now, 10,000 years ago, if you had stood at the edge of Renegade Canyon at night and looked west, you could have seen something more inexplicable and disturbing than anything you might dream of lurking behind a military base's border of rusted barbed wire. A frail light glowing down in the dark hallway of the canyon. It would appear to flicker, like bolts inside a distant thunderhead, a dying camera flashbulb—an animal eye glinting with reflected fire. But the flame gutters out. Clack, clack. Frozen in place, staring transfixed, you'd wait and listen. You'd see the light again before the noise returned. Clack, clack. And by the time it hit your ears, all would fall dark again. Clack, clack. Clack, clack. You'd think, for a moment, that you heard your own heart clattering up your spine, a sound like bighorn hooves trudging some narrow bony ridge. Clack, clack. But when you swallow you can feel that the sound emanates from elsewhere, down there—the canyon. You notice that when the light flickers, it seems to rock back and forth. Clack, clack. Back and forth, ever so slightly. Clack, clack. But what the hell is it? In all the barren blackness, only this sad speck blinking in the foreground of infinity. And then you hear the lungs, the tongue, a human song, it seems, wafting across the invisible night floor. A warm threnody intoning in rhythm. Clack, clack. Clack, clack. And the walls of black basalt radiate the cold press of space, and the stars shine like caves of cruel teeth, galaxy upon galaxy twisting and grinning white with laughter so dead in its ecstasy that it's hard to breathe in all this ferocious ageless night. Clack, clack. But he whose hands you cannot see holds the glowing stone. He is the Master of the Spirits.* He has already ascended heaven and butchered bright Aries. Invisible below, he hammers at the canyon door, beating shut the abyss inside himself by a pair of carved ram horns.

"Quartz is triboluminescent," Whitley said. "When struck, it glows. Tell me how the hell they figured that out."

I slide the card in the door and the light flashes green.

I drop our bags on the floor and stand in the dark. The room smells like a thrift store.

"Look," Mom says.

Beyond the motel blinds, far above the mountains, like a handprint on swollen smacked skin, the red autumn light drains from the sky, leaving behind a pale bloodless twilight.

"Isn't that pretty?" she says, flicking on the light.

Many people in the United States enjoyed remarkable sunsets following the eruption of Russia's Sarychev volcano in 2009.

"It smells like hell in here," she says.

Glaring lavender skies lasted around the globe for years after Mount Pinatubo's 1991 eruption.

People in Europe saw vivid crimson sunsets after the Eyjafjallajökull volcano blasted in Iceland three years ago.

"It's pretty," I say.

Perhaps there will be one benefit to geoengineering.

Sulfur aerosols, like volcanic eruptions, will create not only a planet-cooling haze but dramatic evening skies.

"Help me undress," she says.

We'll go up on the roof and lay out a beach towel. We'll drink beer and smoke pot. We'll stare west and watch the red glow fade to a deep and starless mauve. We'll go inside and jam our ears close against the loudspeaker and listen to the screaming light of Beethoven. For "he who understands my music can never know unhappiness again." The eruption of Krakatoa ejected 20 million tons of sulfur into the earth's atmosphere in 1883. The explosion provided the inspiration for one of the world's best-known works of art. The suicidal painter Edvard Munch later reflected on that sunset over Oslo:

> I was walking along the road with two good friends one day.
> The sun had just gone down, the evening coming slowly. I felt
> a heavy weight of sudden sadness in the sky: it had become a
> seething red. I stopped, leaned against a railing that was bor-

dering the harbor and looked out at the flaming clouds that were hanging there like swords, their blood-red blades reflected in the water. My friends had already passed. But I was frozen there. A loud and piercing scream was shaking through the air.

I try to pull the pillow out from under her neck.

"Ow!" she cries, lifting her head.

"Just stay still."

She stares at the ceiling as I lower her head to the mattress and turn the lamp to dim. I glance at the door chain again before I return to the desk chair, lift the hydraulic knob, and sink down, no longer hiding my e-cig. But the tip starts to flash. I unscrew the cartridge and plug the battery into the USB port on my laptop and continue clicking.

Anthony Barrett writes: "YOU KEN AND YOUR SO CALLED SCIEN-TISTS, ARE RESPONSIBLE FOR THE DESTRUCTION OF GODS WEATHER PATTERNS ON GODS EARTH YOU SIR ARE THE MOST EVILIST HUMAN GOING IF YOU ARE A HUMAN WHY WOULD A HUMAN KILL HIS ONLY PLANET TO LIVE ON."

In the YouTube comments posted below the lectures of David Keith and Ken Caldeira, thousands of people seem to want their heads. Nobody understands the logic. You have to kill the thing you love the most, the thing most sacred and synonymous with yourself.

Jack Handle: "YOU BASTARD. DAVID KIETH IS A MASS MUR-DERER. HE PRETENDS HES NOT DUMPING ALUMINIUM ON US AL-READY. BURN IN HELL."

SheepleAlert writes: "This guy is a Fucktard! So are any others who believe we should further pollute our air for the alleged sake of helping."

Jana Murray: "Climate Engineer Ken Caldeira playing god with our military industrial complex."

"Are you sure you're not hungry?" I ask my mom.

"No. Thank you."

She doesn't open her eyes. She's lying flat on the bed with her socks on, hands folded at her chest. Her wedding ring floats up and down with her heavy rhythmic breaths.

"You don't need anything?"

"No. Thank you."

Click, click. Below another video, New Age guru Laura Eisenhower tells us how to survive Ken and David's plans: "I focus on Sacred Union and Mother/Father God. . . . Right now with our alignment with the galactic plane, we are connecting to the Mother Womb where everything was birthed from. Mother and Father — get that! Both! I am leading people back to the primordial parents — the androgyny that exists in Source. I have 12 hours of material. . . . The inner work of connecting to Source is not wrong. Stay in duality by encouraging the inner work and connection to Gaia."

ChicagoDreamer5 to Laura: "Wonderful, brilliant presentation. I can and have made chemtrails go away, just by commanding them to go away. 'Go away chemtrails/clouds, I disagree with you.' I make sure to say chemtrails, because I don't want to banish our Gallactic Family."

Dana Horochowski writes to Laura: "FUCK — WHAT A VAMPIRE QLIPPOTH WHORE SELLOUT FOR THE BLACK SUN NAZIS, BURN BITCH."

"Text your dad and tell him we're not gonna be home tonight," my mom says.

"You mean Craig?"

"Text your stepfather."

I ask if she's sure she doesn't want to go to the hospital.

"No. Thank you."

Eyes closed, face pale, mouth drawn. Hands folded at her chest, her body rigid . . . she looks like a vampire, or at least that's what I tell myself. She'll never die. She'll always bounce back. Ever since I was a little kid, her back's gone out. It's happened dozens of times over the years. She just needs a day to rest. She says she doesn't want anything, but I bring her a glass of water anyway.

"Sit up," I say.

She lifts her eyebrows into question marks.

"Yo," I tell her.

"Mmmhh?" she groans, popping her left eye open.

"Here," I say, "it's Coso Sour Water. America's Wonder."

"You're stupid."

I hand it to her. "Cures everything from constipation to VD, high blood pressure, and degenerative disk disease."

She lifts her neck slightly to drink.

"I think I liked Sonoma better," she says.

"You mean Sedona? Is your headache gone?"

She says she can't feel it at the moment.

I set the water down on the bedstand and start picking at the metal cap of a warm beer with the car keys. The bottle hisses and the cap rolls across the carpet. I send my stepdad the text. "Craig, Mom's tired. The vortex didn't work. We're gonna stay in Ridgecrest. Love you, home tomorrow."

Pulling on the sliding glass door, I step out onto the motel balcony. Far away, Venus floats alone like a belly ring pierced in space. Dogs howl after sirens up the highway. Beneath the mountains, the steel power poles stretch silhouetted through the sand. The poet and essayist John Daniel, once a teacher of mine, didn't know that the shamans of China Lake were trying to make rain, but he says what I want to say better than I can at the moment. In *The Trail Home*, Daniel writes: "Anthropomorphic figures are common in rock art, and we too have created many. Ours are of the colossal scale that characterizes many of our marks on the west, standing in perfect straight lines across flats and over mountains, each one identical to the others, continuous lengths of high-tension cable passing between them. Like the Indian anthropomorphs, these are related to the power of nature, but to a different kind of power. They are not made in humility, to connect the makers with the spiritual powers of Earth. These are made to carry away the power of rivers, extracted by dams, and the ancient power of the sun, extracted in coalmines and burned in gargantuan plants whose smoke turns the clear desert distance to haze. These towers made in our image carry the captured life of nature to distant cities — they carry it one way only, out of the land and into the widening mouth of our human craving." Yet John Daniel may be a bit sentimental. I don't think the shamans created their images in perfect humility. The trail home is more complicated, more twisted.

My mom tells me to plug in her phone.

"Don't let it die," she says.

"Are you sure you don't need anything?"

"No. Thank you."

A toilet flushes behind the wall and someone starts coughing. I stare at a hole punched in the drywall beside the bathroom, then refill her water glass and set it on the bedstand. Heavy footsteps thunder down the overhung hallway outside our door.

YouTube user almanulinux writes of David Keith: "I would say that the best this guy should do if he is a bit interested in this planet is to buy a gun and kill himself."

Someone named crudhousefull writes: "Oh my god. Kill me before these idiots do."

Rick Ish writes of Caldeira: "I feel a bit sorry for the people wielding *all this power*—how do they look each other or anyone in the eye? Any sane person with an ounce of humanity would die of guilt being so narcissistic; they have a lot to answer for."

Ria den Breejen writes: "Ken Caldeira lies even more and dares no second to look straight into the camera."

Anthony Barrett writes, again, to Caldeira: "I HOPE YOU AND YOUR UNSCIENTIFIC SCUM MATES HAVE A NICE TIME IN HELL."

When I met Ken Caldeira at Stanford, I found him to be a shy, quiet man somewhat impaired when it came to making eye contact, which didn't particularly surprise me. I wanted to meet Ken because of an especially striking statement he'd made—namely, that his work represented, chiefly, "an expression of despair." Outside of a few of the most misanthropic and bleak metal bands, I hadn't heard too many people summarize their job in such terms. Needless to say, I was impressed, and I didn't expect to greet the most sanguine individual. But I had to ask, "Should I despair as well?" And I thought I had to truly look him in the eye, meet him face to face, in order to know the answer.

Caldeira walks like any man might if forced to bear some portion of total human failure. He looks like my stepfather, except his back's a bit more bent, his thinning hair fizzes out a little further, and when he stands, the slight hunch keeps his gaze focused on the sidewalk two feet in front of his sandals instead of six. I supposed, at first, that his body had simply adapted to long hours crouched over keyboards while supercomputers cranked out their month-long climate models, but it seemed an odd posture, especially for someone supposedly studying how to inject sulfur aerosols 100,000 feet into the stratosphere. But Ken occasionally glances up, and when he does his grin is mostly warm, and his words ring calm. Yet you can still see inside his eyes that his mind never stops working, and while we walked across the Stanford campus, while he kept his hands clasped behind his back in thoughtful professor pose, I couldn't help thinking the entire time that he looked like a prisoner in handcuffs.

"Is there more to it than irony?" he asked, when I told him about China Lake.

It was Friday. Caldeira had dressed casually. A salmon-colored Tommy Bahama button-down, faded blue jeans, and leather sandals. He camouflaged well with the sunny Spanish colonial architecture, the geometrical stands of palm trees, the general privileged, monastic calm that permeates one of the world's top research institutions.

"I was hoping you could tell me. Native American shamans and the US military chose the same place to make rain. It didn't work for either."

"Hmm," he said. "Well, primitive cultures were always concerned with modifying the weather."

I was surprised that he'd agreed to meet me, considering all the death threats on YouTube and my essential anonymity. When I pulled my rental car into the Carnegie Institution parking lot and left it unlocked without a permit in front of a Tow Away sign beside a dumpster and started hurrying past the rows of green houses, my army surplus rucksack slung over my shoulder, eyes darting in every direction, I could easily have been any random inspired psycho embarking on a campus killing spree. But I was already three minutes late. I didn't know where I was going. I didn't want to miss him. And in reality, anyway, geoengineering isn't yet high on the radar of the common citizen. As for the chemtrail people, most seem too caught up in sideline conspiracies involving aliens, Illuminati symbols, and wire systems implanted under their skin to ever focus long enough on a decision-making process that might result in destroying anything other than themselves. But when geo-engineering becomes a true political choice, some scientists might find themselves keeping tighter security.

One of the first things Caldeira told me when I met him was that he planned to quit the subject.

"The bulk of my work on geoengineering is probably done."

"Why?" I asked.

"Well, really, I'm not that interested in it anymore."

He said, as I knew, that he did a lot of the initial SRM computer modeling. When he started, he never intended to enter the field. He'd earned his PhD studying under Marty Hoffert at NYU in 1991. Hoffert was one of the most vocal, apocalyptic, and partially poetic scientific voices calling for global climate change mitigation. His diatribes against fossil fuel corporations painted dismal pictures of a future "feudal agricultural economy in high latitude lands still fertile for crops and habitable in climate" or, in the worst-case scenario, "hunter-gathering capable of supporting perhaps a million or so humans worldwide." He spoke of Carl Sagan and the Fermi paradox. He said the short "lifetimes of technological civilizations," such as our own, were the "reason for the absence of intelligent life in our Milky Way galaxy."

Needless to say, Hoffert's words sounded extreme, not many listened, and Caldeira moved on to better projects. Three years after graduating from NYU, he started running models behind the barbed wire black-budget fences of the Lawrence Livermore National Laboratory, just south of San Francisco, a laboratory with "near-mythological status as the dark heart of weapons research." Caldeira worked alongside Lowell Wood, protégé of Edward Teller, the man who built the hydrogen bomb and inspired, if that's the right term, Kubrick's *Dr. Strangelove*. Wood supposedly still enjoyed the Dr. Evil moniker given him by his Cold War critics; Caldeira, however, a former antinuke activist, did not enjoy all his research at Lawrence Livermore. "We sat around the room thinking of ways to manipulate geophysical systems to use them as a weapon." During one project, they tried to determine whether the United States could shoot tidal waves across oceans by detonating hydrogen bombs underwater. In another, they studied spreading lethal pathogens through clouds. It wasn't cheerful work. And when Caldeira ran the first sophisticated geoengineered climate model in 2000, it was largely to discredit the belligerent pronouncements of his veteran colleague Lowell Wood, who had argued that it was necessary to bypass "the bureaucratic suppression of CO_2," that "mitigation wasn't going to happen," and that the US government should simply go ahead and begin geoengineering for "instant climate gratification." According to Wood, it was simply common sense, no different from anything we'd already done: "We've engineered every other environment we live in — why not the planet?"

Strangely, much to Caldeira's surprise, he found in his initial model that Lowell Wood was basically right. Sulfur aerosol injections actually did appear to cool the planet.

"That was exciting, and we've learned a lot since then," Caldeira told me, "but I want to do new research and identify new problems. That's what keeps me engaged as a scientist."

I wondered if he wasn't speaking offhand, proffering the academy's eternal dictum — Fiat lux! Let there be light! — the command to discover and illuminate new frontiers as some sort of excuse to duck out of the current territory, a broad tableland that seemed to me still awash in shadow and, if not altogether unexplored, at least worthy of more thorough mapping.

"Is it possible that you're quitting now because you no longer want to be identified with the technology? You don't want your name on it if it comes to deployment?"

He lifted his head and smiled.

"No. That's not it. It's just not exciting to me anymore. The field has sort of plateaued. The party has arrived."

I found him upstairs in the Department of Global Ecology, a long two-story building adorned with lateral planks of giant redwood. A stone tower rises from the southwest corner. It looks like it should hold a church bell, but it catches the coastal wind and cools the building without wasting power. I had expected locked gates, a receptionist, security, someone to beep me in, but no one came. I stood alone in the concrete lobby, beneath hip glass garage doors pinned back on their tracks, and listened while water dripped down the hollow cooling tower. The fat plops ticked off the seconds, dropping and bursting on a grate of rusted iron while a breeze blew through the open entrance, lifting magazine pages from a coffee table made of recycled residential doors.

Above the threshold at the back wall, I noticed a camera.

The best option seemed up.

I climbed the stairs and continued down a long hallway. Gray caps of industrial carpet reflected skylights fogged from distant rain and seagull shit. "You must be looking for lunch," Caldeira said, opening the door after I'd paced another minute outside his office, glancing through the chicken wire glass, certain I'd found the face from YouTube.

He ordered food on his computer while I glanced around his office. He had some woven tapestries, bright stuff with a lot of maroon — Stanford colors — brought back from South America, it seemed.

"We're enemies."

He stopped typing and gave me a sudden worried look. His office door was closed, the building quiet.

"Enemies?"

I told him I did my undergrad across the bay at Berkeley.

"Oh," he said, sort of laughing. "Go, Bears."

He stood then and we started down the hallway, back out toward the lobby. A colleague and two students joined us outside. We walked behind them for a quarter mile to a central quad surrounded on one side by a food court. Heavy old oak trees made shade for picnic tables hewn from the same wood. Ken opened a compostable take-out box to reveal a kale and quinoa salad tossed in olive oil and balsamic vinegar. I watched the dappled bands of sunlight filter through the trees, glittering over the dark leaves while he stabbed them.

"SRM has the problem of eroding political will," he said, "but it also gave conservatives this idea of a quick fix, forcing them to look at SRM's science, and when they did and recognized its dangers, they were basically looking at the reality of climate change."

I tore the tinfoil from the blunt end of a grilled chicken burrito while one of Ken's students — a pretty girl in a yellow pleated chiffon dress — sat down beside me with a smoothie. She never spoke or removed her Ray-Bans, and no one ever introduced her. The same was true for the Chinese graduate student who sat across from me. He looked about my age.

"By a roundabout," Caldeira covered his mouth while he continued chewing, "SRM has made some climate deniers reconsider a business-as-usual strategy."

I stuck out my teeth and bit down, and several black beans fell from the burrito and bounced across the table. I wondered how fast I could chew without looking like I was starving to death, insane, or high on meth. It seemed a pitiable waste of time to clog my face with bits of chicken breast when I could fire off questions at one of the world's most influential scientists. But Ken seemed happy to talk. And after his gaze roamed around the table, flitting over the oak branches, past the pale blank faces of pedestrians — students and strangers — he eventually looked straight at me. Perhaps all Caldeira needs to convince the world of his good intentions is a tossed kale salad.

He took another bite.

"You should read Alan Robock's article," he told me.

There was nothing smug or stiff about him, and if his students remained silent, I figured it was because they'd heard all this before.

"It lists all the potential reasons why solar radiation management might be a bad idea. I think there are twenty-five or something close to that. I'm not sure."

The only problem was that Caldeira also wasn't telling me anything I hadn't already heard. Of course I'd read Robock's article. Every academic paper I'd read on the subject eventually said the same thing: solar geoengineering offers a fast, cheap, and fully imperfect solution to climate change. That was why I needed to talk to him. I wanted to know just how fast and how flawed. Behind all the computer models, academic papers, and cautious pronouncements, what did the scientist really think — what did he see when he imagined the future?

"Yeah, I've read Robock. I think he's actually up to twenty-eight reasons now."

Caldeira's colleague sat down beside me then, across from Ken, and pulled out a white-bread sandwich. It fit perfectly inside his

Ziploc bag, and I watched his fingers pick through it carefully, peeling back the zippered plastic like a surgeon stretching tweezers toward a sterile alcohol swab. I wondered if his wife had made it and if she used mayonnaise.

Caldeira asked him the name of the Robock article.

"I'm not sure," he said.

He told me I'd find it online.

I took a bite of the burrito and chewed fast, repeating all my questions like a Buddhist mantra — questions I'd written down the night before in my notebook and then rewritten an hour before sitting in a crowded Palo Alto café, narrowing them down to the ten essential ones that I thought I could memorize — while Ken's colleague started talking about another paper he had to write and Ken advised him not to devote too much time to it.

I cut in at the first pause but didn't ask anything planned.

"Ken, it's not clear to me why you want to stop researching SRM." I moved my tongue over the roof of my mouth, scraping off the stuck tortilla. "We won't begin to see the planet start to cool this century unless," I said, swallowing, "we engage in solar radiation management. Right?"

"Yes. That's basically right."

"So why do you want to quit?"

Wasn't this the most pressing topic a scientist could study? What could be more exciting than potentially saving the world? Or were we so far gone that despair had finally overwhelmed him? Or if he thought the technology might actually stave off the future, wasn't he at least concerned about his own personal safety? I knew that David Keith had already officially reported two death threats to police.

It was strange to realize and hard to believe at first, but Ken Caldeira wants to quit researching solar radiation management because he really is bored. There's nothing really exciting, nothing more substantial, that he can actually learn.

"More small-scale research is necessary," he said, "but basically we won't know what will happen until a full-scale deployment."

I asked if that meant that he disagreed with his friend David

Keith, who argues that field tests are a crucial component of any rationally managed SRM program.

"David's correct that the technology is basically simple and fast-acting, but field tests won't tell us much. We won't actually know what will happen until we're full scale."

If Caldeira isn't lying, then the CIA-funded geoengineering study probably isn't either when it says that "there are no field tests planned for this study." Its authors claim to be looking at how the public might react—the social response—and beyond that at the moral, historical, and political precedents that might illuminate the complexities of any actual deployment. They're doing social science. Gathering intelligence. No testing.

"Well, I know some scientists have called for a US geoengineering research program on the scale of the Manhattan or Apollo Project. Do you think . . ."

He smiled again and cut me off.

"A Manhattan-like project is unnecessary. The US government doesn't need to spend forever researching and developing. There's already a company—Aurora Flight Sciences—that says they could do it for $8 billion annually."

I knew this already. David Keith managed the Aurora study, and Bill Gates' FICER fund paid for it.*

"So if the US government really wanted to deploy an SRM system, how soon could it start?"

"We could have a full-scale operation ready to go in one year."

Jesus, I thought. Caldeira balanced some quinoa on his plastic fork while the girl in the chiffon dress rubbed her finger across the face of her cell phone.

Caldeira's colleague then said something very strange. Perhaps he was merely testing me, baiting me to see if I'd grab at the conspiracy hook and destroy whatever small credibility I had in their circle. Perhaps he was merely joking. Perhaps he was serious. He spoke of the SPICE experiment attempted in Britain, the one that protesters shut down in 2011.

"The SPICE experiment was a failure, but it did prove one thing," he said. "The public will be dead set against the technology."

He stared across the table at Caldeira.

"If I was going to do it," he said, "the research has to be top secret, and you deliver the aerosols in secret. Otherwise, the public will never allow it to happen."

The thought crossed my mind that if the technology could be ready to go in one year, maybe that year was last year. If it was so cheap that any determined billionaire could feasibly deploy it rogue, maybe a government $18 trillion in debt with a history of unilateral preemptive action could also go rogue if it really believed in the possibility of rapid and catastrophic climate change, if it really wanted to block, as Princeton's Stephen Pacala called it, the monster behind the door.

I asked the two men if they thought that the US government should go ahead and begin sulfur aerosol injections in secret.

Caldeira's colleague had made his point.

He stared at Ken, and Ken sat poker-faced, and I watched his eyes sift through his skull, his gaze rubbing along the table's wood grain, past the handle of the plastic fork that had fallen into the salad until he blew a sigh, made a grimace, and scratched the hair behind his wristwatch.

He stared back at his colleague.

"I don't really think people are going to be that much against it," he said.

Sitting there, it occurred to me that David Keith's strategy of gradual field tests would work brilliantly as public distraction. We could do a few tiny, insignificant trials, squirt a few drops of sulfur from a weather balloon, and after five or ten so-called experiments, from which nothing whatsoever could be learned, scientists and government alike could concur that the technology didn't work, or that it was far too dangerous, or that it was still too early to take any levelheaded steps. With the public so soothed, the spraying could commence — or continue — in secret.

"Mining operations in the United States have put so much barium in the air progressively over so many years," Caldeira said, "that the levels today are astounding. But nobody said anything as it was happening, because it occurred gradually. The same could work with geoengineering. People might not say anything because the initial effects could appear negligible."

I asked him if the sky would turn white.

"I don't think so," he said.

"Really?" I said. "Alan Robock . . ."

He cut me off and continued.

"Whatever whitening may occur will probably be negligible to the human eye. You wouldn't likely notice any difference."

"What about the stars?"

He said the same. "You'd still be able to see the stars. You wouldn't detect any noticeable change."

"Alan Robock says the sky will turn white and we'll lose the stars."

"Does he?"

I asked Ken if he thought it was possible that Robock might be overstating the aesthetic impact because he didn't want to see the technology ever go to deployment.

"It's possible," he said. "I think Alan Robock and I disagree about the importance of the social response."

"What about the termination problem?"— the idea that if the system ever shuts down, temperatures might rise fast enough to turn our species and all others to toast.

"The termination problem gets too much attention and is far overstated."

I asked him if he thought we'd actually do it.

"There will have to be a climate emergency."

This was one of the questions I had memorized.

"What exactly will constitute a climate emergency? I mean, given the natural variability of the earth's climate system, isn't it impossible to pin a single weather-related event on climate change? Even with computer models, it would take decades, maybe hundreds of years, of data to definitively attribute a single specific event to climate change. Right? So how exactly will we know when we've reached an emergency?"

I stared at them.

Ken and his colleague burst out laughing.

I looked around the quad, thinking that someone must have tripped and fallen. Perhaps two squirrels stood embattled above us on the arm of an oak bough.

But they were staring back at me.

The girl in the chiffon dress wrapped her lips around the smoothie straw.

I sat smiling, waiting shamefaced for some loud censure of my futility. It was as though the entire conversation had been resolved by a statement spoken beyond the bounds of absurdity. I hoped they'd clarify the joke or at least answer my question, but no one ever did explain my stupidity.

It was disconcerting. But I think now that perhaps the objective caution, the practiced detachment that urges scientific minds away from stating what they might actually think or imagine — or truly hold in their hearts — found a sudden accidental expression. Scientists like Ken Caldeira don't earn their daily bread confessing their emotions before bed in a diary. They don't win lifetime research positions at Stanford by painting blurry pictures of recurrent dreams. Their imagination does not get paid until it produces something practical. They make good money and forge solid careers upon highly crafted computer models, from which they export expert data, and they interpret their numbers in peer-reviewed papers carefully — conservatively — if they want to appear reasonable and remain reputable and comfortable on the academic job market.

But what happened at that moment, what their laughter spoke to, I think, was the absolute poverty of my imagination. I couldn't see what they'd seen. For me a climate emergency was still an abstraction, just some vague platonic ideal of perfect destruction, but they'd been there a long time, circled around the world, sorted through the endless monotony of recurrent climate simulations, and they'd gathered enough good, solid, reputable data to convince themselves that they'd seen something concrete, an impeccable picture developing in the dark rooms of their brilliant minds, clarifying as they carried it across the continents, decades, and carpeted halls of government, growing steadily into a reality that so violently outstripped the bounds of all natural variability that only man or

God could have created it, and now they couldn't shut it out, now it had arrived complete and luminous, it came bounding through their lips in a sudden bright burst of terrible hilarity, a booming laughter that was itself an expression of staid wonder, stored grief, and familiar boredom, a boredom born from the fact that here they sat supposedly talking to some sort of writer, a creative type, and not even he had permitted his mind to picture it — but I could hear it — the monster behind the door, the calamity we'd carelessly fed and religiously furthered for far too long, so long now that if they broke down the door we could only, possibly, buy time by poisoning ourselves with a solution so brutal, ugly, and unsophisticated that it could only constitute an affront to their genius.

I suppose it was hilarious. The ice sheets of Greenland don't slide out to sea several times a season like monsoons in Southeast Asia. Such an unprecedented catastrophe defies the imagination, and yet it had already begun. Ken and his friend were laughing for all of us, I guess, laughing, as Nietzsche says, "in order not to die of the truth." And what was the truth? They were trapped. They were scientists. Not poets. And neither could change the world. If they painted a metaphoric picture more complex or disturbing than the platitude of monsters, if they spoke of their nightmares and visions, if rather than laughing they started screaming insults and empirically based prophecies, people still wouldn't see, and of course they wouldn't believe. They would only end up discrediting themselves. They and others like them had already presented the data, and in spite of all the evidence, emissions continued to rise.

No wonder Caldeira was bored. No wonder he laughed.

And yet, "I think we'll muddle through it, or at least the rich will make it okay," he told me, sitting beneath the oak trees that Leland Stanford had planted with the cash left over from the railroad. The railroad that he persuaded Congress to pay for and that made him billions in his day. The railroad that finally closed, in the American mind, the imagination of a limitless frontier, the narrative that you could leave everything behind, forget your past, and carve a new life in the wilderness of the West.

"Adaptation is a nonelective course," Caldeira said.

He closed his lunch box and threw it away, and I followed him down a path different from the one we'd come in on. I struggled to recall my mantra of questions. For some reason I kept picturing the painting from my childhood bedroom, *Westward the Course of Empire Takes Its Way*. The original, a brazen twenty-by-thirty-foot congratulation of America's manifest destiny, towers over the western staircase of the House of Representatives where several years ago Caldeira, then advocating for more geoengineering research, asked Congress: "What if we were to find out that parts of Greenland were sliding into the sea, and that sea-level might rise 10 feet by mid-century?"

I wondered if he'd glanced at *Westward* before he spoke and what he'd thought of it at the time. Did he see the long-suffering pioneer woman still sitting at the center of the painting, still staring cross-eyed in the wrong direction?

"What if rainfall patterns shifted in a way that caused massive famines?"

Did he see the birds flying like griffins to devour the men at the summit's platform?

"What if our agricultural heartland turned into a perpetual dust bowl?"

Did he see the dramatic evening sky over the Promised Land? The scattered clouds lending the texture and patina of pyrite, a scarred quality, to something that should be so soft and yet seems ready to topple?

"And what if research told us that an appropriate placement of tiny particles in the stratosphere could reverse all or some of these effects?"

I wanted to ask him.

"We do not want our seat belts to be tested for the first time when we are in an automobile accident," Caldeira told Congress. "If the seat belts are not going to work, it would be good to know that now."

Did he see the barren hills of Berkeley, the future site of the Lawrence Livermore National Laboratory, rising misted at the bottom of the painting?

There is the "potential," he told Congress, "that direct intervention in the climate system could someday save lives and reduce human suffering."

The title of Leutze's *Westward* refers to the final lines of a poem written by George Berkeley, a poem that, years ago in college, I used to recite silently, almost unconsciously at times, while I sat between classes on a brick stairway beneath the campanile listening to the late afternoon bells toll as Tool blasted on my headphones.

Westward the course of empire takes its way;
The four first acts already past.
A fifth shall close the drama with the day:
Time's noblest offspring is the last.

Berkeley wrote his poem in 1726 as an ode to America, the continent where he'd hoped to establish a prestigious new university, but his daughter died and funding dried up. Things didn't work out. At least not initially, not while he was alive.

For a time, I thought the university still subscribed to his theory of immaterialism. "To be is to be perceived," Berkeley wrote. He'd argued against John Locke that reality was made up solely of minds and their ideas, that the body, as an external substance, and all its physical surroundings — trees, mountains, people, and animals — did not really exist. Apparently, as an undergraduate himself, Berkeley decided he wanted to experience nonexistence firsthand. He told his friend to cut him down only after he'd passed out. Then he hanged himself from a rope. I guess George Berkeley was pretty metal. Perhaps the blackout served as inspiration for his later philosophical works. I remember thinking it obscene that for $15,000 a year I couldn't take a proper piss when I wanted one. In reality, though, it wasn't Berkeley's philosophy that had inspired the university's founders but his famous poem, and the library bathrooms were often locked that semester not because anyone suspected that our bodies weren't real but rather that they were — and so too a few minds with certain ideas. That same spring a kid at Virginia Tech pulled a Glock 19 from his backpack and killed thirty-two people before turning the gun on himself, and security was tight.

But there were still plenty of bushes and fountains and a few scattered redwood groves. Even at a school with more than 30,000 students, you could always find an isolated place to reflect or relieve yourself in silence. It wasn't just a large campus with a pretty view. It was lonely and inspiring, very badly inspiring, especially around sunset. Especially late in the spring of 1866 — 140 years after Berkeley's poem and 5 years after Leutze's *Westward*—when the future University of California trustees stood gazing west through the Golden Gate out to the Pacific Ocean. Inspired by the burning sunset, the intersection of sea and land, heaven and earth, hard work and inheritance, the trustees honed in on a name that would pay tribute to the college as the culminating institution of an age-old process of westward expansion and gradual enlightenment. They named the school after the philosopher, poet, and theologian George Berkeley, settled on the motto "Let there be light," and began clearing the dense stands of redwoods.

The grizzly bear, shot nearly to extinction, became the school's mascot.

Ornate buildings rose up among the hills, each aligned for sightlines through the bridgeless headlands of the Golden Gate out over the final plane of expansion, the Pacific, and it was this view I'd contemplate in the afternoons beneath the concrete obelisk of the campanile, whose hollow carapace housed the bones of tyrannosaurs and buffalo and beside which stone grizzlies the size of guinea pigs sat on carved benches, their heads hung low in remembrance not of themselves but of the brave sons of California who died in the Great War, and before that in the Philippines, and then later in World War II, their bodies shipped back across the Pacific during that century when military training was still compulsory on campus, and as I sat on the red brick steps, fact and myth wrestling for footing, it was this same sea that the pilgrims painted in Leutze's *Westward* saw like the glittering eye of God as they stood agape upon mountain peaks, and it was this sea that lay reflecting the molten dusk every day beside the stalagmite projection of downtown San Francisco skyscrapers while the smog hovered like campfire fumes above the city and the cars honked their way across the bridge and the subway slithered down beneath the brown bay water, part of a panorama that filled me at once with awe and dread and a vague inspiration as the final lines of Berkeley's poem droned inside my brain, like some sort of secret encoded across time, something that might allow me to trust the absurd sense of freedom and possibility I felt here as a freshman over the pessimism I'd armored myself with since childhood, if I could only figure out what Berkeley meant by "time's noblest offspring is the last," if only today it didn't sound so cynical, so mocking from every angle, if only I could turn it around again, somehow, unlearn something I didn't yet know I already knew and haven't understood still, but I couldn't and probably won't and it was Berkeley's poem, the words "westward the course of empire takes its way," that inspired the university's trustees, and it was this poem—"On the Prospect of Planting Art and Learning in America," it's called—that I wanted to ask Ken Caldeira about now as we turned and continued down a narrow path tunneled through the grove of pepper trees that led back to Stanford's Carnegie Institution.

I decided to rephrase the question.

"Scott Barrett of Columbia University has called climate change the most difficult collective-action problem in human history. As Americans, *what are we learning* about ourselves in the course of confronting this massive problem? Are we sadistic, bent on destruction? Is it human nature to procrastinate?"

"If Congress had put huge taxes on carbon emissions," Caldeira said, "the economic incentive would have been so great that we already would have had carbon capture and storage and we wouldn't be in this position."

I wondered how long this position could last and if it wouldn't end up worse after more men like Caldeira generously volunteered their expert opinions before Congress. But I couldn't really blame him. I think he was really trying to help—he'd always foremost recommended mitigation. Nonetheless, be it the oil lobby, the fetish of the growth economy, or the innate hubris of humankind, our government had not taken the supposed rational steps necessary to prevent climate change.

Caldeira was like a doctor still prescribing exercise after diagnosing cancer. A doctor who could only console the future with the promise that chemo was cheap.

"What are we learning?" Caldeira said. "I like to think of something my friend Marty Hoffert says. The reason we haven't solved this collective-action problem is because we basically still have these caveman brains left over from prehistory. In a nutshell, we've built a technologically globalized world that our brains are no longer adapted to. Most people can't think in terms of some geographically isolated event or some scenario a decade away."

We stopped to allow a gardener in a golf cart to pass. I pulled out my e-cig, cupped the tip, and inhaled.

"That's why someone's cute dog today gets more of an emotional response than news of havoc on some faraway continent."

This was the basic premise of Berkeley's philosophy.

Regardless of whether anyone takes the doctrine "to be is to be perceived" seriously, the idea contains a disturbing psychological truth. Things tend to not really exist until they disrupt our day, impose on our lives, and in doing so enter firmly into our consciousness. "Things that are temporally and spatially remote," Caldeira said, "things we can't directly perceive . . ." He went on for a while about the vision of his teacher Marty Hoffert, but it's better to let the man speak for himself:

> Stepping back from the immediate moment, one could say that all this is implicit when naked apes with a big brain adapted to live short brutish lives of hunter-gatherers on the African Savannah stumble upon agriculture freeing some to develop writing and culture and eventually the scientific and industrial revolutions leading to their explosive growth, like a cancer, over the entire planet Earth. We invented the technology which extended our lives and changed everything about what we need to survive, but never adapted in a genetic Darwinian sense to the new global environment we created. Some might say this is necessarily a time bomb, that we have all the wrong instincts to live with our technology, and that climate change is the leading edge of a wave of destruction needed to restart the process. The fact that people aren't willing to make the personal sacrifices to combat the climate change they created is interesting and true but it isn't in my opinion the most important question. The most important question is whether *Homo sapiens* can adopt a narrative leading to the sustainable existence of high tech civilization on Earth.

In 2003, Ken Caldeira authored a paper with Marty Hoffert and Gregory Benford. They called for "a concerted Apollo-like program" that would "conquer the technical problems of global warming mitigation." They found it "heartening that *Apollo 11* landed on the moon less than a decade" after JFK declared it a national goal. Their article recommended "running a renewable energy theme exhibit at Disney World exclusively on solar and wind power." Unfortunately, however, Disney did not accept this advice, and needless to say, a decade later the United States and the world have failed to institute any Apollo-like programs that would transform our energy and transportation systems. Instead, Hoffert said later, "the US, China and India" forcibly built "the wrong energy infrastructure for the second half of the 21st century with their 900 new conventional coal electric power plants." Policy makers "have no inkling how dangerous these plants will be."

Today it is probably too late to prevent the planet from warming by 2°C, the maximum amount we might be able to manage to prevent the most severe effects of climate change. It's probably too late to avert even worse warming.

Caldeira sees only irony at China Lake, but his teacher, Marty Hoffert, sees further. We are carving a primitive future for ourselves. We may soon begin making petroglyphs again.

> If we fail, I can imagine a thousand years from now a small fragment of humankind barely surviving the new planetary climate huddled around a fire in some remote northern latitude observing the night sky, subsisting perhaps as hunter-gatherers on a vastly different and biologically depleted planet listening to a tale vaguely recalled in ancestral memory by the local shaman.

I stood with Ken in front of the Carnegie Institution's Department of Global Ecology. The sun had swung around to hover behind the trees somewhere over the Pacific now.

"So basically we won't know if geoengineering will work, or what it actually might do, until we have to deploy it at full scale, and we don't know if we'll have to do it, and we don't know how bad climate change is really going to be, but it might be bad. Is that right?"

Ken smiled. I could see that he wanted to get back to his work. He'd talked to me for an hour and a half, and I didn't want to waste any more of his time.

"Yes. I think that's basically where we're at," he said.

I could hear the water dripping down the empty bell tower, plopping on the rusted wrought iron.

"So everything is uncertainty?" I said.

I felt like I was eight years old again.

"You shouldn't be surprised," he said. "That's the human condition. It's always been this way."

I knew more than I had before, and yet I still knew nothing at all. It was possible they were spraying now, possible they weren't and would never have to, possible that throughout my lifetime the checkerboards carved by geoengineering could allow me to continue checking my e-mail. It was possible we'd all muddle through it.

Other things were possible as well.

"It's all uncertainty," Caldeira said. "You've read the existentialists."

It was like talking to my father, the conversation we never had, him telling me to deal with it, be a man, I cannot help you, good-bye.

"Do you have a girlfriend?" he asked me.

"Yeah."

"Well, when I married my wife, I didn't know what she'd be like in twenty years. You can never predict the future. But you have to continue living. It's the human condition," he said again.

"The human condition," I repeated.

I didn't ask what his wife was like now, or if they'd actually spent twenty years together. I thanked him for his time, we shook hands, and he climbed the stairs.

She smiles in embarrassment, caught in the bright net of the digital flashbulb, while my mother snores. I don't want to think anymore, but there's nowhere to go, no way to turn off my brain. I shouldn't have saved these pictures of my ex-girlfriend, shouldn't be here. Green eyes. Long legs. Red lips. I can hear her voice still. "Goodnight," she says from a bedroom in Portland. I switch the laptop to hibernate, close the screen, and unplug my e-cig before crossing the room and turning out the lamp. The room is dark.

I refill the glass of water on the nightstand and crawl in bed with my mother. The motel had only single queens left.

"Do you remember our first house?" she says suddenly, her voice graveled, low.

"The apartment?"

I stare at the ceiling and try not to move.

"Yeah."

"What about it?"

"Nothing. I've just been thinking about it. I think I had a dream."

When I hiked through the Coso Range with David Whitley, I remember asking him if there were any petroglyphs that represented the black magic work of sorcerer-shamans. He said there were several. "There are a handful of vulva motifs in the tablelands to the north."

"The first time my back went out," she says, "you were a baby, and I was totally alone. I turned off the vacuum and crawled down to the floor, and when you started crying in the morning I couldn't make it up the stairs."

"You've told me before."

"That house was nice, though. It was old, a little run-down, but I kept it nice, or I tried to. I was so proud of you."

"Mel Manor Dive," I say.

She laughs through a sigh.

"It wasn't really a dive."

The apartment where I lived for the first four years of my life was on Mel Manor Drive. The Mel Manor Apartments. It was supposed to be temporary.

"When I moved in there, I was six months pregnant with you. I felt lost and afraid."

She only ever referred to the house as Mel Manor Drive. Whenever she said it, I always heard Mel Manor Dive, and that's what

I called it as a kid. I thought there was a pool somewhere with a diving board, but I never went looking for it, and there wasn't one really. I never got the joke.

"It wasn't too expensive, and it had a nice little yard where you could play."

Some of my earliest memories are of lying in the grass and hugging our dog, a twelve-year-old cocker spaniel named Sunny.

"And you were such an adorable, beautiful child. You were so well cared for, and I was so proud of you."

She clears her throat and takes a drink of water.

"I'll always remember at night getting your little teeth brushed, combing your little hair. It was a ritual. You never fought at all. And I'd sing, 'Looking so good, looking so fine, that's my Barr, and he's mine oh mine!' and you'd get so tickled. Do you remember that?"

"Not really."

I sit up in bed, look around for a clock, and find my cell phone in my jeans. A band of yellow light covers the carpet beneath the door. I walk over and recheck the locks.

"What's wrong with you?"

"Nothing," I say, "I'm just tired."

Behind the drapes, the sky glitters, smashed with stars.

"And I'd pick you up and bring you to the rocking chair and read to you and sing. Sometimes you picked out your own book. You loved *Goodnight Moon*. You held on to me until you fell asleep and I'd set you in bed and go downstairs and collapse on the couch.

"And then on Fridays, I'd get you up early, take you to day care, work all day, and pick you up again. And I'd sing on the drive home, 'It's Friday . . . it's Friday . . . our favorite day of the week—boom, boom—tomorrow we get to sleep—boom, boom. It's Friday . . . it's Friday.'"

"I don't want to talk about this right now."

"Come on. Do you remember our Friday-night song?"

"Yeah."

"I'd stop and get a bottle of champagne and I'd get you ready for bed and then I'd psycho clean the house till one or two in the morning. You were asleep so I wasn't interrupted. And the house needed to be cleaned. No one was going to clean it but me. You slept

so well. I could vacuum your room sometimes and you wouldn't even wake up. And I'd play music, and as the evening wore on and the champagne took effect, I'd get to feeling kind of chipper. I'd wake up feeling like a princess in the morning because my house was clean. I didn't have anxiety over something that needed to be tended to. And we'd lounge around and you'd watch cartoons and I'd make you pancakes, and then we'd drive to the laundromat and go grocery shopping. We'd stop by your grandma's. She loved you so much. And your grandpa used to always make you laugh and laugh. Sometimes you'd help him mow the lawn."

I stare at the ceiling and try to picture him, but it's mostly a face frozen in black-and-white photographs.

"Do you remember him at all?"

"Not really."

The only living memory I have of my grandfather is bringing him beers. I would run out to the garage and grab him a Budweiser and a grape soda for myself, and later, in order not to look at the green tubes that fed his face, I'd lean over the kitchen table and study the Budweiser can — a white-and-red foundation with the colors blue and gold carving out all the occult signs of empire — while the evening news thundered in the background. At the center of the can, a compass dial inlaid with pyramid gems circumscribed the known world. They all pointed outward like so many flames from a tiny blue sun that took its bearing from AMERICA, a single continent stamped at the dial's base. The compass housing was gold, and within it, squaring the circle, rested a white diamond. Along each of its sides and across the four golden segments, blue capitals spelled AUSTRALIA, EUROPE, AFRICA, ASIA. Inside the diamond, a fastened belt held the keys to mastery, looping a glowing scroll that displayed two letters, AB for Anheuser-Busch and my grandfather's initials: Adam Baumgart. With all the ornament and latticework, twisting hop vines and ripened wheat germ, griffins bearing capybaras over a sea of calligraphy I couldn't read — the cans were cut to inspire grandeur and always reminded me of American money. I remember asking my grandfather why we couldn't flatten them and turn them in at the bank. He liked to drop his cigarette butts in them when he was done. Rewarded by the pound for aluminum, he got more money from the recycler that way. I remember thinking that if I made lots of money, I could keep him alive. I had no idea then that there were already companies that would have stored his severed head in liquid nitrogen for $40,000. Too bad though that the cancer had already eaten through his upper esophagus.

"You were so precocious and adorable," my mom says. "I'll never forget you looking at me one day in the car, you were probably two, and I'd said something, and you asked, 'Mom, are you being facetious?' You were so awestruck by everything. You always wanted to see smoke coming out of chimneys and you liked looking down storm drains. I had to tear you away."

She mostly remembers the good times. And the bad times, the fights, she mostly glosses over. "You were hardheaded sometimes. But we're German. It's genetic. I had my moments, too. Once when you wouldn't eat, I wanted to strangle you. I stormed up to your room and slammed the dresser and that snow globe — the big one that played "When You Wish upon a Star"— it fell to the floor and shattered. I felt so bad." She doesn't remember the times when she told me that she wished I'd never been born, that she hadn't kept me.

"Do you remember that house?" she says.

"I have a few vague memories."

"It looked a little run-down on the outside, but when you came in it was nice and it was clean. It wasn't a dive. And you had a play area. You could go out in the front and I didn't have to worry about you. I could just look out the patio door and see the gate was locked."

Standing at the window, I can see the moon rising over the mountains to the east, just the tip, glinting like polished bone.

"Goodnight moon," she says. "Goodnight stars, goodnight air, good night noises everywhere."

"Do we have any more beer?"

"There's some vodka in my suitcase."

It's funny that she remembers me always sleeping soundly. When I think back to being tiny, I can only remember lying awake, the hours passing like epochs, each night a terrible new experiment. I never knew if she'd still be there in the morning when I woke up. I had to crawl back to her bed in the middle of the night to make sure she hadn't disappeared. I still feel it now but less so. You can never know what stands once your glance withdraws, what will continue to grow, if your lover survives somewhere, if a mother will return, if the sun will circle back to shower the world in warm morning light. That's the one thing that you can't teach a child — that they must not know. That living things must suffer. That it takes a long time to acquire the calluses that dirty the filters of perception. *Where did we come from, Mom? Where are we?* Please leave the TV on, the nightlight, too. I won't be afraid but please, *Where was I before I was born?* Why am I not someone else? When the moon rises, does it make a sound? I'm sorry. Will we live forever?

"I'll be glad to get home," she says, yawning.

"Me, too," I say.

But I've always found something depressing about returning to the place where I started. Traveling on foot, I always take a different route to and from my apartment in Iowa. Whenever I go backpacking in the Sierras, I prefer to do a loop. I never walk very far down San Diego beaches. "How far we all come," James Agee writes. "So far, so much between, you can never go home again. You can go home, it's good to go home, but you never really get all the way home again in your life."

"I'm going out," I say.

"Out?"

"Outside. I can't sleep."

"Be careful."

When she starts snoring again, I pour the vodka into my water bottle and unlock the door. A blue glow reflects on the stucco walls and shuttered windows at the end of the walkway.

But where is home? Is it back up the canyon, at the end of the freeway, over the mountains, the circling planes, and roving satellites? Do we belong to another world somewhere beyond the sky, a bright palace with a father in heaven, or is our proper home in fact beneath our feet, upon the earth that bears our weight, the oceans and soil to which our bones succumb?

The duality between the sun and dirt — sky and earth — prevails across all cultures: in the Chinese yin-yang where the female darkness and the male light interpenetrate; in the Native American cosmology of chaos and order, good and evil, kept in check partly by the shamans; and in the warring forces of irrationality and reason represented by the Greek gods Dionysus and Apollo. Dionysus was heir to the early Aegean chthonic religion. *Chthonic*, "of the earth," referred not to the surface of the globe but rather to its dark interior, in which churned the superabundant forces of procreative nature, the rot and womb of life that the Apollonian sky cult later tried to repress. Throughout the world, following the advent of shamanic trance and the organization of supernatural experience into cults of worship, the initial deities were most often feminine.

In Aegean Greece, before Zeus, Apollo, and the entire Olympian pantheon, human beings worshipped the Great Goddess, the Universal Mother. Above all, she symbolized fertility. She made the rains come, the crops grow, the sun turn. She gave birth to humans, the stars, the wild animals, and the roaring oceans. The early Aegean equation of woman and nature is nearly universal throughout the agrarian and hunter-gatherer societies of prehistory, which endured only at the mercy of Mother Nature's reproductive cycles.

In Native Californian mythology, the first god was also a woman. Ocean Mother and her daughter lived together at the center of a massive inland sea. It was Ocean Mother, like the Aegean Great Goddess, who gave birth to the first living creatures by mixing her own chthonic mud into the coherent shapes of bighorns, rattlesnakes, and coyotes. Yet Ocean Mother, like all the goddesses of prehistory's earth cults, wasn't simply a creator — she was also a destroyer. She and her daughter had vagina dentata — a toothed vagina. Together they survived as cannibals devouring the animal children of their own creation.

Similarly, in Aegean Greece, the Great Goddess was not only the guardian of life but also the sovereign of death. She didn't just nourish the children on her surface but also, whenever she deemed fit, devoured them in her own chthonic depths. The revival of Earth Mother imagery in today's New Age movement largely suppresses the monstrous half of prehistory's earth cults. As critic and historian Camille Paglia writes, "The femaleness of fertility religions is always double-edged. The Indian nature-goddess Kali" is always depicted "granting boons with one set of arms while cutting throats with the other. She is the lady in ringed skulls."

In later Greek mythology, the Great Goddess transformed into Gaia or Earth, and her supreme power diminished after she slept with her son, Uranus, the starlit sky, giving birth to the first race, the Titans. Gaia's importance decreased further during the Classical period, when her shrine at Delphi, the chief religious center of the Greek city-states, was rededicated to Apollo. Originally, the temple belonged to Gaia. According to myth, Zeus wanted to find the center of his Grandmother Earth and released two eagles from opposite ends of the globe. The point of the eagles' convergence determined the omphalos of the earth, the navel of Gaia, the primordial source of all life. During the Classical period, however, sometime around 500 B.C., Greek religion transferred the Oracle of Delphi to Apollo after he supposedly killed a dragon named Python that lived at the temple, guarding the earth's womb. After killing the toothed dragon, Apollo pitched its corpse into Gaia's depths and rebuilt the temple in his own image.

This myth represents a profound turn in the intellectual history of the Western world. After Apollo's conquest, the center of the earth, the procreative source of all life, passed from the dark and diffuse flux of Gaia's universal earth cult into the concentrated grip of Apollo's white marble hands. In the words of Paglia:

> Western culture from the start has swerved from femaleness. . . . From the beginning of time, woman seemed an uncanny being. Man honored but feared her. She was the black maw that spat him forth and would devour him anew. Men, bonding together, invented culture as a defense against female nature. Sky cult was the most sophisticated step in this process, for its switch of the creative locus from earth to sky is a shift from belly-magic to head-magic. . . . Man, repelled by his debt to a physical mother, created an alternate reality, a heterocosm to give him the illusion of freedom.

The cult of Apollo, which championed light, logic, and physical form, constituted the first and most definitive step in our quest to transcend nature, to surmount the contingency and chaos of our terrestrial birth and mortal imprisonment.

Today's Judeo-Christian tradition, wherein God the Father says, "Let there be light," survives as a vestigial Apollonian sky cult, shifting the world's productive source away from chthonic Mother Nature and into the head of masculine rationality. Christ never passed through the womb. In the cult of the Virgin, woman, stripped of all carnality, loses her fearsome double-edged aspect. "For the first time in human history the mother kneels before her son," Simone de Beauvoir writes, "she freely accepts her inferiority. This is the supreme masculine victory."

A similar conquest occurs in the Native American mythology of eastern California and the Coso Range, where Coyote, the father of man, uses the vertebrae of a bighorn sheep as a penis sheath to forcefully break the vagina dentata of Ocean Mother's daughter and, by their union, create the first humans, which Coyote in turn spills across the earth from an empty water jug. His use of the bighorn bones is no accident. In Native California, male bighorn sheep, like Apollo, were associated with light, the sky, and solid forms, the supposed antithesis of femininity. In the Paiute-Shoshone cosmos, spiritual power climaxed at the topmost layer of the sky, a realm of pure white, the exact sphere through which bighorn sheep, with their muscular white rumps, traversed daily in their perilous mountain ascents. Their elongated powerful necks, like the projecting light of Apollo, represented the ultimate symbol of masculinity. Male bighorns ram heads before mating, producing a sound like thunder. Their sturdy necks guarantee access to females and, as a metaphor, granted men the courage to break woman's vagina dentata, destroying her uncanny power, and transferring creative energy to the solidity of enlightened masculine ego. In the Coso Range, the sky cult of the bighorn sheep gave the shamans the power to make rain and, in turn, the power to fill the rivers and make plants grow — power, that is, over Mother Nature. Although the metaphors remain consistent cross-culturally, nowhere have they translated into such awesome practicality as in the Western intellect. The artistic and scientific achievements of Western culture are the direct outgrowth of the Apollonian mind, that is, of humankind's relentless attempt to escape the chaotic flux of nature. But repression does not erase reality, it merely buries unpleasant thoughts. And not for long. Today, amid our enormous environmental anxiety, we contemplate — against our will — the steady resurrection of Ocean Mother, Kali, Ishtar, Cybele, Astarte, and Isis, the great Earth Goddesses turning over in their graves, grinning as they rise in all their cruel and fang-whorled glory. Whether real or not, a figment of our imagination or true physical threat, the ghost of Gaia returns dressed in the guise of climate change, haunting our memory, commanding our fear, and welcoming us home. Our scientific instruments only flatter our ego. We built them, and all their data tell us we're to blame — if we conceived these monsters, we might abort and bury them again.

Since the inception of Western philosophy, the human mind has fled from terrestrial origin. "To live — that means to be sick a long time," Socrates said before committing suicide. Death was a cure for being born on the wrong plane — a material plane.

Plato, Socrates' pupil, posited the only reality as a series of ideal forms, an Apollonian "sky of ideas," as the philosopher Hannah Arendt writes, "where no mere images and shadows, no perishable matter, could any longer interfere with the appearing of eternal being, where the appearances are saved and safe, as purified of human sensuality and mortality as of material perishability."

Christianity, following the Platonic tradition, defined the earth as an illusion, a valley of tears quickly transcended as the soul rises in death, climbing toward the eternal rarefied light of heaven. Home was elsewhere. "Yes we are fully confident," we read in 2 Corinthians 5:6, "and we would rather be away from these earthly bodies, for then we will be at home with the Lord."

The language of the church preserves our fundamental repulsion. So far no one has noticed the connection — none of the etymology dictionaries supports my claim. The words *terror* and *terra*, Latin for "terror" and "land" or "earth," are synonymous. To be born, to enter the world, is to stand upon a mound of dirt trembling in fear. The word "awe" traces back to an ancient Proto-Indo-European root *agh*, a primal groan attesting to depression and fear. Traveling upon this terrestrial plane is torture — though modern industrial civilization would conceal the fact. The word "travel" derives from *travail* and traces back to *trepalium*, an obscure ancient three-pronged torture device.

Western science, following in the footsteps of Apollo, Plato, and Christianity, could master the earth only by alienating itself from it. Galileo wrote in awe of Copernicus and Aristarchus — two men separated by 1,700 years who, alongside Kepler, constitute the forefathers of the heliocentric worldview — that their rational thought was able "to commit such a rape on their senses, as in despite thereof to make herself mistress of their credulity."

The birth of the modern world began with Galileo's telescope, a tool that revealed directly to human perception the reality of Earth's circling the sun, a reality entirely contradictory to all appearance.

Before Galileo's discovery, Kepler had described the sun as "the most excellent of all bodies in the universe whose whole essence is nothing but pure light" and, therefore, the proper home of "God and the blessed angels." Similarly, Copernicus' imagination, as Hannah Arendt writes, "lifted him from the earth and enabled him to look down upon her as though he actually were an inhabitant of the sun."

But neither could prove the heliocentric theory so heretical to human perception. These Apollonian dreams obtained reality only through the telescope, that long phallic extension that projected our gaze away from Earth and into the stars. Galileo's discovery ushered in the Scientific Revolution, the age of empiricism, experiment, and the attendant enlightenment of humankind. After his revelation of Earth's insignificance, nothing occurring in our atmosphere could be viewed as a special event. Rather, all terrestrial phenomena became subject to the eternal laws of motion, universal forces that prevailed over not only humanity but also the sun, the moon, the stars, and heaven. Hannah Arendt writes in *The Human Condition*:

> In the experiment man realized his newly won freedom from the shackles of earthbound experience; instead of observing natural phenomena as they were given to him, he placed nature under the conditions of his own mind, that is, under conditions won from a universal, astrophysical viewpoint, a cosmic standpoint outside nature itself. . . . Earth alienation became and has remained the hallmark of modern science.

Science has proven what religion and philosophy always sought, namely — given humankind's ability to consider all phenomena from a standpoint outside the planet — proof, independent of theology, that man is "not, cannot possibly be, of this world, even though he spends his life here."

Or in the words of Ken Caldeira's colleague, Lowell Wood: Why not "terraform" other planets? Why not geoengineer Earth and Mars? "It is the manifest destiny of the human race! In this country we are the builders of new worlds. In this country we took a raw wilderness and turned it into the shining city on the hill of the world."

On September 21, 2003, the *Galileo* spacecraft completed its thirty-fifth and final orbit of the planet Jupiter, crashing just south of the gas giant's equator after 6:56 p.m. Before dissolving, the spacecraft sent its final transmission, a measurement of the mass of Jupiter's third moon, Amalthea, the foster mother of Zeus.

When the Russian *Sputnik* satellite first orbited Earth in 1957, the press described the event as the first "step toward escape from man's imprisonment from the earth."

The *Apollo 11* spacecraft landed on the Sea of Tranquility on July 20, 1969. Buzz Aldrin and Neil Armstrong together collected forty-seven pounds of moon dirt and left behind a plaque signed by Richard Nixon: "We came in peace for all mankind."

Yesterday, when I checked my Aries horoscope, the *Washington Times* said: "Here's another day that's astrologically perfect for letting the world know just how good you are at your chosen area. This doesn't mean you have to make enemies, but you also don't have to deliberately shun the spotlight."

And tonight, NASA's *Cassini* spacecraft continues to orbit Saturn. This morning it discovered an ocean of water the size of Lake Superior on the planet's sixth-largest moon. "Definitely Enceladus," scientists involved in the study said, "there's warm water there right now." If there's any life outside Earth, "it's our best bet."

Is it beautiful or appalling? At the beginning of the twenty-first century, at the apex of our technological and scientific evolution, in our age-old flight from Earth, today, if we are to survive as a species, we can perhaps do so only by slaying Apollo. The sky cult climaxes in blocking out the sun. Solar geoengineering will deflect the light back out into the void of space, turning the sky white, and dimming our days. This can be accomplished only with sulfur aerosols, the same dark chthonic matter ejected from Earth in massive volcanic eruptions. We choke on the dust of our repressions. We return to the place where we started. The cure is neither impressive scientifically nor viable politically, but it's divine in its symmetry.

The Oracle at Delphi achieved a state of hallucinogenic trance through the toxic volcanic sulfur vapors that Gaia continued to breathe between the cracks in Apollo's white temple.

This poison allowed her to predict the future.

"Now your statues are standing and pouring sweat. They shiver with dread."

"Your presence here outrages the god you seek."

"Go back, matricide! The number 73 marks the hour of your downfall!"

But there are no more oracles today, only computer models.

––––––––

"I'm sorry I got mad at you," she says.

"It's okay. It's my fault."

The drive home feels longer.

"The canyon was nice."

"Yeah, it was."

"And the art was interesting."

FOREVER

Summer, Middle America . . . midday, with dark gray clouds closing over the horizon, raindrops dotting the deserted sidewalks while streetlights change for cars that aren't there, a hooded figure draped head to toe in black appears in the distance chanting as he steps out from behind the blind corner of an office building and, beating the skin of a small plastic drum, he continues to the street and halts in the intersection just as another figure appears behind him, her red hair blowing as she drops her hood, crosses the asphalt, and reaches for his hand, holding it tight as together they turn and watch the others hobble out into the street and push past them, a sudden ragtag band of seers, saints, and shamans, visionary pioneers of a new world, the next great awakening, brothers and sisters, vagabond friends and lifelong lovers, the elect few who have recognized the truth and feel called upon to sing, to chant, and to shout and witness, boys and girls and grizzled elders looking skinny and limping but singing proud beside their fathers and daughters, grandparents, sons, and mothers pushing baby strollers, dragging overstuffed suitcases and carts with creaking wheels as they march east and chant in unison, others in the company lugging rucksacks, drums, and mandolins, half of them wearing neon green traffic vests while others hold aloft the golden regalia of their homeland, the heavy reflective highway signs that

still line every roadway from Los Angeles to Washington, D.C., signs beneath which they break bread, pray aloud, and bed down, except that the few they carry no longer warn of divided highways, winding roads, or dead ends but rather imminent extinction, and as their bright vests begin to billow in the driving rain, like the calm emissaries of some flickering world built just beyond the uttermost interstate off-ramp, the pilgrims press on up the length of Main Street and out to the perimeter of the city, and their shapes begin to dissolve into the distance as they take once more to the highway, leaving those in their wake to wonder whether they were even real, and whether or not they should follow, and where that would lead them, what fate they might find tomorrow on that narrow road far beyond the mountains.

They left Los Angeles a thousand strong not long after the governor of California declared the drought a state of emergency. Reservoir levels had hit an all-time low, and some cities were completely out of water. Scientists described the situation as the greatest absolute reduction in water availability ever seen. Farmers were cutting their losses, selling their cattle, and leaving their homes while others started drilling new wells, sucking up such a volume of water from the ground that they made mountains rise and triggered earthquakes. And still the fields lay fallow. It seemed a miracle, but on the first day of the pilgrims' journey torrential downpours flooded southern California, bringing an end to eighteen rainless months. But it didn't last. Optimistic meteorologists predicted the return of El Niño as they passed over the San Andreas Fault near Palm Springs and continued up into the Mojave Desert, just south of China Lake. But El Niño never came.

They walked the highway shoulder at night to escape the sun. In the mornings they doctored blisters, boiled oatmeal packets, and kept marching blindly into the heat haze. In Arizona, Navajo leaders blessed their journey and offered gifts in the form of sacred stones, and when raindrops began to dot the desert once again the elders declared it a sign: great sacrifices often bring rain, and their sacrifice was perhaps the greatest. The leaders of Zuni Pueblo met with them in New Mexico. They received eagle feathers and a special message, which they carried forth across the border of

Colorado, marching twenty miles each day and bivouacking along roadsides and in whatever basements and churches would house them. When they reached Nebraska, they neither heard the dawn chorus nor saw the monarch migration, but curious onlookers stopped to talk to them in towns. Everyone always asked the same question — why? — and their answers seldom varied.

"It was a sense of being commanded by a higher power," their leader said.

Others testified, "It's a prayer of sorts."

"I'm praying for generations that may not exist."

Those who had taken a vow of silence let the signs speak for themselves, "As for us, we can't stop speaking about what we have seen and heard. Acts 4:20."

And what had they seen? "What I have seen is, out of suffering comes great love."

Other pilgrims summarized the grueling 3,000-mile march, "Surrender your heart and follow what's good."

"Pilgrimage may be thought of as the experience of finding a holy place. But it is not a journey to Eden. Transcendence does not come without the understanding of suffering."

"We hope the heart and mind of the people will be awakened."

It's the day after Halloween. I'm hungover, sitting in the rain, staring over the grass at a small party rental stage where a woman stretches trash bags over a pair of PA speakers. She fastens them with duct tape, crouches back behind the cabinet, and swaps some wires. Her face looks unhappy. Several men stand alongside the tiny stage, shaking their heads as she taps the microphone, makes a grimace, and switches out more cables. It's hard to tell if she's afraid of electrocution or the opposite. But as her lips continue mouthing silent words, as she drops the mic and picks up a megaphone, stretching the strap over her shoulder, I decide the PA isn't working.

"Please do not leave bags unattended. They will confiscate them or worse."

She stands on the little stage at the center of the grass, sole cap-

EXTINCTION HAZARD

tain of the raft, while the wind shifts and drives the rain in at a westward angle.

"Bags need to remain on your person," she says.

One of the trash bags flaps out from the duct tape, inflating like a wind sock, as she stares toward the traffic lights blinking on H Street. Unzipping my hood, I gaze over my shoulder, scanning the green lawns, but they spread spotless between the flower plots and the bricked paths of bored tourists.

"The police have been very accommodating," she calls again.

I try to light a cigarette and look inconspicuous. The thought crosses my mind that I could stand and leave, just walk away, and that I probably should. But I want to see them. There is something about their journey, its symbolic gesture, that moves me. Anyway, I drove a thousand miles to be here.

"Please do not leave bags unattended!"

Reaching under the park bench, I drag out my rucksack, the same faded army surplus issue I'd been holding the first time I watched the pilgrims pass in Iowa City. The ATM wouldn't accept the eight-dollar check from the restaurant job I'd recently quit, and I kicked the machine while it beeped and then I turned as the drums, chants, and cheers drifted up the block. The procession crossed peacefully along Clinton Street and out onto the pedestrian mall, and I followed after them, comforted by the thought that I could kill time before I went back to George's Buffet and started drinking again. They formed a circle beneath the stucco walls of the Sheraton Hotel, and I stood at the periphery, staring fascinated toward a doctored road sign while students and shoppers stopped to ask questions.

A pretty girl with dimples came out from the vintage shop. I'd seen her around. She worked there. Whenever she looked at me, I always felt certain that she wanted me to die. She lifted her phone and pointed up the narrow promenade toward two young boys, maybe five or six, sitting calmly inside a sky-blue covered wagon. They were both eating sandwiches. Along the side of the carriage, someone had scrawled the words "Catastrophe Ahead." The boys watched as a woman twirled around the plaza on a pair of old roller skates, her long red hair bouncing in bright phosphorescent waves as she lifted a black sign high above her helmet: "The only way to combat our extinction is extraordinary action FROM THE HEART."

"They must be having fun."

I pointed toward the children.

A man, probably sixty, about my mother's age, turned toward me and nodded. "Mmm," he said. "How many kids get to see the country at that age?" He combed a gnarled, granite-colored mustache with a long fingernail and smiled. "They're blessed. We're all blessed."

The man introduced himself as Don and explained that he and the others had already been on the road for six months. "We have a woman in her eighties," he said, squinting as he pointed across the ped mall.

"They don't have to go to school?" I gestured toward the children.

"Their parents are teachers," he said. "They were teachers."

He said he was from Arizona. He'd walked here. "Join us," he said.

"I can't." The university had recently awarded me a position teaching prison convicts creative-writing classes online.

"Okay," Don said. "Next time."

Among the pilgrims stationed that afternoon in Iowa City, there was a girl named Sean. She'd recently left college, shaved off most her hair, and just started speaking again. She said the 109-day self-imposed silence helped alleviate her depression, a despair born from the fact that 150 species vanished daily. "I could be present and listen to all those who have important things to say," Sean said, "the birds, the wind in the trees, the cars zooming by, the songs of all my friends." I was amazed to learn that Sean had walked most of the journey without any shoes. "You have a whole new awareness when you are barefoot and feeling what you are walking on," she said. Not wearing shoes brought her closer to the earth. "I am massaging her and she's massaging me back. Sometimes it hurts, but it's always good."

Despite the New Age vibe, I liked Sean. I want to see her again — I want to see that her depression has passed.

Across the grass now, a spare trash bag rips loose from the corner of the stage. "Announcement, announcement . . ." It tumbles out, a slither and a roll; then the wind hits it harder, lifting it over the grass, and it hovers like a ghost, drawn magnetically toward the iron bars along Pennsylvania Avenue, and no one chases it.

"Come meet us at the finish line," Don had told me in Iowa.

"Where's that?"

"Washington, D.C."

He gave me his e-mail address and cell phone number and told me to keep in touch. I'd written several times over the intervening months — I wrote Sean as well — but neither ever wrote back.

The lady onstage continues bleating through the megaphone, "Don't place things on the ground and walk away. They will probably be gone when you get back!"

The anxiety in her voice is palpable, electric — despite the broken PA.

But it's hard to tell whom she's talking to.

According to Ed Fallon, the main organizer of the Great March for Climate Action, the most beautiful aspect of their journey was talking to the American people. "We are on a pilgrimage," he said. Walking in and of itself "is not going to change anything," Fallon told reporters in December, but it does represent "the commitment that hundreds of people are willing to make to get the rest of the country thinking about, talking about the commitment we all need to make to move beyond this crisis."

"We want the challenge of seeing this march grow," Fallon said. "When we get to Washington, D.C., we want to see thousands of people, tens of thousands of people descend upon the White House with the clear message that we want climate action and we want it now."

I was expecting huge crowds, hundreds of curious onlookers waiting at the finish line to greet the pilgrims, to mock and jeer and cheer their historic march. But so far neither party has arrived.

Another megaphone starts in across the park. There's a circle of ten or so people assembled in front of the White House. I can't read their signs, but I hear the words. "Unite! Unite! Unite against ISIS!" Were they referring to some primordial Earth Goddess or the Islamic state? Standing up from the park bench, I stub my cigarette on the wooden armrest and watch as the smoke curls and lifts away into the canopy of yellow autumn leaves, thinking, while I pace, of a few days ago inside the US House of Representatives, when I'd gazed up at a ribbon embroidered in blue and gold and read aloud for the first time the words *Westward the Course of Empire Takes Its Way.* For some reason, staring at the original artwork, some of its characters nearly life-size, I noticed something at the center of the painting that I hadn't ever seen.

And it made me smile.

In his summary of the painting, the artist too showed fondness. Emanuel Leutze described "a young vagrant with a fiddle on his back assisting his equally young partner for life up to the rock to peep at the distance." The two, Leutze wrote, "express careless happiness in spite of their scanty equipments." The term "partner for life" I find particularly touching. It is, I think, the only true optimism in the piece. I don't know why I never noticed these two carefree, sane individuals. These two urchins, headed together toward life's summit, are bewitched not by gold but by each other — she by the light in his eyes, he by her body's fitness. All of earth, sky, and human coin would mean nothing if you were not here to help me waste it.

"Is that your bag?" a cop asks me suddenly.

"Yes, it's mine. Sorry."

I want to tell him that of all the characters, of all thirty-two people painted in Leutze's *Westward*, only one walks without shoes — it's the girl climbing up the rock ledge beside her partner for life to peep at the distance. She expresses careless happiness in spite of the fact that she's barefoot. But I refrain from insanity.

"Here they come," the cop says. "Bunch of fucking bums."

Blue sirens flash along the flanks of white motorcycles as the police brake, dismount, and stand in the intersection, blocking the traffic along H Street. They're all wearing reflective neon traffic vests, same as the marchers, whom I can hear now — drums, pots, and pans clanking, boot heels beating on cobblestones as they lift their voices high, like the road signs, flags, and banners I can't yet read behind the walls of the Hay-Adams Hotel.

"Welcome, marchers!" the megaphone screams.

In my mind, in the mental image I'd formed of the Great March, it was the opposite of Emanuel Leutze's painting. People were pulling covered wagons in both, trekking overland across America in search of a better life, but one route led west, the other ran east. One congratulated something false. The other warned of something true.

"Hello! Hello! Marchers!"

The Great March for Climate Action was going to be the greatest cross-country march in US history. Tens of thousands of people crossing the country together, rising up from the darkness of the past, out from the Valley of the Shadow, and gaining momentum every month, every mile, every minute. Soon they'd flood Washington with a democratic force so colossal in its weight that Congress, the courts, and the president could only bow before progress and save us from extinction.

Neon traffic vests flap over dark rain jackets as they cross the grass and circle around the stage, chanting ancient folk songs from the 70s: "This pretty planet spinning through space . . . you're a garden, you're a harbor, you're a holy place." The covered wagons are gone now, as are the two boys and Don from Iowa. But there's the redhead on roller skates, twirling in green glitter spandex pants, lifting her road sign, and singing beside her friends, "golden sun going down . . . gentle blue giant spin us around." HBO is here. A special human interest story. "All through the night, safe 'til the morning light." There's an obese man in a jean jacket that says Earthman on the back beating a drum. A white boy in a Redskins beanie. An old woman wearing round-rimmed glasses and clapping her gloves. A radio host in a checkered golf cap. My black hair tied back in a bun. HBO zooms in on the flushed, shining faces as they keep cycling through the rhyme —"golden sun going down . . . spin us around!"— four times, eight times, twelve times, until the rain abates and the song empties into silence.

The megaphone from the competing protest idles through the oak trees.

"Unite, unite, unite against ISIS!"

A girl in a white beanie lifts a road sign and parries, "This Little Light of Mine!" and the other marchers fall in line.

"Right here in D.C. . . . I'm gonna let it shine!"

Camera flashes flicker over the wet grass.

I scan around the circle, searching for Sean, but I don't see her.

In reality, only four Americans walked across the country.

The core four are joined by a small support staff that drove cars, plus twenty or so other marchers who hiked most of the way but ducked out here and there for personal reasons.

"For climate justice . . . I'm gonna let it shine."

"Over the earth . . . I'm gonna let it shine."

I had wanted to talk to Sean. But now, in a way, I feel happy she isn't here. I have no idea what I would possibly ask her.

"For poor and hungry folk . . ."

"All around the town . . ."

"Trusting in the Goddess . . . I'm gonna let it shine."

But Sean was there. I saw her later, but I felt too bad to talk to her. She had her shoes on, and she looked sad. "I know now," she told a reporter, "that marches are not going to save us. I still struggle with this desire to save humanity, though I'm not sure if that is our natural course."

She said all things must come to an end.

"We humans are no exception. I just hope we come to ours with grace."

A woman named Cathy steps onstage and introduces herself, patting her gray, shaved hair before she taps a Buddhist prayer bell. Scanning the circle, I do see a difference in tone between the young pilgrims and the old. It's hard to identify, to name the divide exactly, but there's something restive in the eyes of the millennials. Disappointment or anger maybe that nobody is here. Or perhaps it's self-consciousness, resentment at the fact that many of the aged marchers outdid them in miles. Or maybe I'm just projecting.

The bell's warm resonance fades, and Cathy stands smiling, exuberant, calm. "All of you, welcome. All of you have participated in the Great March for Climate Action. It doesn't matter where you joined us. Even if you joined us today, we are all participants in the Great March for Climate Action."

Her invitation is generous. I'd like to feel serene, calm, part of the collective — a positive, adamant, and accepted member — but I really just feel tired, wet, and useless now. I need to get drunk again or drink more coffee. Besides the marchers dressed in neon traffic vests and official green t-shirts, perhaps twenty others, including myself, turned up at the finish line. All told, maybe seventy-three people.

"At this time," Cathy says, "I would like to introduce Miriam, our mayor, our special person, and our spirit walker."

Whistles and cheers whirl around the circle as a woman in her seventies slowly mounts the stairs at the side stage. It seems pretty clear that the old people run the show.

But Miriam doesn't have much to say.

"I would like to say: we made it!"

And that's all she says.

"We made it!" the crowd affirms.

"I want to show everyone," Cathy says, "what was given to us that I have carried across America." Her hand makes an A-OK sign as she presses her thumb and index finger together, but I can't see anything. "I bring a stone from the elders of the Navajo pueblo, who said, 'Take this to Washington and tell them they need to protect our sacred land.'"

She reaches back inside a crumpled Ziploc.

"I bring an eagle feather from Zuni Pueblo with a similar message, 'We must work together for Mother Earth who has brought us forth and whom we must love and care for.'" She lifts it high overhead and shuffles slowly in a circle for all to see. I wonder if Cathy knows that it's a federal offense for a nontribal member, a white woman such as herself, to carry an eagle feather on her person. "An eagle feather," she says, "from . . ."

She has to pull her note card back out and read the name.

"From Zuni Pueblo."

At this time Cathy introduces Pat.

Pat jumps onstage, gesticulating wildly while she holds the megaphone tight against her lips. "Washington, D.C., doesn't see climate action happening every day," she warns, waving her hand toward the White House. "But today they do!"

Pat is much younger than Cathy and much more aggressive. I turn my head and close my left forefinger carefully over my ear.

"I want each and every one of you," she screams, "to think of one action, one idea that you will take, and bring that idea to mind!"

Pat allows a generous moment's pause, and in that fragile time frame I attempt to summon to consciousness some action, some minor coup d'état I might discover that could meaningfully affect climate change mitigation. But nothing really comes to mind. Maybe I shouldn't have burned fifty gallons of gas driving here. I told the man at Starbucks yesterday that my pumpkin spice latte only needed a single paper cup's insulation. Perhaps I could do that again. I don't need three to keep the skin of my palm from melting off. I've been drumming in metal bands for the past fifteen years and still have plenty of calluses.

"A couple years ago," Pat shrieks, "there was a man who had an idea!"

She might do well as an MC during the karaoke blackout hour.

"The idea was to convene a coast-to-coast climate march for climate action!"

Her head hangs and her bangs block her eyes.

I wish I was still as drunk as she is.

"His name is Ed Fallon!"

Fallon is a former Iowa congressman. He's in his late fifties and wears a checkered golf cap and a jumpy smile. In 2006 he made an unsuccessful run for state governor, receiving a noble quarter of the vote. He now hosts an Internet radio program called *The Fallon Report*. A sandwich shop in downtown Des Moines advertises gluten-free paninis before each episode.

"Technology is not my forte," he says, raising the megaphone.

On YouTube, most of Fallon's radio shows have between zero and fifteen plays.

"Um, hey," he says. "This is really . . ."

He stares beside me into the face of a young kid from Colorado, or at least that's what the flag patch glued to his messenger bag seems to indicate.

"'Surreal' maybe is the word that comes to mind."

I scoot my heels over the wet grass, following the front line of marchers as they inch closer to the stage. Despite the paltry Internet clicks, Fallon speaks in the frank, husky, even-volumed voice of a man accustomed to an audience. "I'm walking down the streets of Washington, D.C.. and somehow I still feel like I'm walking down the streets of Los Angeles. Something about this climate march just kind of . . ." His eyes cast about for the right expression. "Time warps," he says. "It does such strange things, and it goes fast and it goes slow. It becomes meaningless."

He pauses for a breath, but it looks more like a wince — "meaningless" is probably not the exact punctuating term he'd hoped to land on during his opening remarks. But he recovers. "You know though that when it comes to this issue, time is not meaningless. We have a lot of work to do, and we plan to do it. And what's exciting to me is to see how this march has unfolded." He starts to say more about time and narrow windows, and I zone out for a second, remembering yesterday again, after the Starbucks barista apologized and took the cups back. It was late afternoon, and a thick band of cold October light filtered through the glass beyond the cash register, firing the tiny flecks of quartz inlaid over the tile floors. I tipped the barista and stood beside the window. Outside several male couples paced the manicured paths of a central courtyard, gesticulating in silence. As I perched on the elevated concourse, gazing down behind the thick glass, it all felt like some kind of strange zoo exhibit, except the primates below wore expensive wool suits, ignored the magnolia trees, and actually held within their empty hands — some of them, I wanted to believe — a significant portion of human destiny.

"These windows are two inches thick."

I turned to face my guide, Barry, who had evidently returned from the restroom.

"Each piece of glass weighs 2,500 pounds."

Barry was the uncle of my ex-girlfriend, and he hadn't seemed particularly thrilled to tour me around. But the more questions I fired, the more I confirmed my absolute fascination, the more Barry seemed to relax, and I was almost starting to feel calm myself.

"Part of the renovation?" I asked of the windows.

"Yes," he said.

Another group entered the courtyard and began to drift toward the gazebo.

"They're shatterproof?"

"Resistant," he said. "Nothing is foolproof." Barry pinched the corner of his thumbnail between two canines and watched an airplane mount the cloudless sky. He asked me how my coffee tasted and I told him sweet, as men in uniform kept funneling down the long hallway, shooting careful glances at the bright orange visitor button pinned to the pocket of my flannel. "Why does your cup say George?" he asked.

"It's just easier that way."

He adjusted his tie and slid his hands back in his slacks.

"They always spell my name Barry," I said.

"Such a tragedy."

I asked him if he liked working here and he smiled. "Oh, sure," he said. "It's just me and 23,000 of my closest friends." His hair was cut GI-short, but I think he just crunched numbers in a cubicle. I don't know what he actually did. But my awe at being inside the world's largest office building helped make the place fresh for him.

"Here, I want to show you something," he said.

The barista began to bang the portafilter against the bar top, and I flinched. A splash of milky espresso barely missed Barry's shoe. I stepped onto the escalator and grabbed the rubber handrail behind him. I normally drink my coffee black and I seldom go to Starbucks — it's one of those infinitesimal daily decisions that helps bolster my ailing individuality — but I figured I wouldn't ever have the opportunity to order a pumpkin spice latte on Halloween inside the Pentagon again.

"When I started this march . . ." Fallon adjusts the volume now as the wind rips west across the square, denting the red leaves of the oak trees. The tedious drone of megaphones always reminds me of fire drills, preparation for a catastrophe that never came, the PE coach congratulating the high school on its evacuation time, his voice booming over the basketball hoops and handball courts as he reminds the student body: but next time you'll have to be faster!

"When I started this march, it was impossible to get any media coverage of anything happening on climate change. In fact, a study showed that coverage of climate action had declined by 30 percent. And yet this year we've seen a huge uptake in the interest not just among the national media but at the local level as well."

In many of the small towns Fallon passed through, local papers published a few paragraphs on the march. They often reproduced the same joke. "One benefit of walking 2,500 miles: Fallon has picked up $53 in coins and a few dollar bills."

The national media published nothing.

"On an average day, I would talk to ten or fifteen, sometimes twenty people one-on-one. With ranchers in Colorado and farmers in Nebraska and Iowa. With Indian people in New Mexico. With people affected by fossil fuel industries in Wilmington, California, and Gary, Indiana, and elsewhere. We already know people out there are experiencing this, but what they need is an understanding that there is a force developing, a power beginning to move forward, that is going to make sure that the White House and the US Congress and the legislative chambers all across the country know that we need and demand climate action now!"

Another trash bag tears loose from the duct tape and starts thrashing.

"And I really do feel optimistic," Fallon says.

After I crossed through Pentagon security yesterday and picked up my visitor button, Barry and I passed the 9/11 quilt, and then he pointed at the wall. "Look," he said. A small plaque glued to a concrete column had a picture of an oak leaf with the acronym LEED — Leadership in Energy and Environmental Design — stamped across its face. "When they remodeled, they used a lot of recycled materials," Barry said. The Pentagon's recent $8 billion renovation in the wake of the September 11 attacks complies with all new federal regulations and executive orders for energy conservation and environmentally friendly construction. Several sections of the 583-acre office complex are certifiably sustainable, according to the US Green Building Council. And the Pentagon facility is not alone. Living quarters at Naval Base Guam recently won a LEED Gold seal. The visitors' center at Tinker Air Force Base in Oklahoma earned a LEED Silver. At West Point, the Thomas Jefferson

Library got a Bronze. China Lake is also helping out. The base celebrated Earth Day in 2010 by breaking ground on a new solar panel project that would reduce energy costs by $13 million over the next twenty years. Nellis Air Force Base in Nevada helped shrink the Pentagon's sizable environmental bootprint in 2007 by installing 70,000 new solar panels. Tooele Army Depot near Salt Lake City is spending more than $9 million on wind turbines. A program at NAS Corpus Christi pledged to help green the earth by recycling city sewage for its golf course at a cost of $2.5 million.

All throughout the DoD, you'll find cheerful evidence of a fast-sweeping green revolution. Last year CBS News 8 announced that "Naval Base San Diego is continuing its commitment to help the environment by installing an electric vehicle charging station outside its navy exchange retail store."

Barry and I walked south across a broad mezzanine past a nail spa, a gourmet chocolatier, an electronics store packed with laptops and thumb drives and headphones, a luggage store, a sushi café, and a barbershop. It was like a mall. The only things missing were a movie theater with its aromatic trail of diacetyl popcorn butter, anesthetic smooth jazz trickling from skylights through the fronds of fake palm trees and bouncing softly off clearance signs, and the cries of small children strapped to the backs of merry-go-round horses. Barry opened a door, and we walked into an empty room paved with purple carpet.

"I like bringing people here," he said. Folding chairs faced a tiny stage at the front of the room. "You'll notice that as time goes on, fewer were awarded." All along the walls stretched the names of the 3,491 men and 1 woman who had earned the nation's highest military prize, the Medal of Honor. More than 1,500 were handed out during the Civil War. Only 4 during the Iraq War.

"Are we becoming less brave?" I asked, but Barry didn't find the joke funny.

"No," he said.

"It took them a while to sort out the criteria?"

"Yes."

I studied the plaques and then he opened the door and I followed after him. I noticed that he didn't bother to turn out the lights.

Perhaps it would be all too easy to criticize the Pentagon's energy conservation efforts. Especially with such bases as Guantanamo Bay—which hasn't yet earned a LEED green building award but according to the US Department of Energy has four wind turbines that slice taxpayer energy costs by more than a million dollars each year, "save 650,000 gallons of diesel fuel and reduce air pollution by 26 tons of SO_2 and 15 tons of N2O, demonstrating the Navy's commitment to energy conservation and environmental steward-ship"—was it appropriate within the Pentagon to talk about the possibility of green torture? "This way," Barry said. We left the Medal of Honor room and crossed toward a long concrete ramp, like something you might see in the corner of a stadium, something built for semitrucks, a football field long and fifty yards wide and ca-pable of installing the Super Bowl halftime show. Change bounced inside Barry's pocket as he leaned forward and we marched uphill alone.

"No elevators or escalators. Not back then," he said. "Not initially."

Construction for the Pentagon broke ground on September 11, 1941.

"They had to conserve every scrap of metal for the war effort."

In reality, the Pentagon's energy conservation efforts are no joke. "The Department of Defense is the largest single consumer of energy in the world. Isn't that right?" Barry glanced back over his shoulder and nodded brusquely. "That's correct," he said. "The DoD energy bill totaled over $20 billion in 2012. Ninety percent of the energy consumed by the federal government gets used by the Department of Defense."

That might not sound significant, but it puts the DoD, that is, the Pentagon, a single department within the federal government of the United States, on par with the annual energy use of coun-tries like Denmark or Nigeria, a nation with more than 160 million people.

"But we're trying to change," Barry said.

He told me, as I knew, that the Department of Defense planned to obtain 25 percent of its energy from renewable sources by 2025. The easiest way for the Pentagon to realize this goal lies in an aggressive deployment of a broad network of renewable and energy conservation strategies at all its bases and installations. Facility energy generally accounts for about a quarter of the DoD's energy bill. "Operational energy," on the other hand, according to the Pentagon, "or the energy required to train, move, and sustain forces, weapons, and equipment for military operations, accounted for 75 percent of all energy used by the Department of Defense in 2012." Operational energy, in short, the energy derived from burning fossil fuels, constitutes a much trickier fix than facility energy.

At the top of the ramp, Barry and I passed a display case packed with pictures of soldiers recently killed in action, dozens of men and women, young and less young, some smiling, some serious, some black, others white, others brown. All of them no longer living. According to a 2011 Pentagon report, "Energy for the Warfighter," between 2003 and 2007 more than 3,000 army soldiers and contractors were killed or injured protecting oil and water convoys in Iraq and Afghanistan. One positive side effect, the Pentagon believes, of a more energy-efficient US military may be fewer convoys, fewer casualties, and greater national security. According to Sharon Burke, assistant secretary of defense for operational energy plans and programs, the Pentagon can "reduce risk by reducing reliance." The Pentagon plans to spend more than $9 billion over the next five years "to boost the efficiency" of all operations and "transform the U.S. military from an organization that uses as much fuel as it can get to one that uses only as much as it needs." According to Burke, "Every little bit helps."

"Are you hungry? Thirsty?" Barry called over his shoulder. He continued walking quickly along the windows of the inner ring. We passed a Burger King and farther down, after several turns, I saw the Starbucks in the distance. I felt bad and wanted to contribute something, so I told him that I'd probably purchase a coffee.

"Okay," he said.

Every hundred feet the walls to our left opened, revealing two diverging corridors that burrowed away into the stone interior, stretching a disorienting distance past an uncountable series of closed and locked doors as the hallways seemed to narrow and the tile floors slowly coalesced with the fluorescent lights reflected in their polish. Down one hall I saw a cart loaded with brown paper bags. "You guys get groceries delivered?" I asked.

"No," Barry said, but he almost smiled. I wondered what could make him laugh. Maybe I didn't want to know. "Those are burn bags," he said.

"Burn bags?"

"Shredded classified documents go in burn bags," he said.

"You don't recycle your correspondence?"

"The incinerator's on-site." I watched his hand make a hat brim as he squinted through the sun toward the chalkboard menu. He suggested I try the pumpkin spice latte. "It's quite good." We stood in line and he looked at his watch and I pulled out my credit card and then he turned to me and asked what I was actually researching. At China Lake I'd wanted to know what if anything the military was doing to alter the atmosphere, but as I stood inside the Pentagon the question seemed almost ridiculous to me now. Barry had already answered it. The US military, as the largest institutional consumer of fossil fuels in the world, had already succeeded, perhaps more than any single human entity in Earth's history, in dramatically altering the composition of the atmosphere. That much seemed obvious. But I guess they were trying to change. I wanted to know why exactly, and if they were truly serious, how they planned to pick up after themselves. "I guess I want to know what the Pentagon actually plans to do about climate change."

"That's a good question," Barry said. "But weren't we just discussing that?"

I guess I wanted to know more specifically if the Pentagon planned to add any new particulates to the atmosphere. This seemed as good a time as any. "Have you heard of solar radiation management?"

Barry shook his head. "Is that a company?"

I told him no and explained the concept as quickly as possible and while my mouth moved he shook his head and his face knotted and he stared at me as though I were the source of some appalling odor and then he said no he'd never heard of or read about anything like that and then he excused himself. The bathroom door thudded shut beside the drinking fountain and I stepped up to the counter. "What can I get started for you today?" the barista asked.

The sky darkens while the megaphone booms. Raindrops as fat as thumbs keep sporadic time as they tap the neon traffic vests. "I'm going to support those who are engaged in political action," Ed Fallon says onstage. "And I'm going to support those engaged in direct action. We all need to work together to defeat the corporate co-opting of democracy."

The clouds look like giant bags of concrete as they roll inland, low and heavy, over the Washington Monument, and the obelisk seems to sway.

"Moving forward from this, there will be plenty of additional amazing things happening," Fallon says. "I know it's going to happen."

I'm curious to know why Ed Fallon and his fellow marchers don't mention the military. Like many other activists, he seems to skip a crucial step. The federal government is not simply a regulator, a tax collector, or a fount of private research funds. It's also a massive consumer, the largest consumer of energy in the US economy, in fact, and therefore a massive polluter. "Therefore," there is a chance, as Sharon Burke points out, that "a more energy-efficient U.S. military may well help drive the innovation so urgently needed in the civilian economy, too." Or maybe Fallon already knew this, maybe he liked being coy, maybe the force he'd referred to, the giant "power beginning to move forward," wasn't the march but the military. "Assembling a march of this size is mind-boggling," Fallon said ten months ago, when it still looked like thousands might join him. "You think about the challenges of moving troops around, for example," he said. "Here we're moving a small battalion of climate warriors, if you will." A very small battalion, certainly, but every little bit helps.

In 2009 the Honorable Ray Mabus, secretary of the navy, encouraged the audience at a Naval Energy Forum to think of themselves as energy warriors: "We must be no less bold in our thinking when it comes to energy reform, no less willing to embrace risk. I am not asking you," Mabus said, "to do the impossible." The mission will be difficult, but "we're already doing this at China Lake," he pointed out, referring to the geothermal plant at the Coso Hot

Springs, "where our on-base systems generate 20 times the load of the base."

Mabus spoke that day inside the banquet room of the Hilton in McLean, Virginia, a stone's throw west from CIA headquarters. The bold venture he referred to sounded mind-boggling to many in attendance, but he wasn't joking. The Pentagon was going to go green, beginning with the navy. "By 2020," Mabus said, "half of our total energy consumption for ships, aircraft, tanks, vehicles, and shore installations will come from alternative sources."

That meant facility energy *and* operational energy.

To confirm his seriousness, Mabus announced that the navy would organize a carrier strike group called the Great Green Fleet — consisting of the nuclear-powered USS *Nimitz*, two destroyer ships, a guided missile cruiser, a fuel tanker, and roughly seventy fighter jets, helicopters, and transport planes — equip the fleet "with hybrid electric alternative power systems running biofuel and aircraft flying only biofuels," and "by 2016," according to Mabus, "deploy it."

According to experts at MIT, the navy's renewable biofuels have the potential to emit 50 percent fewer greenhouse gases than conventional petroleum products. Further, unlike corn ethanol, they won't affect food markets because they'll come from old cooking oil and algae-based fat. "The Navy is mindful of not trading one fuel problem for another," says Captain James Goudreau, Mabus' acting deputy assistant. "Our alternative fuels can't compete with food crops."

Mabus' speech at the McLean Hilton managed to blend both devastating understatement and a stunning amount of truth: "The carbon that's emitted from our ships, aircraft, and vehicles is a contributor to global warming and climate change. According to the projections endorsed by our own Task Force on Climate Change, global warming could result in an Arctic Ocean free of summer ice within 25 years. The security implications of this are dramatic. In short, we have not acted as very responsible stewards of our environment."

No statement from anyone in the history of the US military's leadership had ever approached this degree of direct acknowledgment. However, Mabus was optimistic. "But you know," he said, "our Navy and Marine Corps have never backed away from a challenge."

How was this possible? Who had convinced the Pentagon that such an aggressive green agenda was a necessary, or even a possible, national security measure? As Miriam, the Great March for Climate Action's mayor, special person, and spirit walker, testifies, "It's important to get people's attention. Leaders need to do the big things. If enough people demand it, things will change." Apparently, when the price of crude oil more than doubled between 2003 and 2007, enough people inside the Pentagon began to demand change. Their protests helped pave the way for the Great Green Fleet and advanced biofuels. As a 2012 Congressional Research Service report states, "Just a few years ago, fears of 'Peak Oil' production drove policy discussions on U.S. energy security." These frantic discussions about dwindling oil reserves and growing dependence on foreign oil produced some truly fine literature, classics like Lieutenant Colonel Dennis Tewksbury's 2006 "Preemptive Energy Security: An Aggressive Approach to Meeting America's Requirements." Tewksbury spoke fondly of climate change activists. "The public's understanding must transcend the anti-capitalistic chants of 'no blood for oil' and public distrust of oil corporations." Hence, Tewksbury argues not only for energy reform but also for educational reform. "The President must address the issue of energy security by educating the American public about the importance of oil with regard to the economy and explaining that we must prepare to use military force to guarantee access to oil. Oil is this nation's economic lifeblood. . . . We must act unilaterally if the circumstances warrant such action."

Another 2006 paper, this one by Thomas Kraemer, commander of the United States Navy, praised the president's recent educational efforts. "In his 2006 State of the Union address, President George W. Bush proclaimed that 'America is addicted to oil, which is often imported from unstable parts of the world.' He announced it was time for the United States to 'move beyond a petroleum-based economy and make our dependence on Middle Eastern oil a thing of the past.'" According to Kraemer, "most rehabilitation programs follow a 12-step process. The Bush plan is Step One in weaning America from its addiction . . . to this evil commodity." However, Kraemer warns, "America must realize that the greatest threat to global stability is not too much American power, but too little."

God grant me the serenity to accept the things I cannot change, the courage to change the things I can, and the wisdom to know the difference, or as another paper titled "America's Strategic Imperative: A National Energy Policy Manhattan Project," written by Lieutenant Colonel John Amidon of the United States Air Force, puts it, "Failing to take urgently required economic steps now will necessitate far more painful economic steps later and likely require protracted military action." Colonel Amidon adds somewhat ominously, "It is highly doubtful that any military, even that of a global hegemon, could secure an oil lifeline indefinitely."

The three authors, respectively, called for "a national effort on the scale of the Manhattan Project"; a new Apollo program, that is, "a 'Kennedy-esque' edict . . . to wean America off its addiction"; and finally "a comprehensive plan to achieve energy independence — a type of Manhattan Project — to deploy as many conservation and replacement measures as possible." What had to change was our dangerous addiction to foreign oil, a finite and fickle resource controlled by a fundamentalist Saudi dictator that undermined our economy, our military, and our national security.

In short, pity for Mother Earth and her children was not the primary impetus behind the Pentagon's pursuit of fossil fuel alternatives.

James Goudreau puts it bluntly, "Alternative fuel for the Navy is not about being green, it's about combat capability." Marc Kodack of the Office of the Assistant Secretary of the Army for Installation, Energy, and Environment strikes a similar note. "Unless the concepts of 'sustainability' or 'Net Zero' allow the Army to do its mission better, I don't care. The question is how do I create a narrative that allows me to do more — the Army to enhance its mission."

The mission is the bottom line, and the core mission of the US military is protecting national security and its prerequisite, energy security, which as defined by the US Congress in Title 10 of the US Code means "having assured access to reliable supplies of energy and the ability to protect and deliver sufficient energy to meet mission essential requirements."

Nevertheless, as Secretary Mabus is fond of mentioning, another piece of the narrative puzzle — a further positive spin-off of increasing the navy's combat capability via advanced biofuels — may be climate change mitigation. Even if the navy's advanced renewable biofuels don't end up emitting 50 percent fewer greenhouse gases than conventional petroleum fuels — even if it's only, say, 18 percent or 10 percent or even 1 percent — every little bit helps.

The Pentagon purchases and consumes more petroleum than any other institution in the world. Unsurprisingly, in utilizing this so-called operational energy, the Pentagon produces more greenhouse gas pollution than any other single entity on Earth. Such emissions necessarily threaten national security and the prospect of any future life in our solar system. In 1999, even before the wars in Afghanistan and Iraq, the Pentagon purchased 110 million barrels of petroleum products for $3.5 billion. The Defense Energy Support Center (DESC), the agency responsible for securing all fuel products for each branch of the military, tried itself to make these numbers intelligible. "That's enough fuel for 1,000 cars to drive around the world 4,620 times — or 115.5 trillion miles." That's a distance roughly equivalent to 1,700 round-trip flights to Mars. Except for a handful of nuclear submarines and aircraft carriers, everything runs on oil.

In 2003, the army estimated that its branch alone would need more than 40 million gallons of fuel for the first twenty-one days of the Iraq War. In training for the invasion, any F-16 fighter jet flying at peak thrust over China Lake consumed as much fuel in one hour as the average US driver does in three years. At the beginning of Operation Iraqi Freedom, forty-two F-117 fighter jets each flew more than 1,300 combat sorties totaling almost 191 million miles. It would take a Boeing 747 more than 328,000 trips between LAX and JFK — twenty-three years if you assume forty commercial flights a day — to produce the same 52 billion pounds of carbon pollution.

Besides the F-117, sixty other types of plane flew sorties over Iraq during the start of the war.

"I already see the seeds being planted," Ed Fallon says onstage now. "This march is done in terms of its 3,000-mile journey, but the work is just beginning."

On this point, the crowd seems reluctant to cheer.

Someone lets out a soft "woo" and Fallon's voice dips into a lower emotional register.

The HBO man flicks the black tarpaulin back over his camera and takes a knee.

"Every action you do, even if it might seem insignificant, it's most important that you do it," Fallon says. "We need all hands on deck. We need all tools in the tool chest being rolled out."

The DESC reported that it bought 144 million barrels of petroleum fuel — or 2.8 billion gallons — in 2004 for $8.5 billion. In 2008, after the spike in the price of crude oil, it paid nearly $18 billion for more than 132 million barrels of oil, double the money for less energy. As Navy Vice Admiral Philip Cullom admits, "When your fuel bill goes up that much, you've got to ask yourself, 'What are you not going to do?'" Despite the colossal scale of such numbers, the Pentagon's official reports omit several important sources of fuel and several fuel types. It's not implausible that the military may actually consume more than double what it claims. If such were the case, only fourteen countries, including the United States, would surpass the Pentagon's annual oil intake. As the US Energy Information Administration acknowledges, "Estimating, even roughly, the quantity of oil consumed for overseas military operations is an uncertain procedure." It's thought that the United States is responsible for 25 percent of the world's greenhouse gas pollution. But the US Department of Defense likely cannot account for how much operational energy it consumes or how many greenhouse gas emissions it produces, and even if it could . . .

Executive Order 13514 requires all federal agencies to develop an annual Strategic Sustainability Performance Plan "to meet GHG emissions, energy, water, and waste reduction targets." As President Obama said after signing the order in 2009, "As the largest consumer of energy in the U.S. economy, the Federal government can and should lead by example when it comes to creating innovative ways to reduce greenhouse gas emissions." Well said, Mr. Obama. However, if you take the time to read the Pentagon's own 150-page plan, you'll find the following crucial phrase quietly buried near the start of the document: "Operational energy is *necessarily exempt* from the targets of this Plan and Executive Order (EO) 13514."

But as Secretary Mabus says, "I do not seek to chastise anyone or to repent . . ."

The Pentagon is trying to change.

God, grant them the courage and the wisdom.

I tried to ask Ed Fallon later, after all the speeches and songs were finished, about all the tools in the toolbox. Again, it wasn't a terribly nuanced question, but it seemed necessary to ask him and his colleagues, those who were to all appearances the most committed climate change activists in the country, about the possibility of a large-scale direct intervention in the global climate system. "I'm not gonna —" he looked pretty annoyed. "I don't have the time or energy to talk about it now." But it didn't really sound like he knew what the term "geoengineering" referred to. "The big picture is motive," Fallon said. "I don't see the motive for it." He handed me his *Fallon Report* business card. "I'm just wondering," I said, "if mitigation —" Cathy cut in as he started to walk away. "Well, mitigation, certainly," she said, "and adaptation are the two things we're pushing strongly." Cathy touched the top of my hand and began walking me over toward the White House, where the other pilgrims began to pose for pictures as the ISIS protesters circled around them chanting, "End sexual slavery! Unite against ISIS!" The pads of Cathy's fingers felt soft and warm, like my grandmother's hands, far too thin and fragile, but her voice sparkled with a visionary enchantment. "And the other part of it is the opportunity now for creativity," she said. "This has got to be solved with a million different approaches, thousands and thousands of special, specific community actions."

Cathy's encouraging words seemed to echo, strangely, the more nuanced assessments of the defense community's recent green revolution: "The Military-Environmental Complex is not about developing a single 'magic bullet,' but rather describes a web of interaction

among different institutional actors working together to develop multiple technologies that reduce energy demand and develop or promote alternative energy generation." The report in the *Boston College Law Review* goes on to say that "a multi-faceted approach to climate change . . . is essential in light of the practical reality that a single, global regulatory program is unlikely to materialize."

Cathy stands on the stage now with her arm outstretched, ready to take the megaphone back from Fallon. "And I really do feel optimistic," he says again. "There are people, by the tens and thousands, all across the country whose hearts and minds we have changed."

Two weeks before I arrived in Washington, the Pentagon came out with yet another climate change report — there have been three this year — called the "Climate Change Adaptation Roadmap." Secretary of State Chuck Hagel, following the release of the road map, described the challenges ahead at a Conference of Defense Ministers of the Americas in Arequipa, Peru. "Droughts and crop failures can leave millions of people without any lifeline, and trigger waves of mass migration," Hagel said. "Two of the worst droughts in the Americas have occurred in the past ten years . . . droughts that used to occur once a century. In the Caribbean, sea level rise may claim

1,200 square miles of coastal land in the next 50 years, and some is-lands may have to be completely evacuated. . . . Our coastal instal-lations could be vulnerable to rising shorelines and flooding, and extreme weather could impair our training ranges, supply chains, and critical equipment."

The *New York Times* wrote on October 14, "Today, Mr. Hagel's efforts to lay the groundwork for a new global climate deal signal a remarkable shift." Hagel was the coauthor of the infamous 1997 Byrd-Hagel Resolution, which the US Senate endorsed by a vote of 95 to 0. The resolution stated, in the lead-up to the 1998 Kyoto conference, that the United States should not sign any international agreement to limit greenhouse gas emissions that "would result in serious harm to the economy of the United States."

The *New York Times* praised Hagel's remarkable change of heart. "The Pentagon's increased emphasis on the national secu-rity threats of climate change is aimed in part at building support for a United Nations agreement, to be signed next year in Paris, that would require the world's largest producers of planet-warming carbon pollution to slash their emissions."

The *Times*, however, fails to note an important issue that won't be on the bargaining table in Paris. The Pentagon is not only ex-empt under US law from reporting any emissions related to its op-erations to the federal government, it's also exempt from reporting any emissions to the United Nations Framework Convention on Climate Change.

During the 1997 Kyoto negotiations, the United States demanded, as a condition of ratifying the treaty, absolute military exemption from greenhouse gas emissions limits. "America's national secu-rity requires that its military forces remain ready," Defense Secre-tary William Cohen told Congress in 1997. "While global climate change may be a serious threat to the nation's long-term interests, there are other threats we must not forget." A Marshall Institute report written a year later by former Dick Cheney speechwriter Jef-frey Salmon praised the Pentagon's remarkable exemption, which, according to Salmon, "includes multilateral operations such as NATO- and UN-sanctioned activities, but it also includes actions related very broadly to national security, which would appear to comprehend all forms of unilateral military actions and training for such actions." Salmon quotes Undersecretary of State Stuart Eizenstat, the leader of the US Kyoto delegation, "every requirement the Defense Department and uniformed military who were at Kyoto by my side said they wanted, they got."

After securing every possible exemption, the United States refused to sign the treaty.

So far none of the IPCC's assessment reports has made any mention of the Pentagon's exceptional exemptions nor, clearly, have they counted its emissions. In light of such facts, the Pentagon, an institution charged with protecting the security of a nation that consumes more than 25 percent of the planet's oil, appears to offer the world in its recent climate change road map the following pragmatic recommendation: adapt.

"I know it looks like we have to do everything we can and we have to do it now," Fallon says onstage. "But we also have to brace ourselves for a long, hard fight. So don't burn out."

It's the end of the highway, and many among the repair crew do look tired. Several sit with their traffic vests removed, packed between jeans and the wet grass. An old man at my feet taps the skin of a toy drum. Printed on his vest is the command: Clean Energy.

"We need you," Fallon says. "The young people, we need you. *We need you so bad.* Take a little time off if you need to, but come back and be ready to continue in whatever way you feel called to help save this planet, to deliver the message that we are going to fight until we win climate action and climate justice. Thank you."

He really does look optimistic as he waves and bows, lifts his checkered golf cap, and walks off the stage. He rejoins the circle and stands behind a group of bearded men holding some kind of tattered rope.

"Now," Cathy says, "we want to deliver messages to President Obama written by Americans young and old that we met along our route." A twenty-foot chain of handwritten messages folded in half and taped in thin strips along a length of twine stretches behind the stage. "They're double-sided, by the way," Cathy says.

I suppose this was her idea of the kind of multifaceted creativity we need. A kindergarten art project. A giant Hawaiian centipede composed of hundreds of different talking legs crawling across America. Perhaps one day someone will staple it along the wall above the eastern staircase of the House of Representatives.

"We promised to bring their messages to Washington, D.C." Cathy says. "And we are going to do it now. We are going to hear from over thirty of these messages. And we will now be able to say that these messages have come home. May I please have our first speaker, please?"

Somehow I managed to feel more optimistic inside the Pentagon yesterday. Something about the military is if not altogether inspiring then at least remarkably consistent. Power is like energy. It cannot be created or destroyed. And if you have as much power and energy as the Pentagon, you can never relax your vigilance when it comes to identifying a possible threat—even if that threat is yourself.

Pat plucks a message, mounts the stage, and reads calmly, "God bless. Love from the mountains. Northern New Mexico."

Another marcher steps up to read and the two swap the megaphone.

Someone behind me whispers, "God, this protest is gay," and I turn to watch the young kid in the Redskins beanie walk away with his girlfriend.

The marcher reads in a stuttering voice, "Please take . . . global . . . warming seriously. Science is . . . not fiction. Fort Collins, Colorado."

While many right-wing policy makers remain skeptical of climate change science, the pronouncements of their DoD counterparts ring increasingly blunt. The department remains unwavering in its assertion that climate change is happening and will harm the world. And while the Pentagon's greenhouse gas emissions exacerbate the problem, the verbal admissions of military leaders are, steadily, helping America face the severity of its future. This is because "the military, the Pentagon," as Defense Secretary Chuck Hagel speculates, "has maybe, at least perceived by many people, a more serious look at the world."

"I take it you've read the *Quadrennial Review*?" Barry asked me yesterday as we stepped off the escalator and started down a long corridor. He pointed ahead and said that generals and other big-wigs had offices with windows in the distant outer ring. I asked him if Secretary Ray Mabus, the brains behind the Great Green Fleet, was anywhere around. "I don't think so," he said, but he told me, as I knew, that the Pentagon considered climate change a threat multiplier. The Pentagon's 2014 *Quadrennial Defense Review*, the agency's primary public document summarizing current military doctrine, examines the coming crisis.

> Climate change poses another significant challenge for the United States and the world at large. As greenhouse gas emissions increase . . . pressures caused by climate change will influence resource competition while placing additional burdens on economies, societies, and governance institutions around the world. These effects are threat multipliers that will aggravate stressors abroad such as poverty, environmental degradation, political instability, and social tensions — conditions that can enable terrorist activity and other forms of violence.

Senator James Inhofe of Oklahoma has condemned the Pentagon's biofuel program and its increasing endorsement of climate change reality. "ISIS is still gaining ground," Inhofe said, "and causing havoc in Syria and Iraq," with militants traveling from more than eighty countries to join the fight. "It is disappointing, but not surprising, that the president and his administration would focus on climate change when there are other, legitimate, threats in the world." Inhofe refers to climate change as a hoax and a conspiracy. Recently over a morning radio program for children, he attempted to make his point of view more intelligible. "My point," he said, "is that God's still up there. The arrogance of people to think that we, human beings, would be able to change what He is doing in the climate is to me outrageous."

Unlike certain members of Congress and their conservative constituents, the Pentagon, with more than 6,000 home installations and a network of more than 700 bases in strategic locations across the globe, many of them on coastlines and islands now facing inundation, cannot afford to be naïve about the science. Chuck Hagel confesses that "our coastal installations could be vulnerable," but he probably means they *are* vulnerable. Already, 150 miles south of the Pentagon at Norfolk Naval Base, the world's largest naval station, rising tidewaters are disrupting daily operations. As Naval Rear Admiral David Titley puts it, "Ultimately, the data wins; the observations win. The ice doesn't care about politics or Democrats and Republicans; it just melts." According to Titley, "This is the adult way to think about climate change."

Nor can the Pentagon any longer afford to be too naïve about its own role in the coming catastrophe. I asked Barry about Ray Mabus' ice-breaking speech in 2009. "It's true," Barry said, "we have not always acted as very good stewards of the planet." We turned and started down the outer ring. A woman in uniform eyed my visitor button as she hurried down the hall, briefcase dangling, heels clicking. "But the speech annoyed certain people," Barry said. "They thought it sounded off-key. The reality is that for the US military the immediate life-or-death stakes inherent in defending our national security must always, by necessity, trump the more abstract concept of environmental security." But Barry said Mabus wasn't disputing that. "He was saying that the pursuit of alternative energy has the opportunity to tackle a number of security issues, one of which and the least pressing of which, many would argue, being climate change."

The Honorable Ray Mabus spoke carefully into the microphone at the Hilton. "I do not seek to chastise anyone or to repent on procurement decisions made over the last decades when the dangers of fossil fuels and their effect upon the environment were not as well understood or as fully recognized. Nor am I naïve enough," he said, "to believe that we can simply flip a switch and go off fossil fuels overnight. But I believe the Navy and Marine Corps have an obligation to do something now about our impact on the environment, and that we can take substantive measures to improve our core warfighting capabilities while improving our energy footprint."

Barry and I turned again and continued down another corridor, and I wondered if he actually had anything to show me. We seemed to be walking in circles. "The central question," he said, "is whether or not a domestic biofuel industry is necessary for national security. Some people will tell you it's a terrible waste of taxpayer money."

In 2012, the Great Green Fleet strike group performed at the Rim of the Pacific Exercise, the world's largest international maritime war game, where it consumed, in the words of the navy, "the single largest purchase of biofuel in government history." Together, all seventy-six ships and planes except the nuclear-powered *Nimitz* burned a 900,000-gallon 50/50 blend of bio and conventional fuels. The navy paid up to $150 a gallon for the biofuels—fifty times the average price of conventional fuel—to demonstrate the efficacy of its renewable Great Green Fleet, which succeeded in sinking two obsolete retired war vessels. Russian and Indian dignitaries cheered. Total biofuel costs for the one-day demonstration amounted to $12 million.* According to the Pentagon, "All systems performed at full capacity."

Unsurprisingly, certain members of Congress have tried to block the Pentagon from buying more biofuels—the navy needs an additional 37 million gallons by 2016 if it's going to deploy the Great Green Fleet. "Adopting a 'green agenda' for national defense, of course, is a terrible misplacement of priorities," Senator John McCain said. He described the program as proof that "the president doesn't understand national security." Senator James Inhofe said the Pentagon "should not be wasting time perpetrating President Obama's global warming fantasies or his ongoing war on affordable energy." Ray Mabus, however, insists that "if we establish the market, the price is going to begin to come down."

"Mabus' statement is utterly ridiculous and reflects an absolute lack of understanding of America's, and the world's, energy realities," says Thomas Pyle, president of the Institute for Energy Research. "People have been working on biofuels for over 125 years and they are still incredibly expensive."

But the navy and marine corps have never backed away from a challenge. Mabus invoked the Apollo program in 2009 during the announcement of the Great Green Fleet: "When President Kennedy said in 1961 we would go to the moon and return within that decade, most of the technology required was not even invented. Bold steps are in our nature as Americans and what make us a great nation; no one has ever gotten anything big done by being timid."

Barry scanned a card and opened a door, and we stepped into the waiting room of a small office. There was gray carpet, a coffee table with magazines, and a receptionist. She smiled and continued typing while Barry introduced me as a family friend. He swiped his ID again, and we stepped into a small room crammed with cubicles. Fluorescent lights burned brightly overhead.

He flicked on a light switch.

I stood there in silence, bewildered and speechless, while a battery-powered magnetic detective siren twirled at the center of the room. Barry walked me down the aisle, between the rows of cubicles, but no one was home. We stood beneath the little red light while it circled impotently among the fiberboard ceiling tiles above our heads.

"What's that for?" I asked.

It was like something you might find overpriced at the mall in one of those party-gag gift shops that sold dildos, classic rock posters, microphones, fog machines, and magic tricks with silk thread and wax from China. I waited for something to happen.

"We have to turn it on whenever we have visitors," Barry said.

He showed me his desk. There were pictures of his kids and a few sticky notes stuck to the computer monitor. He said the work was classified but boring stuff. "A lot of numbers. Money. The budget."

Another marcher reads another message through the megaphone, "Dear Michele Obama, dear strong woman, we are all working hard to stop the insanity of the Keystone Pipeline. It should not happen and America should go forward to do everything we can to stop climate change. Please ask your husband to stop the pipeline. Tracy, Indiana."

Ed Fallon hoists the megaphone once again. He smiles and reads, "We humans are simply a part of the whole web of life, not the master. Kevin."

There's a girl standing just off to my left. "Let's go," she says. Her yellow windbreaker blows as her friend nods and follows. I feel sad watching them walk away, but there's probably nothing to stay for, nothing more to see. A deep rumbling rolls across the square as a marcher yells into the megaphone.

"The single most important issue facing the civilization today is saving our planet Earth. Stop Keystone Pipeline! Nebraska."

Far beyond the trees, a tiny jetliner cuts through the vault of clouds piled over the Potomac.

"Sorry about the siren," Barry said yesterday.

He'd walked me back down the long white corridor, and we stood before a bright display case full of pictures, facts, and quotes about the navy's Great Green Fleet. Inside I read the oft-quoted phrase, "Energy Security is National Security," and the frequently cited numbers, "A $10 increase per barrel of oil increases the DoD's energy costs by $1.3 billion per year."

It's like a mantra.

Ray Mabus says it, "Every time the cost of a barrel of oil goes up a dollar, it costs the United States Navy $31 million in extra fuel costs." Sharon Burke says it, every "$1 rise in the price of a barrel of oil translates to approximately $130 million during the span of a year" for the military. Former Defense Secretary Robert Gates says it, "Every time the price of oil goes up by $1 per barrel, it costs us about $130 million." But repetition doesn't change the facts. The cheapest biofuel the navy has yet purchased, a Tyson chicken fat–based hydrotreated renewable jet fuel from Dynamic Fuels, costs $26.75 a gallon. Fuel from California start-up Solazyme, the navy's top choice for advanced biofuels made from algae, runs as cheap as $61.33 a gallon and as much as $427.63 a gallon. One company, Albemarle, sells the navy jet fuel from n-butanol at $4,454.55 a gallon. Honeywell UOP, a company that converts isobutanol to jet fuel, charges $11,248.99 a gallon. Does it make sense, in the best-case scenario, to pay nearly $27 a gallon for a fuel because you're supposedly concerned about the price volatility of a fuel that costs $3.26 a gallon? Perhaps if you assume that the United States is dependent on foreign oil and the world is running out of oil.

"As a nation and as a Navy and Marine Corps," Ray Mabus says, "we simply rely too much on a finite and depleting stock of fossil fuels that will most likely continue to rise in cost over the next decades. You know the statistics better than I do: the United States consumes 25% of the world's oil but controls the production of only 3%." According to Mabus, "We know oil is a limited resource. We buy from volatile areas of the world. Over time, the price keeps going up. . . . To a certain extent we have ceded a strategic resource — one that is difficult to guarantee — to other nations. We have ceded this to other nations who are allowed to exert disproportionate influence as a result. This creates an obvious vulnerability to our energy security, and to our national security, and to our future on this planet."

In 2011, Mabus told an audience at a National Clean Energy Summit in Las Vegas that "we buy our energy from people that may not be our *friends*." In 2012, he told the audience at the Pacific Rim demo that "today shows we can reduce our dependency on foreign oil." In 2013, he reiterated the mantra that "the Great Green Fleet will signal to the world America's continued naval supremacy, unleashed from the tether of foreign oil."

What the Pentagon doesn't volunteer so frequently, however, is the fact that almost 40 percent of the oil consumed in the United States comes from the United States. What we can't get at home we have to import. Where do these imports come from? Where do we get that other 60 percent? According to the University of Texas at Austin's annual energy poll, the average American believes that 58 percent of our foreign oil comes from Saudi Arabia. Who gets the silver medal? The average American, terribly cynical, imagines that Iraq supplies our second-largest source of foreign oil at 15 percent. As political scientist John Duffield says, "People have tended to exaggerate how much oil we imported from the Middle East."

In fact, less than a quarter of the oil that the United States imports comes from Saudi Arabia, Iraq, or even the greater Middle East combined. According to the US Energy Information Administration (EIA), 50 percent of our foreign oil comes from Canada and Latin America, with Canada supplying the brunt at 28 percent. Canada provides the United States with more than twice as much crude oil as Saudi Arabia. But we may not even need Canada. President Obama recently announced that "we produce more oil here in the United States than we buy from the rest of the world." According to a recent American Petroleum Institute report, "In 2011, the U.S. became a net exporter of petroleum products for the first time since 1949." If Obama or his successor approves the Keystone Pipeline and lifts the ban on the export of crude oil, the United States could remake West Texas Intermediate the international crude oil benchmark. The headlines from the EIA read unequivocally, "U.S. Oil Import Dependence: Declining No Matter How You Measure It."

Of course, we have no way of guaranteeing such favorable conditions over the long term — right? What Ray Mabus, Sharon Burke, and the other purveyors of the Pentagon's sustainable biofuel mantra don't often volunteer is that the idea of a finite and rapidly depleting stock of fossil fuels — the fear of peak oil production that drove policy decisions over a decade ago — has largely been debunked. We know that oil is a limited resource, but hardly to the extent that one might hope for or fear.

Marion King Hubbert, a geoscientist working for Shell Oil Company, first proposed the theory of peak oil in 1956. Hubbert famously prophesied that world oil production would achieve its maximum level of extraction, that is, its peak, sometime around 1970 and then sink into terminal decline with catastrophic consequences for the world economy. Later he pushed the peak back to 1995. In 1997, British petroleum geologist Colin Campbell predicted a peak by 2007. Kenneth Deffeyes, a geologist at Shell Oil, said he was "99% confident" that peak oil would hit in 2004. In 2007, Germany's Energy Watch Group announced that world oil had peaked in 2006. "Anticipated supply shortages could lead easily to disturbing scenes of mass unrest," the report stated, a situation that "could spin out of control and turn into a complete meltdown of society." A complete list of botched peak oil predictions could take forever.

"While opinion-makers, decision-makers, the academy, and the financial market seem to be caught up in the 'peak-oil' mantra, and an excessive enthusiasm for renewable energy alternatives to oil, oil prices and technologies are supporting a quiet revolution throughout the oil world," Leonardo Maugeri, an oil executive and senior fellow at the Kennedy School's Belfer Center for Science and International Affairs at Harvard, wrote in 2012. Nowhere is this revolution more dramatic than in the United States, where new oil-extraction technologies such as horizontal drilling and hydraulic fracturing, or fracking, have opened up new reserves like North Dakota's Bakken Formation, a shale deposit that may, according to one estimate, contain as much oil as Saudi Arabia. "The shale/tight oil boom in the United States is not a temporary bubble," said

Maugeri, "but the most important revolution in the oil sector in decades."

Today, the lowest estimate for the total volume of oil contained in the Canadian tar sands alone is greater than the 1.3 trillion barrels that Marion King Hubbert thought remained worldwide in 1956. The lesson is not that the world is running out of oil—technological innovation has changed that—but, rather, it is running out of only conventional oil, the light sweet stuff you find in Saudi Arabia. Even depleted conventional wells might yet yield many more generations' worth of barrels due to the new drilling methods developed in the United States. "The lesson," according to Maugeri, "is that oil is not in short supply. From a purely physical point of view, there are huge volumes of conventional and unconventional oils still to be developed, with no 'peak-oil' in sight." The lesson, says Christof Rühl, chief economist at BP, is that "peak oil has been predicted for 150 years. It has never happened, and it will stay this way." It is unfortunate, however, he adds, that the "human capacity of digging hydrocarbons out of the ground and burning them and turning them into energy seems to be much larger than the atmospheric capacity to absorb the resulting CO_2." It is an unfortunate and grizzly irony that our species' gift for exploiting the liquid dregs of countless living worlds routinely erased over untold aeons itself furnishes our reckless march toward oblivion. "That is likely to be more of a natural limit than all these peak oil theories combined," says Rühl.

The environmentalist George Monbiot observes with some cynicism, "There is enough oil in the ground to deep-fry the lot of us, and no obvious means to prevail upon governments and industry to leave it in the ground. Twenty years of efforts to prevent climate breakdown through moral persuasion have failed. . . . I don't like raising problems when I cannot see a solution. But right now I'm not sure how I can look my children in the eyes."

"Dear Barack and Michele and girls, please don't leave our kids and grandkids in hell on Earth. Climate change is real. Katy, Illinois," another marcher reads.

"Don't forget us little people. Marvin, New Mexico."

The marchers, George Monbiot, and other environmentalists, however, may soon have to face up to a further disturbing irony.

The Pentagon, the patron saint of fossil fuel energy, antihero of international climate accords, god of greenhouse gas pollution, and protector of our national security, is trying to change.

According to the Pentagon's own grim realpolitik perspective — its "more serious look at the world," as Chuck Hagel describes it — the military's domestic biofuel program doesn't make sense. We are not running out of oil or depending on Middle Eastern oil; nor do biofuels appear to cut the Pentagon's energy costs. Why doesn't the military keep it simple and burn the cheap stuff from our good friends just across the border in Canada? The Pentagon recently moved against Congress to retain section 526 of George W. Bush's 2007 Energy Independence and Security Act. Section 526 prevents federal agencies from buying fuels that produce more emissions over their life cycle than conventional petroleum. Military exemptions to the section would have allowed the Pentagon to purchase oil from the Canadian tar sands and accomplish its mission of energy independence. But the Pentagon successfully negotiated to keep section 526. Why? When pressed, Sharon Burke responded to the flaws in the Pentagon's biofuel narrative. She offers what is officially the last and least motivating factor in the Pentagon's pursuit of alternative energy. The memo is brief: "As we seek energy security and independence, we don't want to trade one security challenge for another."

The other security challenge she refers to is climate change.

As the *Boston College Law Review* observes, "The synergy between the military's interests and energy conservation may provide political cover for those who otherwise might not"— and, I might add, *cannot*—"support investment in clean energy technology solely for civilian purposes or environmental reasons." Is it possible that the Pentagon is offering a series of flawed arguments about improving its ability to wage war as political cover when, in fact, it may have already embarked on the long-famed and elusive Apollo-like program needed to transform the entire nation's operational energy? Is improved "energy for the warfighter" really a euphemism for the improved life span of *Homo sapiens*?

I stood inside the Pentagon, before the bright Great Green Fleet display case, and stared at the navy's flowing green energy security logo. "It's a lot like what you saw with DARPA in past years," Barry said. "Military demand funded the R&D that produced innovations not only for the military but all Americans."

A rising tide lifts all boats. The ice doesn't care about politics or Democrats or Republicans: it just melts. This was the adult way to think about climate change. Or as Sharon Burke summarized more broadly this year in *Foreign Affairs*:

> The benefits of the Pentagon's drive for energy efficiency go well beyond improving the U.S military's energy security and lowering its costs. Through coordination and technology transfers with the private sector, the effort to create a more energy-efficient and secure fighting force could also stimulate innovation beyond the military and help reduce the carbon footprint of many businesses. Some of the world's most important technologies, from semiconductors to the Internet, have resulted from collaboration between the U.S. military and private industry, and the U.S. energy sector will likely benefit from that pattern, as well.

I really wanted to believe this was possible. But the idea that at bottom the military might actually be developing biofuels out of some consideration for the health of Mother Earth and her children sounded so counterintuitive that it seemed to me either that too many people inside the Pentagon were totally drunk on corn ethanol or that biofuels had a further and darker unstated purpose. Perhaps climate change formed yet another cover. One had to wonder if the biofuels weren't being developed, like cloud seeding, as some kind of future weapon. In a certain obvious sense, they were. The navy's cutting-edge biofuels would power and were already powering instruments of death. But the blade was double-sided. And its other edge seemed softer. The biofuels could also combat climate change. It was the same lesson as at the China Lake labs and the base's technology museum — the harmony between violence and invention, the age-old paradox of war — and I thought of Pierre St.-Amand's words, how quick he was to point out "humanitarian uses of the things we have done in a naval laboratory." And standing in the corridor, staring at the Great Green Fleet display,

I could read the paradox directly off the photograph of an F/A-18 Hornet, the cheerful logo printed just below the cockpit, just behind the right elbow of President Obama, an image of a narrow green leaf growing between the sky and the sea, reaching toward the nose cone of the fighter jet, jutting in the same direction as the missiles strapped beneath the wings, all of it pointing toward this new synergy among military, economic, and environmental defense, asking me to believe, it seemed, for a moment, in a fighting machine that planted not only bombs but seeds, seeds that would help engender a future and more prosperous America.

As Obama reiterated for the crowd at Andrews Air Force Base, "Moving towards clean energy is about our security. It's also about our economy. And it's about the future of our planet." And it's a brilliant narrative, an evolved form of the military-industrial complex, cleansed of its historic toxic connotations — no longer simply a means of providing guaranteed business to American corporations but a means of providing for the future of the planet. And countless other benefits may accrue. Ed Fallon wasn't referring to the Pentagon, but he said it correctly, "I already see the seeds being planted." So what if the military had to exaggerate our dependence on foreign oil and propagate the fiction of peak oil? You have to frighten people to force them to change. "To be is to be perceived," George Berkeley said, and so far while many Americans had perceived a rise in prices at the pump, very few had noticed the oceans climb seven inches over the past century, and even if they had, for the vast majority the imminent threat of rising living costs frightened them terribly more than the thought that their way of life could someday cost the planet its future. Which is not to blame the "bewildered herd." No doubt it is a luxury to study what you cannot perceive directly — you aren't flipping burgers when you're averaging altimeters from satellite radar to estimate rises in global sea levels. But in any event, climate change isn't metaphysics. And the Pentagon knew this. They and many bright minds besides theirs had peeked through the keyhole and seen the monster behind the door.

The question, however, was how to construct a narrative for the rest, for those unable or unwilling to see. "The persistent difficulty," as Walter Lippmann writes in *Public Opinion*, is that "the real environment is altogether too big, too complex, and too fleeting for direct acquaintance. We are not equipped to deal with so much subtlety, so much variety, so many permutations and combinations." Hence "a specialized class" must persuade Americans by appealing to things that are primary, things that they have seen and that they fear, things that have imposed on their lives and entered firmly into their consciousness. "To traverse the world men must have maps of the world," Lippmann says.

In other words, you talk about defending people's way of life, not taking away their car keys, and you provide them with a road map, a narrative — a fiction — because most Americans can neither "understand nor influence the very events upon which their lives and happiness are known to depend."

Siddhartha Velandy, a graduate of Harvard Law and a US Marine Corps major, summarizes the remarkable promise inherent in the new military-environmental complex:

The Green Arms Race has the potential to succeed where existing international and unilateral efforts to encourage efficient energy innovation and address climate change have failed. . . . The progeny of the Green Arms Race, rather than a strategy of mutually assured destruction, will be a more efficient fighting force, a reduction of the worldwide reliance on fossil fuels, new spinoff green energy technologies, and the creation of a new, more stable, world order — a mutually assured sustenance. The once disparate approaches to address climate change, energy dependence, and national security become one and the same: initiate and win the Green Arms Race!

"What do you think of the whole thing?" Barry asked me.

I had thought the race was over. I came to Washington with the assumption that America had failed, and only a sudden and massive democratic force unlike anything ever seen in world history could possibly pull us back from the brink of ruin. But inside the Pentagon, I started to feel naïve, guilty nearly, embarrassed for resenting an institution that I'd always seen as massive, overfunded, and unscrupulous, when in fact it did infinitely more than fire missiles. And I thought that the word "utopia" still meant "nowhere" and we hadn't yet found a cure for the cancer called war and never would and in the meantime the Pentagon wasn't going anywhere and it produced much more than mere bombs — did anyone driving a car in some unfamiliar city ever refuse to use Google Maps just because DARPA developed microchips and GPS? Did they unbuckle their seat belts to thwart the benefit of air bags because they came out of a China Lake laboratory? Nobody switches the channel during the Super Bowl because of a slow-motion replay. Instead they pay closer attention.

I wanted to believe in the progeny of the Green Arms Race. I wanted to believe in a future of mutually assured sustenance.

"War is the father of all things," I said.

"A lot of things," Barry said.

———

I used to be an activist. A decade ago, I was interviewed on PBS during the *NewsHour* with Jim Lehrer. My friends and I handed out a lot of forms at school that got kids off the military recruiter's list. Few people knew this, but the federal No Child Left Behind Act gave more money to public high schools if they turned over every student's name and phone number to the military. The marines used to show up at lunch driving Humvees onto the quad and blasting hip-hop. They set up pull-up bars on the grass and gave rap CDs to the strongest Patrick Henry Patriot. We got to skip class to play first-person shooter games inside massive blue motor homes stamped with bright US Air Force decals. A midterm test in my American history class was canceled junior year for a special assembly on foreign languages. The presenters talked about money for college, the importance of Arabic, and opportunities for travel. I only found out after the assembly when I told them I was interested that they were from the navy. The army used to call me every couple of weeks during senior year and tell me they had a great soccer team. I'd been the varsity goalkeeper since freshman year. "Your friend José says you're the best in the city." A lot of my friends signed up, and I never heard from them again.

"Obama, Turkey is not your ally!" The megaphone from the ISIS protest aligns with my eardrum again. The chant drifts across Lafayette Square as yet another marcher takes the stage and shouts toward the White House.

It's Sean. She's wearing shoes now. "If this is truly a democracy, then why do the real people, the 99 percent feel so powerless to effect change that will ensure the future of the human race? Elise, New Mexico."

Activism is a depressing game—whether they joined today or started in Colorado, I think that's the message coming home to several of the young marchers. Apathy and complacency are death, no doubt, but nobody rewards your passion, your action, or your belief. They call you a bum, a bastard, an anarchist, and anti-American, or they simply tolerate your naïveté. I got kicked out of my high school graduation ceremony for speaking my mind, never received my diploma, and didn't change anything. It's possible, though, that I've been approaching everything the wrong way.

Miriam, the spirit walker, reads through the megaphone, "It is inherently American to speak your mind. Let's approach this as real Americans worthy of the respect of future generations. Pennsylvania."

Another marcher, "Jobs don't matter if there is no clean air or clean water. Nicole, Colorado Springs."

A couple "woos" for that one and then some "shhh" sounds. The redhead on roller skates looks angry. Several small groups hover at the periphery of the march, blabbing at a rude volume. There's a cluster of girls in local high school sweaters huddled beneath an oak tree. I can hear them discussing their next maneuver. More people up front keep looking back over their shoulders. Cathy taps the prayer bell, trying to focus attention, as another marcher mounts the stage and the high school girls turn toward H Street. "Dear Congress . . ." she reads, as another couple debates over lunch. Two boys pick up bikes and a girl with blue hair runs after them.

It's an unkind thought — I generally try to root for the under-dogs, the little people, the losers — but the march and the messages and the chanting and the songs and banners and road signs and many miles behind them constitute only a terrible waste of energy. It seems this way especially while those marchers, the people who just joined today, keep walking away. And who could blame them? The pilgrimage seems to point only to the profligacy of the people present, white people mostly, young and old but mostly old, with enough time and money to waste on the symbolic performance of democracy, a performance that is ultimately self-serving. "It is no longer possible," Walter Lippmann writes, "to believe in the original dogma of democracy; that the knowledge needed for the management of human affairs comes up spontaneously from the human heart. Where we act on that theory we expose ourselves to self-deception." I watch the high school girls walk away and wish more people would as well. We've all done our duty. I'd like to leave now, to no longer contribute to the charade — it's a dangerous ma-neuver given the location — but I unzip my backpack, take out my flask, and while the young kid from Colorado reads a message through the megaphone, I think of that afternoon, mid-June 2005, in San Diego during my high school graduation ceremony when the freshman ROTC came out after the national anthem in full uniform twirling fake rifles covered in football tape and marched toward the fifty-yard line chanting in unison and tossing their guns while the entire stadium full of 5,000 people stood frozen in silence for two whole minutes with their hands over their hearts and at some point I snapped and yelled "Fuck US imperialism!" and security escorted me out and my mother started weeping in the bleachers and wouldn't talk to me for several weeks afterward so I stayed at my friend Kyle's house and his parents were kind and so were all the others. They told me not to feel too bad. "Don't be too embarrassed," they said. I was just young, an idealist, and had to give it time, a few more years, perhaps, they said, to develop a more complex appreciation of geopolitics. "You'll understand when you're older."

I'm still trying to understand the contradictions. I don't know what to believe. But I don't want to be naïve.

"Is the Pentagon hiring?" I asked Barry.

"Probably," he said. "You could apply online."

Barry straightened his tie and checked his watch again. He said he had to get back to work. We turned and started back toward the mezzanine above the security checkpoint. Walking down the long concrete ramp, I contemplated buying something in the gift shop or having a penny crushed into the shape of the Pentagon or working for an important think tank. This was the adult way to think about climate change and the history and future of the world. Protests don't change things. Powerful people do.

Barry stepped behind me onto the escalator above the checkpoint and grabbed the rail.

Only one more question remained.

"Can the Pentagon actually go green?"

On this point Barry finally laughs.

"The most important question," Marty Hoffert says, "is whether *Homo sapiens* can adopt a narrative leading to the sustainable existence of high tech civilization on Earth." As Marc Kodack says, "The question is how do I create a narrative that allows me to do more — the Army to enhance its mission." Or as Sharon Burke says, "We need to fight a war — the question is how do we do that."

How do I create a narrative that allows me to accomplish my mission?

How do I fight a war?

Barry shook my hand and wished me well. I turned and dropped my visitor button in the cardboard box before the metal detectors and walked outside past several soldiers with machine guns. Heading toward the escalators, I slipped on my headphones. Somewhere in the back of my mind, whether learned or hereditary, I've always held on to a certain truth, something I knew certain people inside the Pentagon would subscribe to, and that was the conviction that the complexity of the human world exceeded the calculation of infinity and for all intents and purposes probably has been and will be — even though no one in the government would put it this way publicly — fucked up beyond all recognition. But all those DoD people believed in one thing. One thing held it all in check, one thing preserved the order of civilization, and it wasn't love or kindness, trust or goodwill, but power, particularly the superior economic, diplomatic, and military power of the United States. Speak softly and carry a big stick. For a large portion of my life, I'd devoted a massive amount of personal energy to resisting that stick. Maybe it was something Freudian — I envied and feared its power — but it didn't make sense. It was like trying to will water uphill against gravity or request that evil vacate the world. Power follows certain laws. Like energy, it cannot be created or destroyed. Kill the king, you'll find another right behind him. Dissolve US Central Command and you'll cede control to something far worse. "Every revolution evaporates," Kafka says, "and leaves behind only the slime of a new bureaucracy." And forget the aphorisms; even personally, it was hypocritical. I benefited from that power. And always and everywhere I'd been attracted to it, craved the anxiety and tension, the stakes inherent in its maintenance, the razor-thin line between peace and violence, victory and defeat, light and darkness, and I found it, like most, through sublimated forms, through drum sticks, keeping the beat, holding down some semblance of order in a maelstrom of grinding chaos, and it came once through soccer, as a keeper, protecting the goal line, screaming out commands, organizing defenders, and sometimes getting kicked in the face, in the leg, breaking my arm, my nose, and my tibia in half; I kept my eyes closed for an hour, the time it took to get to the hospital, before they plugged me into a morphine drip. But I've always wanted to feel like part of the winning team. And I've always wanted to believe in this country. But it's hard — I never really had a father and I've never really felt at home. I guess I'll always be a bastard. I yam what I yam.

Underground, beneath the Pentagon, I stepped off the escalator, clicked to one of my favorite albums, *The Destroyers of All*, and added more fare to my ticket. I turned up the volume as the guitars began to drone and whine, and moving toward the platform I pictured structural steel slowly bending, and then the drums started cracking away at the foundation and the album began its long intolerable flight, advancing with all the warmth, comfort, and certainty of a skyscraper lurching toward the earth, and I started walking quickly, following the officers, number crunchers, and other tourists toward the trains, and every twenty feet, all along the walls throughout Pentagon station hung bright neon Lockheed Martin billboards that looked like screenshots from some Xbox *Medal of Honor* TV commercial, and I studied one while I waited on the platform and the crowd piled up behind me, a low-angle shot of a massive Humvee tearing over jagged rocks, tire tread throwing streaks of dirt into a neon gold sky, and to the left clean sci-fi robot script read, "We call it protected mobility, Soldiers and Marines call it a safe ride home," and as the train slid into the station, I stuffed two wintergreen pouches into my lower lip, crammed into the car, and turned to stare at the billboard until the doors slammed shut in my face, and standing there, gripping the rail while the train began to gather speed and the warm bodies bumped against me, I reached into my shirt pocket and clicked the volume up further and the moaning guitars began to blend with the screaming of the train as it ripped along the metal rails, and I studied the face that hovered before me reflected in black glass. And listened to the drum sticks stitch together the gloom like starlight. *It does not grieve.* And closed my eyes. And I felt the long, hard grip of the Pentagon, the cold enthrallment of its sparkling white hallways, melt slowly away. *It will not grieve.* And I turned the volume up louder and thought that the virtue of excellent music was that it permitted the listener, if he or she paid attention, to subsume the noise invading their skull into a narrative of their present experience. *Bring me the comfort of cold inertia.* And in my case, as was often the case, I felt as though

I was en route to my own execution. And I felt happy. Traveling on the subway train, swaying alongside so many strangers, our bony elbows bumping together underground, the screaming discord filling the last alcoves of my memory, I felt perfectly alone, perfectly in harmony, perfectly part of a chaotic world hurtling inexorably toward destruction. *Our extinction seeded in blind avarice.* And exiting at Foggy Bottom, I walked quickly through the Friday rush hour, fed my ticket to the stall, and hurried toward the escalators. *Come dawn no light will be thrown on them.* And a woman in a long black dress made eye contact with me while she descended and I smiled at her while I rose and walking alone, the imaginary hiss of the escalator fading behind me, I finally spit, gazed up at a glowing red sky, and listened as the last track crescendoed at six minutes and thirty-seven seconds. *This vermin, these ingrates, us of the earth, the destroyers of all.* And crossed toward the White House.

Another marcher reads onstage, "There is no more food from plants or meat from game. Our people are suffering from diabetes and cancer. Our water is polluted from uranium and God knows what. What is left for our future generation? Have a safe journey, God be with you all. Lucia, Acoma."

Another marcher takes the stage. And laughs. "This one starts out interestingly," he says, then reads, "Dear God, we are running out of time and soon our planet will be beyond our repair. Awake your people and bless these walkers."

God grant me the serenity to accept the things I cannot change, the courage to change the things I can, and the wisdom to know the difference.

I take another shot from the flask, but I don't feel powerful. I'm still trying to understand the contradictions. I don't want to be naïve, but the Pentagon spends an average of $104 billion annually on the global protection of oil. This fact will not change. Imagine the millions of lost jobs, the total collapse of our economy, the power we would concede to other nations, to other "people," as Ray Mabus calls them, "that may not be our friends." As Andrew Bacevich, a retired US colonel and Boston University professor, explains: "Imagine the impact just on the Pentagon were this country actually to achieve anything approaching energy independence.

U.S. Central Command would go out of business. Dozens of bases in and around the Middle East would close. The navy's fifth fleet would stand down. Weapons contracts worth tens of billions would risk being canceled."

Whether or not the war in Iraq was about finding weapons of mass destruction, defeating terrorism, ensuring Iraqi freedom or an oil lifeline or world economic growth, the fact is that today within that country—even as we're no longer depending on foreign oil or running out of oil—petroleum companies are establishing contracts that will extend the lifetime of their companies far beyond this century. The only obstacle is ISIS, the appalling offal of a failed war, a war we fought preemptively and unilaterally. But imagine for a moment if we manage to rein in ISIS and the oil starts flowing as projected, could a war that killed more than a million civilians and deposited thousands of tons of depleted uranium across a country known as the cradle of civilization, a country responsible for the birth of agriculture and the written word, really be called a failure? It depends upon how you read the ultimate goal of that $1.7 trillion investment. "Iraq holds about 18% of proved crude oil reserves in the Middle East and almost 9% of total global reserves," says the US Energy Information Administration, "ranking fifth in the world." Or as the former chairman of the Federal Reserve, Alan Greenspan, said: "I am saddened that it is politically inconvenient to acknowledge what everyone knows: the Iraq War is largely about oil. Thus, projections of world oil supply and demand that do not note the highly precarious environment of the Middle East are avoiding the eight-hundred-pound gorilla that could bring world economic growth to a halt."

Today, however, despite the growing chaos, the cradle of civilization is producing 4 million barrels a day. Imagine, though, if we did decide to ship our troops back en masse; imagine all the Humvees and the M1 Abrams tanks that get 4 miles per gallon and .2 mile per gallon; imagine the B-52 Stratocruisers that gulp down 500 gallons of oil each minute; imagine the pairs of Apache helicopters that burn 60,000 gallons of jet fuel in a single raid; imagine the F-16s flying tens of thousands of sorties over Iraq for the first year of the war; and imagine all of them burning biofuels; imagine soldiers being diverted to protect cornfields rather than oil fields and their pipelines, ports, and shipping routes; imagine the absurdity of this image and every pillar of the Pentagon's biofuel argument. You can't produce biofuels in a theater of war. The long resupply convoys will remain, and soldiers will continue to die protecting them whether they carry fossil fuels or biofuels from algae, chicken fat, or corn. And imagine once again that at the start of this future war, already present, forty-two separate F-117s fly more than 1,300 combat sorties over Iraq — imagine all these jets burning biofuels. And imagine that instead of producing 52 billion pounds of carbon pollution from conventional JP-5 jet fuel, they produce double that amount from burning advanced algae biofuel.

The true 800-pound gorilla inside the Pentagon today is the fact that biofuels contribute more to climate change than do conventional fossil fuels. "Because biofuels come from plants, which absorb carbon dioxide from the atmosphere as they grow, burning biofuels in vehicles"— or destroyer ships, or guided missile cruisers, or F-117s, or F/A-18 Hornets —"would in theory slow the buildup of greenhouse gases, compared with burning fossil fuels," explains David Biello for *Scientific American*. The problem with this theory, however, is that growing and cutting and cooking and transporting all that plant matter require massive amounts of energy, most of which comes from fossil fuels. A recent report from the Institute for European Environmental Policy found that if all EU member states went ahead with their 2020 National Renewable Energy Action Plans, the "use of additional conventional biofuels up to 2020 on the scale anticipated . . . would lead to between 81% and 167% more GHG emissions than meeting the same need through fossil fuel use." The report concludes that "the use of these additional conventional biofuels cannot be considered to contribute to the achievement of EU climate change policy goals."

The life cycle of corn ethanol in the United States consumes 3.5 times more fossil fuels than the petroleum fuel life cycle, produces more than three times the greenhouse gas emissions, and demands more than 1,000 times the water. "U.S. production of corn ethanol went from 50 million gallons in 1979 to 13 billion gallons in 2010," David Biello writes. "A government mandate to supply 10 percent of the country's passenger vehicle fuel drove that enormous growth, however, and the product has been affordable only because of massive federal subsidies." In 2010, federal subsidies and tax breaks for oil and natural gas totaled $2.8 billion, and biofuel subsidies reached almost $7.7 billion. In return, the federal government collected $56 billion in corporate taxes from oil companies. These taxes helped fund a further increase in greenhouse gas emissions and a decrease in world oil supply through the subsidized production of more corn ethanol, altogether a peculiar strategy if you're concerned about a finite and dwindling stock of fossil fuels, not to mention the future of the planet.

The Pentagon's pursuit of biofuels is an investment not in some cutting-edge innovation but rather in a terribly expensive technology that is older than the written word. Naval Captain T. A. Kiefer, a strategy professor at the US Air Force War College who has deployed seven times and served twenty-one months in Iraq, writes in the *Strategic Studies Quarterly*, the air force's most distinguished journal:

> In the more than five thousand years that humans have been producing ethanol as wine and beer and distilled spirits, it has always been realized that all the invested labor and energy made the resulting products far too precious to use their alcohol fraction as a fuel. Only urban folk in the modern era, blinded by the ubiquitous wealth of fossil fuel energy, could fail to see the negative energy balance of using distilled liquor as a fuel at the cost of all the wood or gas or oil fuel used to distill it. Ethanol has inherent limitations that have made it a perennial loser.

Imagine if the United States were to substitute corn ethanol for all its current transportation fuels — we would need a cornfield triple the size of the contiguous United States. In such a scenario, the United States and most of the world would be left with nothing to eat. Even now, the diversion of arable land to the production of biofuel crops is driving up food prices around the globe, increasing world hunger, and fueling not cars so much as global instability. The population of the world increases by 2.5 people every second,

150 people every minute, 9,000 every hour, 216,000 every day. By 2050, there will be 9 billion people living on the planet. Add to this the facts that the world is already on track for the worst-case warming scenario predicted by the IPCC, and the global water supply is projected to drop by 40 percent over the next fifteen years. Why are we spending water on fuel? Why are we making fuel from food? According to a World Bank lead economist, Donald Mitchell, the main factor "behind the rapid increase in internationally traded food prices since 2002 . . . was the large increase in biofuels production in the U.S. and the EU." A United Nations report, "The State of Food Insecurity in the World," counted 1.2 billion people living in hunger in 2011 and called on G20 nations to abandon their biofuel programs, stating that "any further growth in biofuels will place additional demands on the food system." Peter Brabeck-Letmathe, chair of the colossal Swiss food and drink company Nestlé, sums it up concisely: "This is absolute madness."

If economic realities and moral claims don't cancel the production of corn ethanol in the United States, Mother Nature probably will. "Climate change has substantially increased the prospect that crop production will fail to keep up with rising demand in the next 20 years," says Claudia Tebaldi, a scientist at the National Center for Atmospheric Research and coauthor of a 2014 study titled "Water and Climate Risks Facing U.S. Corn Production." The rising demand, however, refers to the fact that very soon the world will have 2 billion more mouths to feed. The United States, by far the largest producer of corn in the world, has grown 32 percent of the planet's crop since 2010; we are also the largest exporter, accounting for about 40 percent of global corn exports. Were our corn crop to fail, the security implications at home and abroad would be profound.

The Pentagon, thankfully, does not suffer from absolute madness. That's why it's pursuing advanced biofuels, that is, biofuels not derived from food crops. The Pentagon is particularly interested in algae. Algae grows much faster than any other food crop and has a power density hundreds of times greater. Craig Venter, cofounder of the biofuel start-up Synthetic Genomics, estimates that it "would take a farm roughly the size of Maryland" to replace all US transportation fuels with algae biofuels. Compare that to the power density of corn, which would require an arable landmass triple the size of America. What's more, algae can grow in outdoor ponds in hot, dry climates nourished only by sunlight, CO_2, and brackish water — or even sewage. Hence another theoretical benefit: algae biofuels could grow without diverting water away from crops or people and without inflating food prices. It all sounds nice in theory. The problem, however, as a recent European Commission report states, is that "a substantial amount of energy is needed to manage all the water used in the mass cultivation of microalgae for biodiesel. A recent study suggests that seven times more energy is required to manage the water, than is delivered by the biodiesel when it is used as fuel." That figure of seven refers just to the ponds, and does not even take into account the vast amounts of energy required to refine the algae and then transport it to a gas pump in California, Iowa, or Iraq.

According to the Argonne National Laboratory, to place a gallon of nonhydrotreated biodiesel in a gas station pump requires twelve times the total energy and more than two and a half times the fossil fuel energy as regular petroleum diesel. Even this calculation requires several cheerful assumptions. Indeed, as Captain T. A. Kiefer writes, "A critical look at the more optimistic studies that predict the higher EROIs," that is, higher energy returns on investment, "reveals that they depend upon a host of unrealistic assumptions — massive supplies of free water and nutrients, a free pass on enormous environmental impact, and market economics that miraculously transform the huge burden of enormous accumulations of soggy byproduct biomass that has per-ton value less than the cost of transportation into a cash commodity crop."

The problem is that even "advanced" biofuels require more energy and water than conventional petroleum fuel and ultimately emit more greenhouse gases over their life cycle. "You cannot convert biomass, or sugar, into large volume chemicals because you'll never make money," says Alan Shaw, former CEO of Codexis, the first advanced biofuel company traded publicly on any US stock exchange. "Everybody but me is still in this nightmare," Shaw said in 2013 after abandoning the company. "This model is broken."

One corporation, however, San Francisco–based Solazyme, the

navy's top pick for algae biofuels and the winner of a $21-million biorefinery grant from the Department of Energy, seems to be enjoying the nightmare. The company's cofounder and president sits on the board of the federal biofuel advisory committee. The navy pays Solazyme $61.33 per gallon for its cheapest fuel, which according to Ray Mabus "will immeasurably aid this planet, which we call home."

However, there's actually no *solar* in Solazyme.

As Captain Kiefer observes, the company "actually grows their product in dark bioreactors, feeding it carbon and hydrogen energy in the form of sugar. This makes them unique in producing a biofuel 100% dependent upon a food crop and getting 0% of its energy from the sun via direct photosynthesis — a worst case scenario."

According to Jean Ziegler, a former Swiss Parliament member and UN Special Rapporteur on the Right to Food, "The global corporations that produce biofuels have . . . succeeded in persuading the majority of world public opinion and virtually all of the Western nations that energy from plant sources constitutes the miracle weapon against climate change. Yet their argument is a lie."

The Pentagon, admittedly, does not seek to replace all its operational energy with biofuels. And that's a good thing, perfectly in accordance with reality, because no biofuel company could deliver that order without first starving and deep-frying the lot of us. Rather, it's just the navy, and it's only shooting to replace 50 percent of its operational energy. It will need 37 million more gallons of biofuel to accomplish its mission of launching the Great Green Fleet in 2016. To date, the navy's largest purchase of biofuel totaled only 350,000 gallons.

Ray Mabus never said how long the Great Green Fleet would sail. Rather, he simply said, "We will deploy it."

And we certainly will. Perhaps it will float for a few days or a month — maybe a year. In any case, "Leading change is not new for the Department of the Navy. We have done so repeatedly in the adoption of new technologies to power our ships. And resistance to change is not new either," Mabus says, referring to the days when the navy traded wind for coal, coal for oil, and oil for nuclear power. "Naysayers swore at that point that the Navy was giving up a sure means of propulsion in favor of uncertain, dangerous, and probably infernal machines. The naysayers were wrong."

And they still are.

The Pentagon will again accomplish its mission.

The narrative of a green US military is not a narrative leading to the sustainable existence of high-tech civilization on Earth. It is rather a narrative about the changing role of the US military in the era of climate change.

It is not an investment in a weapon that improves the capacity of the warfighter, nor is it an investment that combats climate change. It is rather an investment in a weapon that is purely psychological. And yet it does provide the Pentagon with a sure means of propulsion. That's because it's an investment in a narrative, however fraught, that in the final analysis begins to launch the military forward into a future wherein climate change poses a profound threat to national security, and it further propels the mind of the American public forward to imagine a future wherein the military, with its more realistic look at the world, begins to move ahead to address the pressing security threats posed by climate change; it is a future that demands not only an expanded defense budget but also expanded thinking about the types of military operations appropriate to such a budget; it is a future, already present, in which despite the supposed best efforts of the international community, global greenhouse gas emissions continue to increase alongside a hungry and aspiring world population; a future in which the planet continues to warm and the Pentagon, forever exempt from reporting greenhouse gas emissions, continues to protect the world economy by guarding the infrastructure of global oil; a future perhaps wherein many Americans continue to enjoy a high quality of life relative to the vast majority of the globe; in which the Pentagon continues to consume the fossil fuels it protects at an astonishing rate; in which its operations expand to include a set of risky but necessary armed and humanitarian climate-related interventions; a future in which innovation and courage are demanded and tested; a future, same as the past, in which the world suffers rain and drought, heat and cold, sloth and hunger; a future, same as the past, in which remarkable sunsets sometimes empty into oceans of starless night;

a future, same as the past, in which the world exists within a constant state of tension, turning on a fragile axis between light and darkness, disaster and ruin, terror and ecstasy; a future, same as the past, in which many are born and in which many shall die; a future, same as the past, full of good and evil, gods and devils, doctors and shamans; and yet if all this is to exist, it is a future unlike the past in which a series of US naval bases stationed around the equator supply a fleet of retrofitted Boeing 747s with the petroleum jet fuel necessary to circle Earth, spraying the stratosphere with sulfur aerosols forever or perhaps for a thousand years, or maybe five hundred, or maybe a century, or a decade, or at least until we reach forever, that necessary point in the future in which our planet begins to glisten as bright and cold as all the other rocks and stars drifting in space, one more lifeless light among a myriad observed by no one.

————

The wind rips once more across Lafayette Square. An empty Cheetos bag cartwheels over the grass.

"Dear Congress, I have an eleven-year-old son. Please take action for him and his peers. Sincerely, Dylan."

I take another shot from the flask. Jim Beam. Cheap bourbon distilled from corn. Forty percent ethanol. Thirty dollars a gallon.

Someone tries to rally the group, screaming louder into the megaphone: "Environment over fossil fuels! Colorado."

Cheers and whistles. But not from the kid with the Colorado flag patch standing beside me. He looks to be about high school age. I wonder if he dropped out to follow Ed Fallon here. Would he follow him again? What did he think of democracy and direct action now? I remember listening to a speech online that Fallon gave in Colorado several months ago. "I have been struggling for years," he said, "on what I can do to help bring this crisis to the forefront of the American consciousness." He said there was so much good work happening across the country. He felt optimistic. "We hope the impact will be significant before midterm elections."

And I remembered that speech and that boy from Colorado

several days after the march ended when, driving back to Iowa, I learned over the radio that Republicans had swept the House and the Senate. Senator James Inhofe of Oklahoma — a deeply religious man who has accepted more than $1.7 million in campaign donations from oil and gas companies and the author of 2012's most fascinating work of nonfiction, *The Greatest Hoax: How the Global Warming Conspiracy Threatens Your Future* — would now head the Senate Committee on Environment and Public Works. Even though I wasn't particularly surprised by these results, I somehow felt bad for Fallon and the boy. But I probably shouldn't have. You don't spend eight months walking across the country because you think you're going to win. It's like the Badwater Ultramarathon — like any extravagant and wholly voluntary trial of suffering — you don't do it for the belt buckle. You do it for yourself. To conquer something deep inside you, which could be anything, but it's probably most often fear or pride or addiction or boredom. And that I think was the main difference between the young and the old marchers. They were both on the same team, battling the same monsters, but I think the old hippies and politicos like Fallon already knew at the outset that the race was over. The younger pilgrims, like Sean, did not. "I came to the march knowing a bit about climate change," she said, "but really excited to learn the specifics about what's going on everywhere regarding food, water, and air." When she learned the specifics, she stopped speaking for 109 days.

Another marcher reads another message. "Dear Mr. President and First Lady, I wanted to talk about how it's really hard to recycle here. I was wondering if we could get a facility to recycle glass and aluminum. Sincerely, Lorenzo Hernandez, Washington Middle School, Albuquerque, New Mexico."

Another. "Dear Mr. and Mrs. Obama, I believe that since you are our president it is your responsibility to better our future. By better I mean eco-friendly solar panels, more farmers markets, and bike lanes. Yours truly, Christopher Johnson, eighth grade, California."

Another message from a child. "Dear President Obama, I wish we could be more eco-friendly, more trees, more turning lights off, and more solar power. Thank you from the Turner Middle School kids, eighth grade."

213

It's like standing on the deck of a ship. The hull's already punctured and the lifeboats are missing. The kids keep asking, "Are we there yet?" "Are we home yet?" And nobody answers. Their parents just tell them to go back inside, turn out the lights, go to sleep. For the older marchers, the pilgrimage wasn't really activism. Cathy, Ed, Miriam, and a dozen others, they didn't really want to cure or save and couldn't anyway. They would be dead by the time the wind turbines stopped turning over Guantanamo and the shit hit the fan. They just wanted to put up the symbol of a fight, one last peaceful march while their bones were still strong, and then they could die without a sticky conscience. And if there was any friction inside the group, it was this: more than anything, the march was an act of mourning. And that act was grotesque. They weren't pilgrims but pallbearers, pallbearers now carrying the disembodied megaphone voices of children, children who very possibly wouldn't reach their own old age, home to the nation's capital, to Washington, to the monuments and houses that had, in their minds, already buried their future.

"Dear Mr. and Mrs. Obama, I am concerned about our environment being treated like a trash can with people littering everywhere."

"Dear Congress, I am a Mexican student that wants to help the environment by reducing our carbon footprint."

But for the handful of young people in the group, it was different. Their lives were just beginning. The mourning was harder for them. They had to keep living. And in that sense they had to keep fighting. In that sense they weren't mourners but refugees.

"Dear Michelle and girls . . ."

"You may not have time to read this . . ."

"It may not be in your power to change the whole country . . ."

"How can we save our sacred mountain?"

"Please, please, stop the destruction of Mother Earth."

"We hope you will do this so we don't lose our planet."

"Can we please have more trees?"

"More recycling . . ."

"More solar panels . . ."

It's like a funeral song, even through the megaphone, some ancient recording excavated from a landfill that will never play again but for this moment. The expectant voices of children calling for more recycling, more trees, more clean energy carry across the gray afternoon on the harsh wings of the megaphone toward the White House and beyond that to the US Capitol and the other houses of power, hoping in some small way to influence the supernatural authority once believed to reside there — until Cathy returns to the stage and grabs the megaphone. "We have heard only a few of these messages. Thank you all for participating in the selection of them and bringing them here to D.C. At this time it is a pleasure to introduce Emily, who will sing for us."

The kid from Colorado holds up his cell phone and snaps a picture as a young girl takes the stage, a guitar strapped over her shoulder. "Hey, guys, I'm very excited to join you this morning." Emily speaks with a slight lisp. "This power system's out so I'm going to try and sing loud for you guys." But her singing voice sounds fine.

"Mother, mother . . . There's too many of you crying."

I stand back as some of the marchers perk up, join hands, and start twirling in circles. Ed Fallon nods his head and mouths the words. The kid from Colorado smiles at me.

"Brother, brother, brother . . ." Emily croons loudly, eyes closed. "There's far too many of you dying."

And it occurs to me that the Great March is not the opposite image of Emanuel Leutze's painting. It is just what the painting appeared to depict in the lonely astonished afternoons of my only child's solipsism: people casting a glance of horror into the future of tomorrow. "Time's noblest offspring is the last." We are all participants in the Great March for Climate Action. We will be the progeny of the Green Arms Race. I am no longer an activist or a mourner but a refugee, a refugee from whatever it was those pilgrims actually saw in the sunset of Leutze's *Westward the Course of Empire Takes Its Way*.

We are refugees, all of us — us of the earth, the destroyers of all.

"Father, father . . . We don't need to escalate."

A recent report from a Climate Geoengineering Governance research project sponsored in part by the University of Oxford says that "there are a number of reasons for thinking that the military rather than scientists will run solar geoengineering projects." One of these reasons "relates to current US security policy and doctrine, whereby it is extremely unlikely that Congress would approve the development of the technology and its control by the UN."

"Yes, we are rugged individuals," President Obama told Congress in 2011. "Yes, we are strong and self-reliant. And it has been the drive and initiative of our workers that have made this economy the engine and envy of the world. But there has always been another thread running throughout our history, a belief that we are all connected, and that there are some things we can only do together as a nation."

Or as Victor Davis Hanson, a military historian awarded the National Humanities Medal in 2007 by President George W. Bush, writes in the *New Atlantis*: "Without a national religion or a common race or ethnic culture, Americans are united primarily by shared ideas and commitments, such as equal opportunity and individual merit. . . . Our military functions as a reflection of our national meritocracy, where wealth and breeding do not necessarily guarantee rank and privilege."

Anyone can apply online for a job at the Pentagon.

Such a strict meritocracy allows the navy, as Paul Wolfowitz says of China Lake, "to keep the very best people around."

Yes, we are the restless, the self-reliant. Yes, we are still the progeny of the "frontier experience," as Hanson writes, the progeny of the haunting vastness of the West that "made Americans intent on conquering time and space, explaining why European inventions in transportation and communication came into their own in America on a scale undreamed of elsewhere."

What people better than Americans could dream of or dare to launch a machine that would have to run for a thousand years? Who else could have the audacity to pursue such an unwanted solution? Who are the very best people?

"America's role as a 'receptacle of the unwanted' — an arena where audacious individuals," Hanson writes, "fleeing from poverty or discrimination, were in a hurry to start over and succeed rapidly — only added to the restless fascination with machines that were so disruptive of the traditions and tranquility of the past."

Our machines and scientists built the automobile, the atom bomb, the hydrogen bomb. They lifted man to the moon and annihilated the indigenous people of America, and they will carry us westward still.

"Congratulations for reconfirming the American spirit of exploration," President George W. Bush told the scientists of China Lake a decade ago.

For we thrive in stress, despise repose. We are the engine and envy of the world.

Our spirit of military independence evolved alongside our growing certainty in the unassailable supremacy of our military forces, as well as our increasing sense of being the only power able to preserve order after the Cold War, in a post-9/11 world. "In short," writes Hanson, "the culture of the United States — characterized by an emphasis on youth, individualism, and restlessness — is evident in our manner of making war."

There are some things we can only do together as a nation.

As Sharon Burke writes, "As this young century unfolds, the security of the United States — and most nations of the world — will increasingly depend on *our* natural security."

National security is only natural.

The Climate Geoengineering Governance report goes on: "The perceptions that geoengineering would create a potential doomsday device, which if stopped would rapidly lead to a catastrophic 'termination effect,' could easily be perceived to present a threat to US security. Under such circumstances it would be reasonable to assume that there would be considerable US security interest and a desire to have it under US security control or at least subject to considerable oversight."

Regarding that oversight, the report identifies a tragic bit of irony: "It is unfortunate that a plan to deal with a failure to achieve a global climate policy consensus, itself requires a global climate policy consensus that will be arguably more difficult to achieve."

But consensus isn't necessary. Democracy is not consensus. Neither is geopolitics.

Regarding such consensus, in a concluding section titled "Avoiding Dystopian Futures," the Climate Geoengineering Governance report states: "Current experience suggests it may well be impossible, and geoengineering would have to be imposed."

"Bold steps are in our nature as Americans," asserts Ray Mabus, "and what makes us a great nation; no one has ever gotten anything big done by being timid."

Standing at the side stage, Emily packs up her guitar while Ed Fallon hands me his business card. He starts to walk away. "The big picture is motive," he says. "I don't see the motive for it." Cathy takes my hand, leading me toward the White House, and says that now there is the opportunity for creativity. "This has got to be solved with a million different approaches," she says, "thousands and thousands of special, specific community actions." Cathy releases my hand and we stand facing the White House while she scans the group. "There may be someone here who knows about geoengineering," she says. "Wait just a minute."

I watch as she tries to step around the ISIS protest. Their numbers have grown to maybe thirty or forty people, about the same as the marchers. They keep circling in the gravel along Pennsylvania Avenue, just in front of the iron bars guarding the green grass, as Cathy, Fallon, and the core marchers attempt to insert themselves before the fence to pose for pictures. Federal police stand impassive, arms folded at the periphery, watching while the Kurdish man with the megaphone calls out a series of commands and the group fires back, "Unite, unite, unite against ISIS!"

Of course, climate change is just another issue. The march just another protest. One more daily distraction that Obama might deign to contemplate from his bedroom window upstairs.

"Protect freedom now! Obama, Turkey is not your ally!"

I stand among several indie press people and prepare to take a picture, but the ISIS people circle back and keep pacing between the cameras and the marchers.

"ISIS is the world's enemy! Support Kurdistan! End sexual slavery!"

Part of me wants to stand up for the marchers. I want to say, "Hey, man, a few of these people walked 3,000 miles to be here."

"Just wait a minute." "Back off." "Give them some fucking room." "Just a photo." "Whatever." "Bro." But everyone has an issue, every generation its war, each day an apocalypse. The marchers knew this. Undeterred, they start their own chant, "What do we want? Climate action! When do we want it? Now!" The cries of the two groups begin to blend incoherently, and for a moment it feels a bit embarrassing. Cathy's Buddhist prayer bell materializes out of somewhere, endeavoring feebly to focus the pilgrims' attention. "Marchers, marchers . . ." she calls, but nobody pays any mind. Instead they jump in on the next chorus, "Unite, unite, unite against ISIS!" and the Kurdish man with the megaphone smiles at the sudden concord, calling, "Thank you, friends, I hear you," as he steers his group over behind the cameras. Several dozen flashes reflect off the road signs before the convoy circles back. This time he changes his attack: "Obama, ISIS is the result of the climate crisis!"

Laughter and applause erupt from the marchers, followed by more fervent shouting.

"ISIS is the result of the climate crisis!"

I stand there smiling, mumbling the words for a minute, "ISIS is the result of the climate crisis," until another window opens, and I snap a clean photo, stash the camera, and begin to back away.

Cathy's prayer bell clangs on through the din as it starts to drizzle again.

The sound gradually fades across H Street.

But her words still echo through my mind: "Now there is the opportunity for creativity."

Nostradamus, the famous astrologer and apothecary born in 1503, wrote about the period of history between 1555 and 2055. In one of his most famous prophecies, he mentions a mysterious individual.

> Mabus puis tost alors mourra, viendra
> De gens et bestes, une horrible defaite;
> Puis tout a coup la vengeance on verra,
> Cent, main, soif, faim, quand courra la comete.

For centuries, scholars, quacks, and mystics have endeavored to discover the true identity of the nefarious figure mentioned in quatrain 62 of the second book of *The Prophecies*. His coming signals the dawn of a new age and the end of civilization.

> Soon Mabus will die, and then will come
> A terrible undoing of animals and people
> Then, suddenly, vengeance will appear
> In the form of a comet; hunger, thirst, a hundred hands.

Ray Mabus told the crowd at the McLean Hilton in 2009 that he believed that we have an "obligation to do something now about our impact on the environment, and that we can take substantive measures to improve our core warfighting capabilities while improving our energy footprint."

The Climate Geoengineering Governance report correctly says that "geoengineering will make weather events blameworthy," and that for some states "such as the United States, which are seen to have superior technological capabilities and global influence, that blame may be applied and acted upon, even if the USA does not engage in geoengineering." And the report goes on: "If no-one engages in geoengineering there is a significant proportion of the population who will believe it is ongoing anyway, who often blame the US government, and the sinister hidden organisations they believe are controlling its actions. While these individuals are not part of the current mainstream geoengineering debate, they should not be dismissed."

If I read Nostradamus correctly, it will not be Ken Caldeira or David Keith who is assassinated by some fanatical chemtrail conspiracist but rather a spokesperson from the US military. Ray Mabus may soon die. Following the assassination of Mabus — or perhaps his is a natural death, maybe a stress-induced heart attack — the geoengineering system will commence or continue with destructive results for all human beings and beasts. Gaia will wreak horrible vengeance. And after the apocalypse, perhaps fifty people will subsist in some remote northern latitude, suffering hunger, thirst, and cold as their hundred trembling hands feed a small flame housed in a DIRECTV satellite dish salvaged from the outskirts of Alberta, Canada — or as Marty Hoffert prophesized:

If we fail, I can imagine a thousand years from now a small fragment of humankind barely surviving the new planetary climate huddled around a fire in some remote northern latitude observing the night sky, subsisting perhaps as hunter-gatherers on a vastly different and biologically depleted planet listening to a tale vaguely recalled in ancestral memory by the local shaman.

Time will have passed. A few of us will survive the great population bottleneck of the Late Anthropocene. Our memories will be vague. We won't recall the geoengineering system. But the shaman will paint pictures and carve petroglyphs and pray for rain. He'll tell a story about the sky, about a great comet that struck Earth and fried our friends, our families, and our now-forbidden cities. A narrative about the houses of power long abandoned, left to the winds. And perhaps in dreams he'll travel there, back to his kitchen, to the ease of his morning coffee. Three tablespoons of crude oil contain the same energy as eight hours of hard human labor. It won't be our fault. The sun shines today also. Just as it will in the future, upon a world in which no one remembers anything.

———

"Going to meet our helping spirits makes us feel valued and connected to the spirit that lives in all things. We feel loved by the power of the universe, and we never feel alone again." "During a shamanic journey, you can choose to go to the Lower World, the Middle World, or the Upper World." "During your journeys you can move between the worlds as much as you like." "Everyone can journey and be open to the new dimensions of life that the spirits are waiting to show us."

I'm lying alone on the motel floor now, clicking on my laptop through the pages of an e-book my mom sent me. She bought a hard copy originally, but I left town before she could give it to me. In her e-mail, she said it might help lighten my spirits. She said it might also help my research. Before that, she told me to go to hell.

"Any way that you can get to the Upper World is fine." "You will pass through a transition — such as a cloud or a layer of fog — that will indicate that you have entered the Upper World." "If you are still seeing planets and stars as you journey upward, you have not yet reached the Upper World." "After the change in drumbeat of four sets of seven short beats, you will hear a rapid drumbeat for about a minute." "During this rapid drumbeat, retrace your steps back to your starting place and into the room where you are lying or sitting."

I came back to China Lake because I still have questions. There is still something I'm trying to learn.

"It is important to find a power animal or guardian spirit you can trust who can be your guide through your adventures in nonordinary reality and who can answer questions for you." "During one of my more memorable journeys, I encountered my teacher Isis who asked, 'Do you know what your problem is?' I was very surprised by such an abrupt question and replied, 'No. What is my problem?' She replied, 'You just do not see life as an adventure.'"

The window is open and the lights are off. Streetlight bleeds through the curtains while Beethoven strings glide softly through my laptop. Adagio affettuoso ed appassionato. Only a few fingers of scotch are left in this bottle. I keep clicking through the book, riffling through virtual pages, but I don't feel powerful.

"If you just lie down and listen to the drumming without setting an intention, it is possible that you might have a powerful journey. . . . It is a lot easier to journey in total darkness." "Generally, I find that alcohol interferes with maintaining concentration and staying alert in journeys. . . . True power is being able to use our energy to create transformation for ourselves, others, and the planet."

Two weeks after the Great March for Climate Action arrived in Washington, D.C., the small desert community of Ridgecrest, California, celebrated its first-ever Petroglyph Festival. Unfortunately, I missed it. I did not get back to San Diego until mid-December, and then I didn't stay long. The little dog, Moby, kept blowing out his anal gland on the arm of the new couch in front of the TV, and my mom kept blaming me. She woke up late, drank champagne, watched murder shows, and said my footsteps frightened Moby. She swore the spare bedroom had a smell. I took the Leutze painting down, sprayed the leftovers of an old Calvin Klein Romance cologne across the bedspread, and tried to walk as softly as possible. Thankfully my stepfather wasn't there. The fight reminded me of a miserable formative Christmas more than two decades ago when I asked Santa for the LEGO Mars Space Station and my mom broke down a few days before the twenty-fifth and told me that it was too expensive, that Santa Claus wasn't real, and that she was sorry. This time, however, neither of us cried, and no one apologized or hugged, and I drove away feeling not so much sad as sick, sick at the thought that, in all likelihood, the chances of life on Mars were still greater than a month at my mother's house. Magic cave music blared in the background. I picked up the remote and clicked away from Soundscapes to channel 2635, DOGTV. I wished her a Merry Christmas. "Here is your Eden," I said, and I told her to take her pills.

"Go to hell, my son." She refilled her glass of champagne. The Buddha statue made a sucking sound. "Right now, I wish you were never born."

Four hours later, I parked the car in Ridgecrest.

"It is very common to receive a dismemberment when asking for healing." "Although it might sound gruesome, people report a tremendous amount of peace and love during the experience." "Bear ripped her apart and took out her heart, and then put her back together with a heart that was healed."

A man named John talked to me at Tommy T's Bar. He said he had lived here his whole life. John had worked on the base. Although he'd never heard of geoengineering, he remembered one cold December many decades ago as a child, when the rumor around town was that Pierre St.-Amand planned to seed the clouds over Ridgecrest and give children their first white Christmas.

"That would have been nice."

Outside the bar, I smoked a cigarette. A streetlamp lit a patch of golden grass at the edge of the parking lot, the same shade as the rest of the lawns in Ridgecrest, same as all the grass at my mother's house, my grandma's house, and most of the front yards in southern California. Back inside, I told John that on my way into town, driving north along Highway 395, beyond the Joshua trees of Victorville and the abandoned trailer shacks of Red Mountain,

I had noticed a low billboard on the roadside advertising the new Petroglyph Festival. All it said was, "We've been waiting 10,000 years for this."

"What are we waiting for?" John asked.

He ordered another round.

According to Jay Famiglietti, a hydrologist at NASA's Jet Propulsion Laboratory and a professor of earth system science at Caltech, "California has only one year of water left." Thirty-eight million people live here. It still hasn't rained. What will you drink, piss or whiskey? "We're not just up a creek without a paddle in California," says Famiglietti, "we're losing the creek too." What freeway will we take? Which direction will the refugees run?

"That's where everybody went," Kathy Bancroft, tribal preservation officer of the Lone Pine Paiute-Shoshone, told me the next day. "When the pressure was on here in the valley, and there were massacres on the lake, and they were trying to kill us all off, that's where my family went to hide was in the Cosos." Kathy and I sat together on the outskirts of the reservation inside a bright empty mobile home. "Our people lived here," she said. "We may not have lived in one place in a house. We traveled around in order to survive. But this valley was our home." Her dark eyes studied mine until the table buzzed and we both jumped. The phone rotated counterclockwise between us, blinking. "Go away," she said, patting the screen. "They're not local numbers." I stared out the window through the latticework of a naked sycamore and watched the lights drift north along 395.

Kathy put the phone down. She talked about memory.

"When somebody asks, 'What do the petroglyphs mean?' it's not something simple. And it's not — a lot of them, I don't know what they are." She folded her hands and set them on the tabletop, rubbing her thumbs together. Thinking for a long time. Her round cheeks wrinkled as she clenched her teeth. "I remember being young and asking who drew those pictures. 'The people that were here before us.' That was always the only answer I got. People have taken that to mean that there was another people here before us. But that's not what that means."

Archaeologists have succeeded, thanks in part to this single ethnographic statement, in systematically disinheriting the Paiute-Shoshone's claim to the art of the Coso Range and the greater Owens Valley. As Bureau of Land Management archaeologist Greg Haverstock told me, with some reluctance, in his office the following night, "This is going to sound controversial, but the Paiute tribe — and this is something I don't really discuss in front of them — but archaeologically the Paiute-Shoshone came into the area about a thousand years ago or less than that." Haverstock, a federal agent, spoke bluntly. "The bottom line ultimately is that the petroglyphs are on federal land. It's a resource that's owned by the American government."

I asked Kathy what "the people that were here before us" meant. "It means our ancestors."

The phone vibrated again and set off spinning. "You're blowing up," I said, and Kathy laughed. "I know." Chains rattled in the truck bed out the window behind me, and her dogs began barking. "That's enough!" Kathy yelled, leaning over to press her voice against the screen. "Quit hollering." Earlier she told me that the room we sat in came from Manzanar, the concentration camp just up the road, home to 10,000 Japanese American prisoners during WWII. "The worst thing happening now is the town of Ridgecrest," she said, typing a text now. "They want to be the petroglyph capital of the world." She shook her head in disgust. "I heard that on the local radio station. I heard it and I thought, who said they should do that? This wasn't too long after those petroglyphs were cut out."

It's hard to mold a viable tourist option around the navy's largest worldwide landholding — but not impossible. Weeks before, I read the press release for the first annual Petroglyph Festival on Ridgecrest's official website. "Experience the rituals of Native Americans through song, dance, music, and food," it said. "Kids love these hands-on attractions and professional demonstrations!" I asked Kathy if she'd attended the festival and she said of course not — none of the tribes were involved. "Witness history come alive as Native Tribes create a real Native American encampment!" the press release said. "Learn from nearby tribes and historians as they demonstrate how early natives settled the mysterious desert!"

Kathy asked if I'd attended the festival and I said, no, I couldn't and wouldn't have.

But I, like many others, do find the desert mysterious, and it becomes more so every day as it surfaces beneath our feet, within our once-verdant cities, and keeps pushing past us, expanding along the outskirts of Riverside, Los Angeles, and San Diego to merge with the waterless Mojave, a beautiful landscape that was always there but seldom seen, and as the aqueducts evaporate, as it slowly evicts us, we can only attempt to appreciate its odd vegetation.

"It's a different world," Governor Jerry Brown said recently on April Fool's Day — four days before my birthday — announcing finally, for the first time ever, statewide imposed mandatory water restrictions. "The idea of your nice little green lawn getting watered every day, those days are past."

Apparently Governor Brown was not joking.

"But somebody has to witness," Kathy told me. "Even if it's destruction. You have to be a witness. So you can say, no, you already destroyed this. We're not going to let you do that again."

I met Greg Haverstock's colleague Ashley Blythe, an archaeologist at the Bureau of Land Management, in Bishop thirty minutes before sunset. Ashley apologized for the cat hair in her car and I climbed in and said I didn't mind and we drove out to an isolated volcanic tableland nestled between the 14,000-foot peaks of the Sierra Nevada and White Mountains. We waited at the last stoplight on 395 and watched the wind drag a tumbleweed across the street. We talked about the drought. "Are you a journalist?" she asked. The speedometer hovered over 50 and the road veered east and I said, no, just a writer. "Most people around here don't even know what BLM stands for, let alone what we do." I counted the mile markers while she flicked on her headlights and told me that the bureau was recently ordered to assess the risks that climate change posed to its operations. "Wildfires must be an issue," I said, and Ashley nodded. She touched the bridge of her eyeglasses. Barbed wire posts and dead burrobush whooshed and blurred outside her window. "Alternative energy and water conservation are also big issues." The order was Obama's Executive Order 13514, the order from which the Pentagon's operational energy is necessarily exempt.

Ashley lifted her finger from the steering wheel and pointed straight ahead as we pulled off the pavement and started down a long dirt road. "Those were the most sacred peaks for the Indians."

Silhouetted, the snowless caps of the Sierras brooded through the glowing dusk while the Prius rattled over the graded dirt and Ashley raised her voice.

"I can't remember the names of them. They're not the biggest, but they appear that way from the valley floor."

Ashley slowed, and I watched a slim contrail climb over the mountains, building a long, thin ladder out from the tallest peak toward the sole planet now blinking in space.

"Is that Mars or Venus?"

"I'm not sure," she said.

We parked at the dead end. The door slams echoed vaguely off the low cliffs in the distance; then the air filled with a deathly quiet. Alone, we started across the valley floor, threading our way through the bony chaparral, and the air, brushed with sage, felt warm, heavy, imbued with a particle that prevented sound. "These volcanic tablelands were laid down in a single event. Basically a mountaintop blew, and this is a wave that came down from Mammoth Mountain."

Ashley edged along a screen of blackened shrubs, then stopped.

We picked a course across what had once been the broad bed of a river.

"A wave of lava," she said. "And this is where it stopped."

Beneath the silent vastness of the valley's twilight, the remote table of rock seemed almost entirely cut off, immured, like an island, and I waded toward it across a waterless stream, out to the far banks where the sand began to slope and the bleached and crumbling cliffs rose before us, shadowless in the failing light.

Once, long ago, all the lakes of the valley were connected in a massive inland sea.

"The Chalfant site is different from the Cosos," Ashley said. "The rock is permeable. It's soft. Very light."

"It isn't basalt?"

Like a wave lapping at warm sands, a car sucked down the highway behind us, and Ashley turned to stare. "No," she said. "Volcanic tuff. It's a pale porous rock. That's why it's so easy to carve out here."

A bat tumbled brokenly above our heads and disappeared before the wall of rock.

"The light isn't great," she said.

We stepped into a wide cupped section of cliff, a sort of cove or cathedral, and stared up at the pallid soft rock covered with dozens of deeply indented petroglyphs. The largest, twenty feet up, looked like a sun. "What do you call that?" I asked.

"We call those shield figures."

I took a picture that didn't come out.

"Another difference between the Chalfant site and the Cosos is that Chalfant is totally unprotected. Anybody can walk up to it at any time of day, just as we have."

"Assuming they know where to find it."

"Yes," she said.

Ocean Mother and her daughter lived together on an island at the center of a massive inland sea.

"We have to climb up a bit."

Beyond the concave lip of the wall, the cliff bends south, running straight for another half mile or so. I follow her carefully, clambering along the mess of scree, but it isn't hard to see. The chalky white rocks clink together musically beneath our feet, and overhead, all along the fractured crown of the wall, glow dozens of deeply scored ovals, each one slit down the middle.

Ocean Mother and her daughter live together on an island in the sea, and they feed together, as cannibals, upon their own progeny.

"The thing to keep in mind," archaeologist David Whitley told me, "is that supernatural power was seen as something fundamentally neutral or ambivalent. It could be used for good or evil. Shamans were not just healers but also sorcerers responsible for curing and creating illness."

Another difference between the Chalfant site and the Cosos is that the dominant imagery at Chalfant is not bighorn sheep.

"Are those vulva motifs?"

Ashley turns. A last fragment of dusk pools strangely in her glasses. "That's exactly what they are," she says.

Chalfant is the site north of China Lake where David Whitley told me I'd find the work of sorcerer-shamans. It is the site that, in

2000, Whitley got listed on the National Register of Historic Places and of which he writes, "Given the overall structure of far-western Native American symbolism, beliefs, and metaphysics, it is likely that the vulva-form petroglyphs at the Chalfant site . . . may pertain specifically to sorcery, due to the association between the vulva and evil supernatural power."

In the shaman's worldview, the forces of darkness—evil and death—were equally essential to the benevolent powers of light and life. The shaman's task was not to reconcile these competing forces but rather to move between them, balancing each pole as needed to preserve the order of the world.

Ashley inches closer to the wall. A few more stars peer out over the White Mountains. "I came out with the tribal members," she says. "That was really emotional. It was the first time they'd been out here."

"What was their response?"

"A lot of anger and a lot of sadness. This is a site they still use."

I ask if she knows what type of rituals they conduct here, but Ashley isn't sure.

"They had to use ladders and a generator for the power saws. Anybody could have driven in on them."

Chalfant, unlike the Cosos, is also the site of one of the worst cases of rock art vandalism in recent history. "Altogether six petroglyphs were cut out from the walls," Ashley says. "Some were over 3,000 years old." She points again and my eyes follow the line of her finger upward, squinting through the gloom toward the center of the wall where the tuff begins to bulge, then looking down, at the bottom of the round protrusion, almost like a chunk of seaside sandstone that simply dropped away, dissolved, and vanished with the tide, I see the saw blade incisions, the pale cube they cut, the block of rock, half the size of a household door, missing.

Coyote used the neck of a bighorn to break the daughter's teeth.

"It is considered a generous offering to invite our helping spirits to move through our bodies, as they are disincarnate and unable to experience the pleasure of physical reality themselves." "Traditional ways of entering the Lower World include climbing down the roots of a tree, traveling down the center of a volcano, through a hole in the ground. . . . Isis answers questions for me personally, and she also helps me when I write my books, when I am teaching workshops, and while I am lecturing at conferences."

"Who did it?" I ask Ashley as we start back to her car.

"We don't know. But we don't think it was anyone local."

The first annual Petroglyph Festival included an educational program, an Indian flute concert, and a street fair with more than a hundred vendors. There was also a $20 wine walk and an "inter-tribal pow wow" complete with a traditional Cherokee hog fry — never mind that the Cherokee aren't from California but from Georgia, Tennessee, and the Carolinas. The festival arrived at the tail end of the town's fifty-year anniversary celebrations the year before. Ridgecrest was not officially incorporated until 1963. The navy "brought out a lot of people in the community," Justin O'Neill, a planning consultant for the Petroglyph Festival, said of the prior anniversary celebrations. "I see this as a great thing, just to see that amount of community engagement in a town where, unfortunately, we don't get to have too many shared experiences."

Pierre St.-Amand never delivered Christmas snow to the children of Ridgecrest. The town is known not for cloud seeding but for the fuses it built for the bombs dropped over Hiroshima and Nagasaki. It's known for developing the Sidewinder and Hellfire missiles and for building the landing systems on the Mars rovers *Spirit* and *Opportunity*. It's not known for climate control, for weather modification, or, generally, for the oldest Native American rock art in the Western Hemisphere. But all this will change. And soon perhaps, at least for a little while, perhaps like the rain shamans themselves, the pilgrims will journey from far and wide to experience the heart of the mysterious expanding inhuman desert that was never their home.

"The Petroglyph Festival will be our signature event," Ridgecrest Mayor Dan Clark told reporters. "We're going to *saturate* this community with representations of rock art."

"It's going to be the city's 50th anniversary on steroids," said Denny Kline, a field officer for Mick Gleason, Kern County's District 1 supervisor.

Sponsors for the four-day festival included Coca-Cola, General

Electric, NASA, the Ford Foundation, McDonald's, and Home Depot, among others.

"Sometimes we don't think of Ridgecrest as a destination spot," consultant Justin O'Neill said. "But we forget how appealing the desert can be to European travelers who don't have access to that. ... We're tapping into those markets again and saying, 'If you're going to plan a trip, this is the weekend to plan it.'"

More than 15,000 people, some traveling from as far away as France, Russia, and New Zealand, attended the festival. Sadly, however, none among the several dozen aliens was allowed to view the petroglyphs of the Coso Range during the festival, as navy-guided tours remained confined to American citizens.

But nobody seemed to mind. "Hotels averaged over 60 percent the event weekend," Doug Lueck of the Ridgecrest Area Convention and Visitors Bureau told the city council during a recent meeting. "Some were considered sold-out." In addition, Lueck said that "there was an 80-percent approval rate for the vendors and that over 90 percent of vendors surveyed would attend the festival next year. Meanwhile, attendees surveyed revealed a 95-percent successful rating for the festival."

For the roughly 14,900 people unable to experience firsthand the mystery of the desert via the Coso Range petroglyphs, there was still the Chalfant site, and closer, within Ridgecrest, a substantial and as yet untouched art exhibit.

When I walked around Ridgecrest's new $6-million park, I didn't notice anything remarkable. The grass was brown and dead, though nighttime sprinklers had managed to feed a few new beds of golden poppies. Freshly poured sidewalks meandered between streetlamps and squat palm trees while traffic thrummed along China Lake Boulevard and red ants bubbled among the gravel scattered beneath the narrow monoliths carved with images of bighorn sheep, shamans, atlatls, and abstract checkerboard symbols. I knelt at the base of one of the petroglyphs and read the inscription on the side: Olaf Doud, 2014.

Olaf Doud, a local artist, spent several months carving out the twenty-one images of Petroglyph Park. "I do several at a time so it doesn't get so discouraging," Doud told Ridgecrest's *Daily Indepen-*

dent, explaining that most petroglyphs took around four hours to carve. He said he planned to peck some of the images by hand and use power tools on others. Despite the hard work, Doud insisted that he was "looking forward to showing young people how they're made and what the meanings are as far as we know."

At the center of the park, the padded play structure stood empty save for a blade of noonday sun that cut the length of a plastic khaki slide. A brand-new sign, still graffiti-free, glowed white and spotless beside the bathroom. It said that "while the petroglyphs, pictographs, trails and blinds shown here are artistic representations of the work created by indigenous natives, it is important to know that they are faithful recreations of existing art and *look exactly* as you would see them if you were able to travel to original tribal grounds and habitat."

I bent over the drinking fountain and swished water in my mouth. From where I stood, I could see the distant quaking lines of the Cosos fixed inside the yellow midday haze, like seismic waves pressed into carbon paper, and I thought of that dark lava canyon cutting through the barren mesa, surrounded on all sides by bomb targets, boiling hot springs, and volcanic domes, and of those countless thousands of bighorns no one chiseled for pleasure but rather in pain for 15,000 years, and I thought of that fragile technology blinking down in the dark hallway of the canyon, quartz hammerstones working all night, barely luminescent, like worms of blue static boring through the raveled blankets of rock. And I swallowed. Far away, two tiny glinting jetfighters unfurled a blurry windblown figure eight along a hundred miles of restricted Sierra Nevada airspace.

"The landscapes in the Upper World can be quite varied, and you might find yourself in a crystal city or simply in the clouds. When you are in the Upper World, it is common to feel as if you are standing on something, although you can no longer feel the earth beneath your feet." "From a shamanic perspective, everything is alive and has a spirit — so I also call upon the airplane's power animals and helping spirits to be present to ensure a safe flight."

I walked and watched the contrails drift until I reached the western edge of Petroglyph Park. Here a small rock outcrop faces China

Lake Boulevard and the Chevron station across the street, just several hundred yards south of the main gates of the naval base, a block north of the Dollar Tree. Olaf Doud painted these rocks to resemble the scarred surfaces of Renegade Canyon's desert-varnished basalt. He finished them with several earnest reproductions of bighorn sheep petroglyphs. These rocks, according to Doud, a retired human resources manager, are "artistic tributes to the rock art of the Coso Range and the Native Americans who created them." Unfortunately, however, Olaf Doud is neither a Native American nor a shaman, and his many hours of work did not produce any measurable precipitation. In the thirty-plus years that Doud's been carving petroglyphs, he hasn't had any strange encounters.

"Not any unusual ones," he says, "I've been doing it for a long time."

I did not notice anything more than usual myself until I reached the end of Petroglyph Park. The second-to-last petroglyph did not look exactly like any other I had ever seen, and I wondered where Doud had found the inspiration.

"Is this image consistent with anything you've ever seen in Native American rock art?" I asked Ashley Blythe on our drive back from the Chalfant site. Her eyes flickered between the square of my digital camera and the headlit curve of the yellow road line. "No. That's weird," she said. "I've never seen anything like that." Her colleague and superior, Greg Haverstock, told me later, "I can honestly say I've never seen an image in rock art that resembled that even closely."

But as Ridgecrest's *Daily Independent* writes, quoting Mick Gleason, Kern County's District 1 supervisor, "The park will bring everyone together as a community, brand the area, and 'give us an opportunity to attract businesses.'"

The petroglyph stands at the northern limit of the twelve-acre park, separated by a fence of barbed wire from the post office parking lot, in a batch of petroglyphs labeled "2 — Shamanic Visions or Alien Visitors" on the legend at the park's entrance. Just beyond the petroglyph, one block north of the post office, behind the Kern County Superior Court, you'll find the town's newly remodeled petroglyph museum. This is the place where you mail your tour

application and they, in turn, forward it to the navy. It's also the place where you buy petroglyph-themed coffee mugs, shot glasses, jewelry, and clothing. On one of the t-shirts, several shamans, plucked from Renegade Canyon's most famous panel, stand below the heading "My Life's in Ruins." Another t-shirt says: "Advice from the Night Sky: See the Big Picture • Be a Star • Keep Looking Up • Don't Be Afraid of the Dark."

The museum also sells books. Among the many titles related to Native American shamanism and New Age religion, you'll find one called *Shamanic Journeying: A Beginner's Guide* by Sandra Ingerman. If you cannot journey to the museum, you can buy the e-book online. It makes a fine Christmas gift. The beginner's guide has four and a half stars on Amazon and eighty-eight customer reviews.

Unfortunately, Ingerman has yet to write the expert's guide.

"Many people get caught up in the question, 'Am I journeying correctly?' Remember there is no right way to journey—whatever you experience is correct for you." "It is important to learn to honor and validate your unique experience." "Look for the metaphors. Expand your awareness to include the big picture your helping spirits are trying to show you." "If you are stuck on the meaning of a symbol or metaphor, here are some suggestions." "Try asking more questions about what occurred during the journey to see if any new information arises." "For example, 'How did the presence of the sun pertain to my question?' or 'How did the landscape that I perceived relate to my question?'" "Work with each of the clear elements that were present in your journey to uncover how they provide additional information in response to your question." "If you are still seeing stars and planets, you have not yet reached the Upper World."

Lying in my motel room in Ridgecrest, I click away from the e-book and open the last e-mail I received from Ken Caldeira.

I still want to know whether the stars will disappear.

Caldeira told me they would not, but Alan Robock, another major geoengineering scientist, said they would. Caldeira suggested when we spoke at Stanford that he thought it possible that Robock was exaggerating their death simply because he didn't want to see the technology deployed. When I e-mailed Robock to ask about this, he took it to mean that Ken Caldeira had accused him of falsifying his research, and then, very disturbed, he forwarded my e-mail to Caldeira, who then accused me of falsifying his statements, and through all the squabbling I never did learn whether the stars would disappear. I only learned, according to Caldeira, that "when you write like, 'his responses seemed to indicate that he thought it possible' . . . this is a statement about your psychological state, not a statement about what I said," which is true, I suppose. But what's also true, it seems, is that the scientists whose computer models will determine the future of the world are quite like the rest of us with our hunter-gatherer brains, that is, at times terribly myopic, too focused on the short term, on professional careers, personal rivalries, and past achievements, to appreciate the big picture. Since before the beginning of time, the quiet strangeness of the world has revealed itself most profoundly to humankind by the simple action of staring up at night. We pieced together the gods over aeons of stargazing. Then, through four centuries of telescopes, we killed them. But even now, even if we don't journey according to their coordinates, the stars still help us navigate.

Not everyone born longs to reach another world.

For some, it is enough to have found this one.

Being here may be improbable and mysterious enough. But I fear that whatever home I've ever felt may vanish with the stars. If they cease to shine, we may lose not only their glorious indifferent light but also ourselves.

I am not sure that I'd want to keep living on such an alien planet. "It is important to find a power animal or guardian spirit you can trust who can be your guide through your adventures in non-ordinary reality and who can answer questions for you." "My experience has been that there are two key factors to a successful journey: generating a strong intention and asking the right questions. The best kinds of questions to ask begin with the words who, what, where, or how. When you first begin to journey, it is best to ask one question per journey." "'Why' questions are sometimes fine, although they may not be answered directly."

Why is it in the nature of intelligent life to destroy itself?

"Some things belong to the mystery of life and either cannot be answered or may not be appropriate for you to understand." "This certainly does not mean that you cannot ask 'why' questions." "It is simply important to understand that there are sometimes limitations to the answers you will receive to those questions." "It is also very difficult to get accurate answers for 'when' questions."

When will the stars disappear?

"Remember that you are traveling outside of time; time takes on a different and often mysterious meaning in non-ordinary reality." "This is why prophecies are often inaccurate or unclear around timing, which could also be true of the answers you get to questions about when something will happen."

Sitting in the passenger seat of Ashley's car, I stare out the window at the moon breaking behind the White Mountains, spreading a long, thin pall between the pine-stubble peaks.

Ashley says that archaeologists have found occupation sites at the highest elevations. "Middens mean not just that men were up there but whole families. There were large-scale habitations." During the summer months, the Paiute-Shoshone moved into the cooler alpine climates. They collected piñon seeds, carried them down in baskets, and stored them for the winter on the tablelands. "They had to travel around in order to survive."

We talk about climate, human migrations, and the empires of old America, the Mayans, Aztecs, and Anasazi. "The Anasazi began moving north out of their center in Chaco, New Mexico, when the climate turned dry," Ashley says. This was around the time of the Medieval Climatic Anomaly. "There was inner strife, the people split off into bands, and the culture collapsed."

Most people today who stand beneath the Anasazi cliff dwellings on summer road trips, at sites like Arizona's Canyon de Chelly or Colorado's Mesa Verde, stare up mildly impressed at the peculiar and improbable mudstone pueblos tucked into the crevices of the cliffs, imagining the sturdy ladders, the coolness of the dark desert apartments, and the warm breezes that blew west across the walls, perfuming the rooms with the scent of pine, sage, and juniper, inviting the slow rest of the evening, the vistas of soft midnight stars, and as they snap photos on their smartphones, as they journey back toward their vehicles baking in the national park asphalt, their minds imagine a simpler time, perhaps where peace prevailed, where people lived in small family groups, and everyone had a role, and while the fathers turn the keys in the ignition of their SUVs, as the families move on up the road, the imagination expands, and the children begin to ask what happened, and the fathers say that they aren't sure, that it's still a mystery, and the mothers try to picture the piñon seeds they were told about, still scattered across the mortars, beneath the granite pestles, still sitting there after 700 years, the fact that the families simply dropped everything and left, never to return, and the kids ask why, why did they abandon their homes, how did they disappear, and a minute of philosophical conversation passes inside the car as the families speculate, and the children search on their phones, and the fathers, steering from the fast lane on cruise control, say that they probably found a better place to live, and the mothers — I remember my mother's words when we stopped at Mesa Verde. It was a long time ago. She pulled over into a turnout and we gazed together through binoculars, across the gorge, toward the vacant sockets of the ancient windows. "I don't really know," she said.

There was an episode of *The X-Files* that ran that year called "Anasazi."

"Maybe they were abducted by aliens."

Most people today don't appreciate the fear, the paranoia. They don't see the true wisdom of the dwellings. They don't imagine a smattering of surviving bands embattled over scarce resources. They don't see inside the cramped dark of the tiny rooms perched precipitously above the dying creek. They don't hear the grass-tied ladders lifting with a hiss or feel the weight of the boulders, piled and ready to be hoisted and hurled down, down, upon the heads of hungry invaders, the friends, families, enemies, and sorcerers.

"You're right," Ashley said, lifting her blinker. "There is strong archaeological evidence of cannibalism throughout the Late Anasazi culture. It wasn't a happy time."

"Trees and beings like elves and fairies can also be helping spirits." "You can also have an extinct animal volunteering itself as your power animal, since the spirit of an animal species is eternal." "Therefore, it is not unusual for someone to have a type of dinosaur, such as stegosaurus, as his or her power animal." "It is very common to have a mythological creature as a power animal, such as Pegasus or a unicorn."

I asked Ashley about the meaning of the petroglyphs at the Chalfant site as we pulled into Bishop. "They could have been the work of shamans, or they could have been fertility symbols made by women. That would suggest that not all the petroglyphs were made by shamans."

The day before, I'd asked Kathy Bancroft if shamans had made the petroglyphs. "Some archaeologists suggest that the majority if not all of California's rock art was made by shamans, and that the imagery depicts the visions they experienced during altered states of consciousness."

"How do they know?" Kathy said. "Everyone has a story. A lot of their stuff," she said of the archaeologists, "is just made up as far as I'm concerned."

I explained the hunting magic hypothesis, the original archaeological explanation for the bighorn sheep petroglyphs of the Coso Range.

"Wow. That's weird," Kathy said.

She'd never heard of it.

Her black hair hung over her face and her shoulders heaved as she laughed soundlessly. "I'm sorry," she said. "Sometimes when I talk to these archaeologists, it's just like talking to a little kid. You have to be patient, and just nod, and not get upset."

I didn't bother asking her about the imagery of vulvas.

"I'm not even sure that the current Paiute-Shoshone people can fully account for the cosmology of their ancestors," Ashley Blythe told me, "because sadly so much of it has been lost and so much of it is acculturation. Where would you like me to take you?"

Ashley dropped me at the BLM field office in Bishop, where I talked to her boss, Greg Haverstock. "You know, if you give a four-year-old a crayon and say draw me a picture, you see a lot of circles. You might see squiggly lines. I look at some of my kids' drawings and I think, wow, that looks like rock art." He shook his mouse and checked his e-mail and I was conscious of not taking up too much of his time because it was dark outside and the rest of the office stood largely empty. "You can look at some of these sites as a cathedral of sorts, and you can understand how, let's say, one day it's owned and operated by an Episcopalian church and then one day for some reason that church goes defunct or they go bankrupt and they move out and then the Catholics move in, and maybe that religion dies out or those people move away or something bad happens and they lose their funding and then the Mormons move in."

The lights in the room clicked off suddenly.

"They're on a timer," Greg said. He continued talking in the dark. "The main lesson is that it's just a human thing. Rock art reflects how our cognitive system is set up, how we dream, how we visualize, more than any particular belief system. . . . You have to be careful about interpreting the petroglyphs."

Greg went on to explain his personal belief system, which was that the petroglyphs stood on federal land and that they ultimately belonged to the American government. "Or if you prefer," he said, "they're the property of the American people. They're a resource that we all have a right to as citizens."

Sitting there in the dark, I thought of confessing, of telling him that I was the one who stole the petroglyphs from the Chalfant site.

A woman stopped in the doorway, stared at us like we were crazy, and then flicked the lights back on. Greg nodded in thanks.

To shut down the singsong of his proud patronage would have been one more useless protest. Vain and childish. He was just doing his job.

"The ethnographers in the Owens Valley region," he said, "when they made contact with tribal members that actually had memories, those people denied having any knowledge or being associated with people that made rock art. They always talked about it happening before them."

Time will have passed. Our memories will be vague. We won't recall carving the checkerboard lines that blocked out the sky — that good or that evil we had decided was necessary to inject into the world. A small fragment of humankind, the progeny of the Green Arms Race, will ask, "Who built these ruins?" It won't be our fault.

"Am I making my journeys up?" "My experience has shown that the best way to evaluate the validity of your shamanic journeys is on the basis of your results." "If you keep up the practice of shamanic journeying, you will begin to see useful and beneficial results arising from the guidance you receive." "Remember shamanism has traditionally been a results oriented system and it is important for you to evaluate your results on an ongoing basis." "The important question to ask yourself is, 'Do I get information that makes a positive difference in my life?'" "When you begin to see significant results, your mind will begin to quiet down, and eventually you will find that you are no longer distracted by the question of whether or not it is all happening in your imagination."

Boot heels bang along the overhung walkway now as a body passes silhouetted before the window. I turn the Beethoven down and listen to a bed frame bump against the wall behind me. A long moan bleeds through the drywall and expires beyond the darkness of my laptop. Do I get information that makes a positive difference in my life?

"One of the many definitions of shaman is 'one who sees in the dark.'" "It is a lot easier to journey in total darkness." "Therefore, some people close the shades and curtains to darken the room." "Journeying is very safe, and it is important to learn that you always have full control over where you travel and with which spirits you interact."

I drain the last of the scotch and open my e-mail again, a message from my mother, sent several weeks ago before I returned home for Christmas, a Hallmark e-card. A little blue dog darts toward the center of a black knoll and stands within a clearing. Beyond the darkened branches of pine trees, dozens of cartoon stars begin to dance. A calligraphied script unfurls the words, "A little twinkle, twinkle . . . just for you," and the dog starts singing.

"Twinkle, twinkle little star. How I wonder what you are. Up above the world so high. Like a diamond in the sky. Twinkle, twinkle little star. How I wonder what you are."

The dog hops in place, squeaks "I miss you," then disappears through the trees into the night. The calligraphy floats up over the clearing, and the words "How are you?" hang there for several seconds while crickets chirp.

No control, no direction. An endless chaotic battle with no real point.

How are you?

Physically ill, physically terrified.

The key still fits in the ignition. The dashboard still glows. The gas needle jumps and slurs around half a tank. The steering grinds as I slide out from the parking lot.

Where will you go? Which direction will the pilgrims run?

"Remember that you have complete control. . . . If you are about to drive on the freeway, and you are feeling nervous, you can call to your helping spirits and ask for their protection to help you get home safely."

I feed the dashboard a disk and press the gas pedal down. The streetlights fade behind me and the road narrows into an endless straightaway. Metal blasts louder as the needle climbs, pointing toward the base, where the primordial stars burn brighter, more beautiful, more remote than heaven. If I concentrate, I can still get there. I can still read. The sign says it's seventy-three miles to Death Valley.

There's no more mountain left to get behind.

No more shamans.

"Saying 'goodbye' will help you feel more grounded when you return from your journey."

Only desert.

EPILOGUE

The largest El Niño weather system ever seen was supposed to hit California in the winter of 2015–16. Forecasts for the coming Godzilla El Niño predicted above average-rainfall and increased Sierra snowpack and, in the minds of millions of southern Californians tired of dead lawns and shorter showers, an end to the state's historic drought.

After an initial storm in January 2016, however, Godzilla appeared to have vanished. February brought not record-breaking rains but a record-breaking heat wave. In March, Los Angeles County began cloud seeding for the first time in more than a decade. Despite these efforts, from October to June El Niño delivered only 6.88 inches of rain, nearly an inch less than had fallen the year before and less than half the supposed average for the period.

In early June, after scientists declared El Niño officially dead, 84 percent of California remained in a state of drought—this despite above-average rainfall in northern California and a statewide snowpack that weighed in just below average. At the same time Lake Mead, the largest of the Colorado River reservoirs that provide for more than 40 million people in Nevada, Arizona, California, and Mexico, stood just 37 percent full—an all-time low. To the north Lake Powell, the second-largest reservoir in America after Lake Mead, was only half full. Continued drought and a continually warming world coupled with increasing demand and increasing evaporation will ensure that the Colorado River reservoirs continue to fade. Experts now estimate a 50 percent chance that Lake Mead will run dry within the next seven years.

The National Academy of Sciences released its CIA-funded geoengineering study in the winter of 2015–16. In its report the committee rejected the term "geoengineering" in favor of the phrase "climate intervention." The NAS report distinguished between two forms of climate intervention—carbon dioxide removal and albedo modification, that is, reflecting sunlight to cool Earth—and examined them separately in companion reports. Regarding the former, the committee found what was already known: carbon dioxide removal "addresses the root cause of climate change," but unfortunately "current technologies would take decades to achieve moderate results and be cost-prohibitive at scales large enough to have a sizeable impact." The committee recommended that federal R&D dollars be directed toward lowering the cost and increasing the scale of carbon dioxide removal.

Regarding albedo modification, the committee again found what was already known: any global effort to reflect sunlight "would only temporarily mask the warming effect caused by high CO_2 concentrations, and present serious known and possible unknown environmental, social, and political risks, including the possibility of being deployed unilaterally." The committee recommended that "albedo modification at scales sufficient to alter climate should not be deployed at this time." Rather than immediate deployment, the committee recommended that "an albedo modification research program be developed and implemented that emphasizes multiple benefit research that also furthers both basic understanding of the climate system and its human dimensions."

In December 2015, after nearly twenty-five years of deliberations, 180 nations signed an agreement in Paris to limit "the increase in the global average temperature to well below 2°C above preindustrial levels and to pursue efforts to limit the temperature increase to 1.5°C above preindustrial levels." As part of the agreement, individual countries must decide their own "nationally determined contributions," which are to be "ambitious ... represent a progression over time," and determined "with the view to achieving the purpose" of the Paris Agreement.

While world leaders applauded the agreement as a historic and pivotal moment in climate policy, many scientists expressed doubts about the plausibility of a 2°C goal, not to mention a 1.5°C goal, and urged world governments to rapidly commit to much-steeper emissions cuts. The present commitments offered by nations through 2030 put the world on a path toward a 2.6 to 3.1°C warming within this century. How is this possible? Why did nations pledge commitments that fall short of the Paris Agreement's goals?

National contributions established in Paris relied on a set of modeling scenarios that keep the earth below the 2°C threshold. These modeling scenarios were derived from the last UN International Panel on Climate Change report. Nearly all these scenarios — 101 out of 116 — depended on humanity being able to remove CO_2 from the atmosphere. At present, humankind cannot remove carbon dioxide from the atmosphere on any remotely meaningful scale.

Put another way, unspoken in L'Accord de Paris is the assumption that one form of geoengineering — carbon dioxide removal via CO_2 scrubbing towers or bioenergy plus carbon capture and storage — will keep the world from warming 2°C. The historic and much celebrated Paris Agreement rests upon a technology that does not exist — and hence has not been tested or proved safe or even possible — suddenly coming online and affordably sucking 15 billion tons of CO_2 from the sky every year and then storing this safely underground indefinitely.

A radical decrease in energy demand and an immediate switch from fossil fuels to zero-emissions alternatives — in other words, nothing short of a worldwide revolution — remain the only way to "safely" limit warming to 1.5 or 2°C.

On January 20, 2016, the Great Green Fleet weighed anchor at Naval Air Station North Island in San Diego Bay and set sail westward across the Pacific. To accomplish its mission, the navy purchased more than 77 million gallons of blended biofuel, the largest biofuel acquisition in world history. None of it came from algae. All the ships but the nuclear carrier burned a biofuel blend made from 10 percent waste beef fat and 90 percent conventional petroleum.

"The Department of Defense is the world's largest user of fossil fuels," Ray Mabus reminded the crowd at the Great Green Fleet's kickoff ceremony. But today, he said, "We're greener. Our carbon footprint is smaller."

Several months later, off the coast of Italy, the ships stopped to refuel with a blend of 94.5 percent conventional fuel and 5.5 percent biodiesel derived from palm oil. Biofuels made from palm oil produce three times more greenhouse gas emissions than conventional petroleum diesel, increase deforestation, and compete with food crops.

"We only have three requirements for biofuels," Ray Mabus reminded the crowd in San Diego Harbor. "One is that they be a drop-in fuel. We're not changing our engines. Two is that it takes no land out of food production. And three, that it be cost competitive." All aircraft aboard the Great Green Fleet continued to burn affordable petroleum fuel. "I couldn't be more proud of what the Sailors and Marines have done to free us and give us operational flexibility," Mabus said. "America's Navy shouldn't have to depend on oil supplies from foreign nations to ensure our national defense."

On Tuesday, March 1, 2016, Ray Mabus announced his resignation.

An independent estimate of global recoverable oil reserves released on July 4, 2016, by the Norway-based Rystad Energy found that the United States now ranks first in the world among nations, surpassing both Saudi Arabia and Russia. According to the report, "more than 50% of remaining oil reserves" in the United States "is unconventional shale oil."

On July 5, 2016, a video began to go viral on YouTube in which CIA Director John Brennan, addressing the Council on Foreign Relations in Washington, D.C., shared a couple of thoughts about "some things that I find fascinating." One of these things was "the array of technologies—often referred to collectively as geoengineering—that potentially could help reverse the warming effects of global climate change." According to Brennan, "One that has gained my personal attention is stratospheric aerosol injection, or SAI, a method of seeding the stratosphere with particles that can help reflect the sun's heat, in much the same way that volcanic eruptions do."

Two months before Director Brennan's speech, the Senate Appropriations Committee passed a $38-billion bill to fund the Army Corps of Engineers and the Department of Energy for the fiscal year of 2017. Halfway through the bill, inserted quietly at the bottom of page 86, the following sentence appears: "As other nations have launched research programs on albedo modification, the Committee recommends the Department review the findings of the National Academy of Sciences report entitled, 'Climate Intervention: Reflecting Sunlight to Cool Earth,' and leverage existing computational and modeling capabilities to explore the potential impacts of albedo modification."

On November 8, 2016, four days after the Paris Agreement officially entered into force, Americans elected Donald Trump as the forty-fifth president of the United States. Throughout his campaign Trump described climate change as a hoax, promised to revive the US coal industry, and said he would immediately withdraw the United States from the Paris Agreement. Democratic candidate Hillary Clinton vowed to make America the clean energy superpower of the twenty-first century and strengthen US emissions reductions. On the whole, however, neither campaign made much about a warming world, and over the course of three presidential debates, moderators from NBC, CNN, ABC, and Fox News failed to mention the topic even once.

NOTES AND REFERENCES

Anthropogenic greenhouse gases are causing the earth to warm at a rate unseen in the past 65 million years. It is by no means a stretch of the imagination to say that my generation — us so-called millennials — may be the last. There is no mountain of safety or citadel of technology from which, in our armchairs with our smartphones, we can stare down, watching events unfold, only to tie them up later within the bow of some safe chronology. Whatever will be said must be said now. A definitive history of the twenty-first century may never come. This essay has been an attempt to shed light on the world we are creating as we contemplate imprisoning ourselves, perhaps forever, beneath a web of chemtrails. Gaia awaits.

The references that follow for the most part offer a sequential road map, highly distilled, detailing in broad strokes my journey into this odd and not-too-distant world. Publication information for books refers to the editions that I consulted, not necessarily to the original editions. In an attempt to avoid splattering these pages with unseemly Internet links, I've provided the terms required to access references via search engine. For example, in the first reference below, instead of handing you https://www.youtube.com/watch?v=A3b_MEntOLU, I'm going to ask you to pick a few favorite keywords. Try typing "I run YouTube badwater perry," and you'll find the video at the top of your search. This formula should guide you. This is how you use the Internet. By the time you reach the epilogue — I've deliberately omitted keywords and references there — you'll be an expert.

Of course, the Internet provided only part of my research. Contrary to popular belief, the totality of the world's knowledge is not yet available for free on Wikipedia. Conversations in person or via e-mail and phone calls were essential to my research and writing.

2, "I run because": Badwater AdventureCORPS, "2012: Badwater: I'm Running Badwater," produced by Sasha Perry, online at YouTube, 2012.

3, "Yet another special treat": Arthur Webb, "Mr. Bo Peep Runs Badwater," online at Badwater, 2001.

3, "the most physically taxing competitive event": Chris Kostman, "Medical Risks Associated with Badwater Ultramarathon," online at Badwater, 2010.

3, a belt buckle: The coveted Badwater belt buckle displays three silhouetted peaks (one for each mountain range a runner must ascend) against a long sweep of parched ground so that altogether the whole thing looks like a flatlining EKG. Despite this, somehow in the race's twenty-seven-year history no one has died.

3, its suicidal contenders: The original Badwater finish line used to be at the top of Mount Whitney; it's now several thousand feet lower at the Whitney portal outside Lone Pine, California. Many runners, however, in the brutal spirit of the original race, still voluntarily run to the top of Whitney. Afterward some of them, for some reason, run 150 miles back to Badwater Basin in Death Valley, and some of them, still, after running back to Badwater Basin, turn and run back to the top of Mount Whitney, and some of them, after running back to the top of Mount Whitney, turn and run back to Badwater Basin. This last particular prodigious trial of suffering is known as a Badwater Quad, and the first person to run it — a distance greater than twenty-two consecutive marathons in ten days — was a man named Marshall Ulrich. He no longer has toenails.

4, "As we walked": Dave Bursler, "Badwater 2006," online at Run100s, 2006.

4, "things don't have to be seen to be true": Dave Bursler, "2008 Badwater Ultramarathon Crew Report," online at Badwater, 2008.

5, "waterless desert": Albert Camus, *The Myth of Sisyphus and Other Essays*, translated by Justin O'Brien, Vintage, 1991.

6, "Smoke was still rising": Jack Denness, "Death Valley Hallucinations," online at Badwater, July 29, 1999.

6, "It was still 114 degrees": Barry Spitz, "Ross' Karnazes Running in the Grueling Badwater Ultramarathon for the 10th Time," online at UltraMarathonMan, 2012.

6, "I noticed a figure": Ian Parker, "Ian Parker Running Biography," online at Parker Lab: UC Irvine, 2012. In addition to Ian Parker, Arthur

Webb (quoted above) also mentions hallucinating sheep, as does Kirk Johnson in his Badwater memoir, *To the Edge: A Man, Death Valley, and the Mystery of "Endurance,"* Grand Central Publishing, 2012.

13, killed eight people: Keith Coffman, "Property Losses from Colorado Flood Projected at about $2 Billion," online at Reuters, September 19, 2013.

13, "Is it a coincidence": "Yahoo Assures Readers Colorado Flooding Not Caused by Cloud Seeding," online at BeforeItsNews, September 17, 2013.

13, "You would have to be seeding": Laura Poppick, "Cloud Seeding Not to Blame for Colorado Flooding," online at NBCNews, September 17, 2013.

15, raw spots of burning red: US Drought Monitor Map Archive, online at DroughtMonitor, October 2013. Orange patches depict severe drought, red represent extreme drought.

15, "worst drought since the Dust Bowl": Roddy Scheer and Doug Moss, "Dust Bowl Days Are Here Again," online at ScientificAmerican, June 9, 2013.

16, a lot of concerned calls: Joe Busto and I traded words online in lengthy conversations during October and November 2013.

17, "The goals of this course": "Air Force Academy 'Chemtrails' Manual Available for Download," online at ChemtrailsPlanet, March 13, 2013.

17, "chemtrails": "H.R.2977 — Space Preservation Act of 2001," online at Library of Congress, 2001.

18, "Everything is connected": UN Agenda 21, "Climate Change and Chemtrails Connection," online at ChemtrailsPlanet, November 16, 2013.

18, 4,610 times their normal level: Christina Sarich, "Chemtrail Poisons Are Ruining Your Health from Above, and You May Not Know It," online at Infowars, September 9, 2013. The reference link has since been restored. It takes you to a pdf of the flier I mention finding when I initially searched the claim.

18, "Big 4": "Chemtrail Illnesses," online at GlobalSkyWatch, 2013. The website presents a list of illnesses that I've reordered in places and put in paragraph form. If you don't know what Morgellons is, then you definitely have it.

19, "The nerve toxins": Alfred Lambremont Webre, "Laura Eisenhower: Unity Consciousness Will Collapse Military-Industrial Complex," online at ExoPolitics, December 20, 2011.

19, "Laura is powerfully creating": Online at Cosmicgaia2012. Quoted portions appear on the site's home page; further quotes are from YouTube.

20, "beliefs can survive": Lee Ross and Craig A. Anderson, "Shortcomings in the Attribution Process: On the Origins and Maintenance of Erroneous Social Assessments," in *Judgment under Uncertainty: Heuristics and Biases,* edited by Daniel Kahneman, Paul Slovic, and Amos Tversky, Cambridge University Press, 1982.

20, "Aircraft Contrails Factsheet": Search for "FAA contrails" and at the moment — I'm looking at the bottom right corner of my laptop screen, fact-checking now, and it's June 29, 2016 — the fact sheet should be your top result.

21, 1.75 people die: "World Birth and Death Rates," online at Ecology, 2011. Data are from the Population Reference Bureau and the Central Intelligence Agency's *World Factbook.*

21, population bottleneck of the Late Pleistocene epoch: Stanley H. Ambrose, "Late Pleistocene Human Population Bottlenecks, Volcanic Winter, and Differentiation of Modern Humans," *Journal of Human Evolution,* 1998, online at BradshawFoundation and lots of other places.

21, "Between 1949 and 1978": David E. Brown, "We Will Bury You. In Mud," online at Cabinet, Summer 2001.

21, "We regard the weather": Howard J. Taubenfeld and Rita F. Taubenfeld, "Modification of the Human Environment," in *The Future of the International Legal Order,* vol. 4: *The Structure of the International Environment,* edited by Cyril E. Black and Richard A. Falk, Princeton University Press, 1972.

21–22, The weapon . . . suspended all operations: James R. Fleming, "The Climate Engineers," online at WilsonQuarterly, 2007. The discovery of this essay coupled with a separate essay by David S. Whitley constituted the essential primary philosophical shock that impelled my brain down the written course of this book. Note: James R. Fleming is at present — again it's 1:10 a.m. on June 29, 2016 — the supreme and sole authority on the history of weather modification and the most important critic of its apparent and would-be extension: geoengineering. Fleming's writings contain the essential facts and fictions that planted the initial seeds of this book. Thank you, Professor Fleming, for your impassioned scholarship and dogged skepticism. All readers interested in the past and future of a manmade and manmaimed world should read the above essay as well as his excellent book, *Fixing the Sky: The Checkered History of Weather and Climate Control*, Columbia University Press, 2010.

24, the deck of the *Anderson*: The USS *Anderson* was struck by a Japanese kamikaze on November 1, 1944, during the Battle of Leyte Gulf.

25, calibrating gyroscopes at the base: My grandfather actually worked for a military contractor off the base. But growing up I always heard he worked at the base. Maybe ultimately he did work for the base, just not at the base — in any case, until recently, I thought he worked on-site at Coronado.

26, He killed himself eight years ago: Some members of my family will dispute this claim and perhaps take offense. For that, I apologize. It is difficult for me, however, to see my uncle's death as anything other than a gradual process of extreme and willful self-neglect that eventually, most likely intentionally, resulted in his escape from a life he no longer found dignity or pleasure in living.

26, rug made from recycled Nike shoes: The soccer field at my high school was one of the first in the city to install one of these carpets on a massive scale. I remember some coach told us that the blades of grass and their black rubber soil were made from recycled Nike shoes. I accepted the claim at the time, but it seems suspect now.

26, "projections show": San Diego County Water Authority, "News Release," online at SDCWA, October 24, 2013.

26–27, Under the guise . . . blew up the aqueduct fourteen times: James J. Rawls and Walton Bean, *California: An Interpretive History*, McGraw-Hill Education, 2011. See also Mike Davis, *City of Quartz*, Vintage, 1992.

27, "The people here": Remi A. Nadeau, *The Water Seekers*, 1950, County Life Press, free online at Archive.

27, air pollution–control measures: Kirk Siegler, "Owens Valley Salty as Los Angeles Water Battle Flows into Court," online at NPR, March 11, 2013, and Dakota Smith, "Settlement Reached over Dust Control Measures at Owens Lake," online at DailyNews, November 14, 2014.

27, 50 percent chance: Guardian Environment Network, "Colorado River Running on Empty by 2050," online at TheGuardian, July 28, 2009.

27, killing eleven people: Deborah Schoch, "Clouding the Issue of Drought," online at LATimes, June 16, 2008.

28, evening news: After the newscast I found more specific info from

Kate Mather, Ruben Vives, and Richard Winton, "Two People Found Shot in Trunk after Ridgecrest Chase, Gun Battle," online at LA-Times, October 25, 2013.

28, "I Feel Good": John Coleman forecasted weather for the independent local news station KUSI, San Diego, from 1994 until his retirement in April 2014. Altogether, his weather broadcast career spanned more than sixty years. Coleman was the original weatherman for ABC's *Good Morning America*, founder of the Weather Channel in the 1980s, and winner of the American Meteorological Society's Broadcast Meteorologist of the Year award. Despite these accolades, Coleman remains a fierce climate change skeptic. As he recently told Megyn Kelly during an interview on Fox News: "The media has told the nation over and over again day after day for twenty years that the oceans are rising, the polar bears are dying, the sea is rising, that storms are going to sweep the earth, and that we're all going to die of a heat wave — I mean, this is incredible, bad, bad science." According to Coleman, "Carbon dioxide is not a significant greenhouse gas. . . . Not only is the ice not melting, more polar bears are alive and happy today than we've had in a hundred years. Life is good, Ms. Kelly. I got to tell you, life is good."

29, fresh drinking water: "Drinking Water," online at WHO, June 2015. Almost 2 billion people depend on water sources contaminated with feces.

29, effects of climate change: David Adam, "50m Environmental Refugees by End of Decade, UN Warns," online at TheGuardian, October 12, 2005.

29, The link between weather and warfare: Fleming, "Climate Engineers," and Plutarch, Caius Marius; also see Max Mueller, "How the UAE Is Making It Rain," online at EsquireME, March 10, 2016. See also Walt Whitman, "The Weather — Does It Sympathize with These Times?" Strangely, none of the commentators on the history of weather modification seems to mention Whitman's memorandum.

29, The first scientific account came in 1871: Fleming, "Climate Engineers."

30, Dyrenforth, as it turned out: S. C. Gwynne, "Rain of Error," online at TexasMonthly, August 2003.

31, the ninth wonder: Richard Crawford, "Building the Morena Dam," online at SanDiegoYesterday, originally published in the *San Diego Union-Tribune*, June 9, 2011.

31, "I do not fight Nature": Fleming, *Fixing the Sky*.

31, Hatfield had established: Thomas W. Patterson, "Hatfield the Rainmaker," *Journal of San Diego History*, Winter 1970, online at SanDiegoHistory, and "Charlie Hatfield 'The Rainmaker,'" documentary online at YouTube, 2004.

31, The history of real rainmaking: Fleming, "Climate Engineers."

32, Four months after the discovery: Ibid., and Matt Novak, "Weather Control as a Cold War Weapon," online at SmithsonianMag, December 5, 2011.

33, In 1954 Captain Howard T. Orville: Fleming, "Climate Engineers," and Capt. H. T. Orville, "Weather Made to Order?" *Collier's Weekly*, May 28, 1954, online at UNZ.

33, In 1958 the father of the H-bomb: Novak, "Weather Control."

33, "a weather race" . . . "twenty knots": Fleming, "Climate Engineers."

34, "the decision where to seed": "Scientific Problems of Weather Modification," National Research Council, Washington, D.C., 1964.

34, starve Castro's sugar crop: Betty Segal, "CIA Are the Weathermen?" *Berkeley Barb*, July 2–8, 1976; see also Lowell Ponte, "War of the Weathers," *New York Times*, April 17, 1976.

35, "The most dramatic was one day in Saigon": Neurosis, *Enemy of the Sun*, track 3, "Burning Flesh in the Year of the Pig," Alternative Tentacles, 1993; David Halberstam's words online at LiveLeak, "The Self-Immolation of Thich Quang Duc."

35, Pulitzer Prize: Patrick Witty, "Malcolm Browne: The Story behind the Burning Monk," online at Time, August 28, 2012.

37, would we act as strangers: To a large extent I already knew the answer to this question, but I often fantasized about giving my brother another chance, about taking that day back. For a more detailed picture of our initial encounter, see my essay "The Mountain," *Gettysburg Review*, Fall 2015.

39, I spoke with Ed Holroyd: Joe Busto introduced Ed Holroyd to me via e-mail, and Dr. Holroyd and I spoke over the phone and exchanged several e-mails in October and November 2013.

40, 1974 US Senate hearing: All quotes from the Senate Subcommittee on Oceans and International Environment's (hereafter SCOIE) top secret weather modification hearing have been sourced from the hearing's now-declassified 126 pages of transcripts. Look for them online at the Texas Tech Virtual Vietnam Archive.

40, "developed at NWC": In 1967, the navy began calling NOTS China Lake NWC China Lake. Today China Lake is officially abbreviated

NAWS, Naval Air Weapons Station, although NOTS and NWC continue to find usage on websites and street signs and in documents and conversations. I prefer NOTS because it has no three-syllable *W*.

41, "many elaborate experiments": St.-Amand is likely referring to Project Stormfury and several of its smaller predecessors, Cirrus and Cyclops.

42, a remarkable location: The quote comes from the history section of Commander, Naval Installations Command — Naval Air Weapons Station China Lake, cnic.navy.mil. Bare-bones facts are from the NAWCWD Quick Facts Sheet, 2008.

43, Secret City: "Stories from 'Secret City,'" online at ChinaLakeMuseum; population and income numbers come from the US Census, 2013; sunshine numbers are from the NAWCWD Quick Facts Sheet, 2008.

44, "over 100,000 images by satellite": This isn't true. It's just what I told her at the time and I thought it sounded right. In reality, however, the base has not mapped all the petroglyphs — by satellite or otherwise — and it's unknown how many carvings truly exist within the borders of China Lake. Conservative numbers put the total at more than 100,000. Greg Haverstock, a BLM archaeologist, told me that there might be more than 250,000 images of bighorn sheep. The *Los Angeles Times* recently reported that there may be more than a million petroglyphs in Renegade Canyon (Little Petroglyph Canyon) alone. Apparently the base plans one day to assemble a three-dimensional laser map of Renegade Canyon and its petroglyphs that will be available for study online.

44, navy-guided tour: The tours are actually organized and directed not by NOTS China Lake but by the Maturango Museum in Ridgecrest. However, the navy grants the museum the right to organize tours, has the final say when it comes to who gets to attend or lead a tour, and determines the dates on which tours may occur. All the tour guides I met worked on base at NOTS China Lake. Hence, given the overarching authority and presence of the navy, it seems appropriate to describe the tours as navy-guided.

44, hottest place on Earth: Adam Nagourney, "A Record Worth Wilting For: Death Valley Is Hotter Than . . . ," online at NYTimes, December 28, 2012.

47, When humans first arrived: Thomas Curwen, "Spirited Stories on Ancient Walls," online at CalAcademy, Summer 1997, explains the savanna and giant lake bit. The rest is an imaginative rendering of the environment at the end of the last Ice Age, when nearly a third of Iowa was covered by glaciers.

48, confine your dreams to your own junkpile: A fine analogy for the writer's process.

49, Coso, in Southern Paiute, means "fire": David S. Whitley, *Cave Paintings and the Human Spirit: The Origin of Creativity and Belief,* Prometheus Books, 2009.

49, innovate new weapons faster: Robert E. McGahern, "An Examination of the Navy's Future Naval Capability Technology Transition Process," Naval Postgraduate School, December 2004; also see Ralph Vartabedian, "Lab Opposes 'Gold Plated' Systems: China Lake Weapons Center Battling with the Navy Brass," online at LATimes, May 1, 1986.

51, second top secret Senate subcommittee hearing: All quotes from the 1974 hearing are from SCOIE.

51, I spoke with Brian Heckman: Heckman and I spoke over the phone shortly after Thanksgiving, November 2013.

54, Harmonic Convergence: Paul Raeburn, "Harmonic Convergence: Will Earth Slip Out of Its Time Beam This Weekend?" *Free Lance-Star,* August 13, 1987.

55, miner M. H. Farley: First quotes dug out of the *Daily Alta California,* July 24, 1860, online via the CDNC; Francis C. Monastero, "Geothermal Resource Council Bulletin," September–October 2002, provides the "boiling hot springs" reference; David S. Whitley, "The Archaeology of Ayers Rock," *Maturango Museum Publication,* 2005, provides the final quote and asserts Farley's account as the first written reference.

55, he established a resort: "A Land Use History of Coso Hot Springs, Inyo County, California," *Naval Weapons Center Administrative Publication,* 1979, or GHC Bulletin, "Geothermal Pipeline: Progress and Development Update," *Geothermal Progress Monitor,* March 2008.

55, Coso Hot Springs: Robert P. Palazzo, *Ghost Towns of Death Valley,* Arcadia Publishing, 2014.

55–56, Native Americans . . . canceled everything: Whitley, "Archaeology of Ayers Rock"; GHC Bulletin, "Geothermal Pipeline"; Monastero, "Geothermal Research Council."

56, geothermal energy: See the power section of the US Navy's Energy,

Environment, and Climate Change website. At the time of writing, Navy 1 Geothermal was the second-largest producer in the United States; it's now the third.

56, water's too hot to touch: When I talked with Kathy Bancroft — tribal preservation officer of the Lone Pine Paiute-Shoshone — about the influence of the geothermal plant, she said it had absolutely destroyed the hot springs. "The power plant is huge," she said. "And the water is so hot now, it's mostly unusable. You'd think there should be dinosaurs out there walking around because there's these flumes shooting up mud and you can't even walk up there because you might fall through. It's completely destroyed." Despite all the damage, however, Kathy said, "You can still feel the presence of the site, and it's still sacred to us."

56, more recent NRC report: Fleming, "Climate Engineers," and National Research Council, "Critical Issues in Weather Modification Research," online at NAP, 2003.

57, Colorado and California: See the weather modification page on the Colorado Water Conservation Board website, and click the link "Cloud Seeding." Also see "Optimizing Cloud Seeding for Water and Energy in California," a report prepared for the California Energy Commission in 2007 by Steven M. Hunter.

57, Besides Colorado and California: If you want to learn more about the ten US states that cloud-seed, the Colorado Water Conservation Board invites you to click a strip of blue underlined text on the last page of a brief pdf entitled "Cloud Seeding." I invite you to do so as well. But you should know that as of August 2015, the hyperlink took me to a very odd place. Allow Google to translate the page from Japanese: "Shalt think deeply thinking game if you want enjoy the sex without."

57: China Meteorological Administration: Gwynn Guilford, "China Creates 55 Billion Tons of Artificial Rain a Year — and It Plans to Quintuple That," online at Quartz, October 22, 2013.

58, yet another embarrassment: Fleming, "Climate Engineers."

60, Infowarrior Alex Jones: Alex Jones interviews Ben Livingston in a short documentary, *The Father of Weaponized Weather*, online at Infowars, 2011.

61, The earth is currently warming . . . 5°C by 2050: Dahr Jamail, "The Coming 'Instant Planetary Emergency,'" online at TheNation, December 17, 2013.

62, World Bank: See "Turn Down the Heat: Why a 4°C Warmer World

Must Be Avoided," a report for the World Bank by the Potsdam Institute for Climate Impact Research, November 2012.

62, 3.5°C global average temperature rise: Jamail, "Coming 'Instant Planetary Emergency.'"

62, polar darkness: Howard Falcon-Lang, "Secrets of Antarctica's Fossilized Forests," online at BBC, February 8, 2011.

63, grass is growing: Louise Gray, "Antarctica Going Green Due to Climate Change," online at Telegraph, March 30, 2011.

63, ice-free summers: Nafeez Ahmed, "US Navy Predicts Summer Ice Free Arctic by 2016," online at TheGuardian, December 9, 2013. A 2013 study published in *Nature* said thinning permafrost may soon release a massive methane pulse, triggering catastrophic climate change and costing the world economy $60 trillion. Climate skeptics enjoy dubbing and dismissing such bad news as the irresponsible doom mongering of venal scientists.

63, chemtrails are real: Public Policy Polling, "Democrats and Republicans Differ on Conspiracy Beliefs," online at PublicPolicyPolling, April 2, 2013.

64, "Turn it on": This and the following quotes are from James Agee and Walker Evans, *Let Us Now Praise Famous Men*, Mariner Books, 2001.

65, screaming lyrics: Krallice, *Diotima*, "Profound Lore," 2011, lyrics sampled from Friedrich Hölderlin, *Odes and Elegies*, translated by Nick Hoff, Wesleyan University Press, 2008.

65, astronomers at Berkeley: Scott Neuman, "Scientists Estimate 20 Billion Earth-Like Planets in Our Galaxy," online at NPR, November 4, 2013.

67, CIA is currently funding: Dana Liebelson and Chris Mooney, "CIA Backs $630,000 Scientific Study on Controlling Global Climate," online at MotherJones, July 17, 2013.

67, "both solar radiation management (SRM) and carbon dioxide removal (CDR) techniques": The NAS website where this quote originally appeared is now gone.

67, congressional committee: Hearing Before the Committee on Science and Technology, House of Representatives, "Geoengineering: Parts I, II, and II" (hereafter HOR: Geo), available online at the United States Government Publishing House, November 5, 2009, and February 4 and March 18, 2010.

68, Wood, a student of Edward Teller . . . $700 billion per annum: Fleming, "Climate Engineers."

68, Iraq War: Daniel Trotta, "Iraq War Costs U.S. More Than $2 Trillion: Study," online at Reuters, March 14, 2013.

68, David Keith's study: Justin McClellan, David W. Keith, and Jay Apt, "Cost Analysis of Stratospheric Albedo Modification Delivery Systems," *Environmental Research Letters*, online at Harvard, 2012. See Aurora Flight Sciences, "Geoengineering Cost Analysis," 2011, for the full report.

69, "SRM" . . . "fast and imperfect": HOR: Geo.

69, "air pollution deaths a year": David Keith, *A Case for Climate Engineering*, MIT Press, 2013.

69, turn the sky white: For an extensive list of the known risks associated with solar geoengineering, see Alan Robock, "Stratospheric Aerosol Geoengineering," *Issues in Environmental Science and Technology*, 2014.

73, aliens: Erich von Däniken, *Chariots of the Gods: Unsolved Mysteries of the Past*, Berkley Books, 1999.

73, Carl Sagan: Ronald Story, *The Space-Gods Revealed: A Close Look at the Theories of Erich von Däniken*, foreword by Carl Sagan, Harper and Row, 1976.

76, decrepit bungalow bathroom: The main gates to the base have since undergone an impressive renovation.

77, "I work on the base — Tom": Tom is a composite character derived from multiple tours of Renegade Canyon and numerous interviews with individuals who have worked on base at NOTS China Lake. I created this composite character to protect the privacy of certain individuals in fragile circumstances and at times to expedite the flow of narrative. For the same reason, time has been compressed in some instances.

77, My mother: My mom would like me to tell you, she insists in fact, that she is also a composite character. I find this assessment incorrect. She and I will fight about this later.

79, erosion-control hexagons: I've now been out to Renegade Canyon several different times, and on each occasion I've inquired about the function of this plastic flooring. The last time I visited, a tour guide told me that the hexagons were installed not to control erosion but rather to provide a particular Native American individual confined to a wheelchair access to the rim of the canyon and the tribal rituals performed there.

81, "The petroglyph designs": Robert F. Heizer and Martin A. Baumhoff, "Great Basin Petroglyphs and Prehistoric Game Trails," *Science*, 1959.

82, the acquisition of supernatural power: This definition of shamanism and most of the background information concerning shamanism derive from my conversations with David Whitley. The primary discovery that forms the main substance of this portion of the book and that initiated the book as a whole came from reading his 1994 article, "By the Hunter, for the Gatherer: Art, Social Relations and Subsistence Change in the Prehistoric Great Basin." Shortly after reading this article in September 2013, I realized that I had more than an essay on my hands—I had a book. I then went on to read more of Whitley's work, especially his 1998 "Cognitive Neuroscience, Shamanism and the Rock Art of Native California" and his truly awe-inspiring 2009 *Cave Paintings and the Human Spirit: The Origin of Creativity and Belief.* From there, once I had learned as much as I could, I approached Whitley directly. Hereafter, information pertaining to the archaeology of the Coso Range and the history of shamanism in Native California comes from David Whitley unless otherwise stated.

83, "to the land of the dead, '*for joy alone*'": Mircea Eliade, *Shamanism: Archaic Techniques of Ecstasy,* translated by Willard R. Trask, Princeton University Press, 1994. My italics.

84, The most embarrassing case: Matt Stroud, "The Death Dealer," online at TheVerge, December 4, 2013.

85, "It's a fad": Jessica Ravitz, "Verdict in Self-Help Guru's Sweat Lodge Trial Stirs Reaction among Native Americans," online at CNN, June 24, 2011.

85, 600 years ago: There are few exceptions to this time line. The most famous, however, is the rock art at Ayers Rock, which was made early in the twentieth century.

88, something went wrong here: This paragraph and a few prior phrases appeared previously in an essay I wrote for *Vice,* "How Ancient Native American Rock Art Is Tearing a California Town Apart," January 2016.

89, semantically and linguistically indistinguishable: For more info about the semantic and linguistic associations between shamans and spirit helpers, see David Whitley's captivating essay "Cognitive Neuroscience, Shamanism and the Rock Art of Native California," *Anthropology of Consciousness,* March 1998.

92, "a prairie owl": This and further quotes are from Emanuel Leutze's notes describing *Westward the Course of Empire Takes Its Way.*

97, National Academy of Sciences: Again, the NAS website where these quotes appeared is no longer online.

97, study is superfluous: That is, that climate change is not happening. See Public Policy Polling, "Democrats and Republicans."

97–98, "It is extremely likely": The pdf online suggests that I cite the summary as follows: IPCC, 2013: Summary for Policymakers. In: *Climate Change 2013: The Physical Science Basis. Contribution of Working Group I to the Fifth Assessment Report of the Intergovernmental Panel on Climate Change* [Stocker, T.F., D. Qin, G.-K. Plattner, M. Tignor, S.K. Allen, J. Boschung, A. Nauels, Y. Xia, V. Bex and P.M. Midgley (eds.)]. Cambridge University Press, Cambridge, United Kingdom and New York, NY, USA. Good luck.

98, paleoclimatologist Lynn Ingram: Steve Hockensmith, "Why State's Water Woes Could Be Just Beginning," online at Berkeley, January 21, 2014.

98, A 2013 Columbia University study . . . 60 percent of the West: Richard Seager, Celine Herweijer, and Ed Cook, "The Characteristics and Likely Causes of the Medieval Megadroughts in North America," Lamont-Doherty Earth Observatory of Columbia University.

98, Drought conditions: See the US Drought Monitor map at the time of writing, online at DroughtMonitor, August 2015.

98, The IPCC states: IPCC, *Fourth Assessment Report*, 2007.

99, "We may be seeing . . . in the near term": Andrew Freedman, "Time Is Running Out for California Drought Relief," online at ClimateCentral, February 3, 2014.

99, "worst drought in 500 years": Adam Nagourney and Ian Lovett, "Severe Drought Has U.S. West Fearing Worst," online at NYTimes, February 1, 2014.

99, According to page 1118: IPCC, *Fifth Assessment Report*. And yes, that's page 1118. Dear IPCC, how was it that you hoped to persuade policy makers and humanity at large to take global warming seriously when your primary persuasive document was an overwhelmingly jargon-laden tome that stretched past the thousand-page mark?

100, "In every emissions scenario": HOR: Geo.

100, researchers at Princeton: Morgan Kelly, "Even If Emissions Stop, Carbon Dioxide Could Warm Earth for Centuries," online at Princeton, November 24, 2013.

100, "That's the key insight": David Rotman quotes David Keith in "A Cheap and Easy Plan to Stop Global Warming," online at TechnologyReview, February 8, 2013.

100, "Carbon casts a long shadow": Keith, *Case*.

101, By wrapping the world: You will notice that the following discussion of solar geoengineering culls quotes and data from many different sources. I consider this section and later geoengineering sections basically mash-ups of all the information available to me on the Internet in late 2013 and early 2014, during and immediately after my first tour of China Lake. During this time I read basically everything reputable that existed and have taken my quotes from those sources. Where references are not provided for a factual claim, that claim can be read as a distillation drawn from the many sources referenced around it.

Regarding the mash-ups: in my opinion it was not necessary to spend a great deal of time explaining in belabored scientific terms exactly how geoengineering will work, nor did I feel that it was necessary at this point in the book to conduct my own interviews with the major scientific players involved in geoengineering research. This was because as I make painfully clear later, the science involved is hardly impressive — what is impressive about geoengineering is not the fact that it's scientifically possible but the fact that it may be socially, politically, and environmentally impossible. Further, interviews did not feel essential at this point in the book — and still don't — because the statements of the principal scientific players are remarkably consistent. For example, in every article I read David Keith appears to make essentially the same point, that is, the technology is cheap, fast, and imperfect, and we need to begin testing now to determine if it will work. Conversely, Raymond Pierrehumbert repeatedly says in multiple articles that it would be madness to attempt geoengineering (given the termination effect) and that the technology cannot be tested. In short, nobody disputes the primary scientific claim: injecting sulfur aerosols into the stratosphere will cool the planet. What the various scientists do argue about, however, is the other things that it might do. Hence, my strategy: after introducing the reader to geoengineering by presenting montages of where the scientists stand, I slow down, move closer, and begin my own interviews in an attempt to move past what has already been reported and answer my own questions.

101, According to Jim Haywood: Henry Gass, "Starting, Then Stopping Geoengineering Could Dangerously Accelerate Climate Change," online at ScientificAmerican, November 27, 2013.

101, "such a scenario": H. Damon Matthews and Ken Caldeira, "Transient Climate-Carbon Simulations of Planetary Geoengineering," online at Proceedings of the National Academy of Sciences, 2007.

101, "you're toast": Rotman, "Cheap and Easy."

102, "The expectation that humankind": Gass, "Starting, Then Stopping."

102, "If you ramp it up": Joel N. Shirkin, "If You Start Geoengineering to Halt Global Warming, Don't Stop," online at InsideScience, December 2, 2013.

102, "it would be reckless": Rotman, "Cheap and Easy."

102, "the peaceful use of nuclear weapons": Fleming, "Climate Engineers."

102, "This is not a new concept": Edward Teller, "The Planet Needs a Sunscreen," *Wall Street Journal*, online at Hoover Institution, October 17, 1997.

102, "The inherent unknowability": Fleming, "Climate Engineers."

103, "Back in 2000": Ken Caldeira quoted by Nicola Jones, "Solar Geoengineering: Weighing Costs of Blocking Sun's Rays," online at Yale, January 9, 2014.

103, would-be "Titans": Fleming, "Climate Engineers."

103, "Deliberately adding one pollutant": Keith, *Case*, and HOR: Geo.

103, "For most, researching 'geoengineering'": This reference is a little tricky. I'm not sure exactly how I stumbled on it, but it comes from the conversation thread of a geoengineering Google Group. Italics mine.

103, Nobel Laureate Paul Crutzen: Fleming, "Climate Engineers."

104, "The politics of it": Richard Harris, "Risky Tech Fixes for Climate Becoming Likelier, Critic Warns," online at NPR, February 12, 2014.

104, one trillion dollars: Nicholas Stern, "Stern Review: Economics of Climate Change, Executive Summary," online at Yale, 2006.

104, In 2006, the billion people: Anup Shah, "Poverty Facts and Stats," online at GlobalIssues, January 7, 2013; 2,227 consumer units for gasoline and motor oil in 2006 multiplied by total US consumer units in 2006 = 264.67 million (see bls.gov); Gayle B. Ronan, "Businesses Loving Valentine's Day Ever More," online at NBCNews, February 14, 2006; Gary Bauer, "Do Americans Love Pets Too Much?" online at CSMonitor, May 31, 2007; "Largest Military Expenditures, 2006," online at InfoPlease from the Stockholm International Peace Research Institute's *Yearbook 2007*.

104, "$150 billion": Nikki Reisch and Steve Kretzmann, "A Climate of War: The War in Iraq and Global Warming," online at Oil Change International, March 2008.

104, On November 4, 2013: Alex Morales, "Kyoto Veterans Say Global Warming Goal Slipping Away," online at Bloomberg, November 4, 2013.

104, "2015 agreement": After years of negotiations, 180 nations signed the historic Paris Agreement in December 2015. The agreement is supposed to limit the global average temperature rise to well below 2°C. Unfortunately, achieving this goal remains profoundly unlikely. See the epilogue for more information about the Paris Agreement.

104, first official government acknowledgment: Fleming, *Fixing the Sky*.

104, Lyndon B. Johnson: Naomi Oreskes, "The Long Consensus on Climate Change," online at WashingtonPost, February 1, 2007.

105, Throughout his worldwide industrial civilization: President's Science Advisory Committee, "Restoring the Quality of Our Environment: Report of the Environmental Pollution Panel," 1965, online at the CaldeiraLab at Stanford. I first accessed this document and made the connection via Ken Caldeira's Stanford page. Fleming discusses the document in *Fixing the Sky*, which I got around to reading almost a year later.

105, "Kyoto is": George W. Bush, "President Bush Discusses Climate Change," online at WhiteHouse, June 11, 2001.

106, "would have been riots": Fleming, "Climate Engineers."

106, A Pentagon report: Peter Schwartz and Doug Randall, "An Abrupt Climate Change Scenario and Its Implications for United States National Security," online at IATP, October 2003.

106, "would result in serious harm": Clive Hamilton, *Requiem for a Species*, Earthscan, 2010.

107, my father escaped deployment: Parts of the following section appeared in slightly different form in the *Gettysburg Review*, Fall 2015.

110, "true purpose of autobiography": Vladimir Nabokov, *Speak, Memory: An Autobiography Revisited*, Vintage, 1989.

111, "The US government . . . The US has also attempted": David Adam, "US Answer to Global Warming: Smoke and Giant Space Mirrors," online at TheGuardian, January 26, 2007.

111, "It's got to be looked at": CBS News, "'Geoengineering' to Fight Global Warming?" online at CBSNews, April 8, 2009.

111, Stephen Pacala: Robert Hunziker, "Top Ten Dreadful Effects of Climate Change," online at DissidentVoice, April 6, 2013.

112, "Modeling indicates": IPCC, *Fifth Assessment Report*. Italics mine.

112, 160 civil, indigenous, and environmental groups: Martin Lukacs, Suzanne Goldenberg, and Adam Vaughan, "Russia Urges UN Climate Report to Include Geoengineering," online at TheGuardian, September 19, 2013.

112, The environmental organization: "News Release: Concern as IPCC Bangs the Drum for Geoengineering," online at ETCGroup, September 27, 2013.

112, An article published in the *Guardian*: Lukacs et al., "Russia."

113, $4.6 million from Bill Gates: John Vidal, "Bill Gates Backs Climate Scientists Lobbying for Large-Scale Geoengineering," online at TheGuardian, February 6, 2012.

113, This frustrated Caldeira: Jones, "Solar Geoengineering."

113, David Keith told: Erin O'Donnell, "Buffering the Sun," online at HarvardMagazine, July–August 2013.

113, What scares people: Rotman, "Cheap and Easy."

113, "You can't see": Jones, "Solar Geoengineering."

113, University of Chicago geophysicist: Rotman, "Cheap and Easy."

114, In February 2013: Keith, *Case*.

114, advised two of the four committee sessions: From a now-nonexistent NAS web page.

114, "All my work on this topic": Keith, *Case*.

115, "The ocean continues": IGBP, IOC, SCOR, "Ocean Acidification Summary for Policymakers: Third Symposium on the Ocean in a High- CO_2 World," online at IGBP, 2013.

115, Less water to drink: Alan Robock, "20 Reasons Why Geoengineering May Be a Bad Idea," *Bulletin of the Atomic Scientists*, online at Rutgers, May–June, 2008.

115–16, A 2013 study . . . "Pick your poison": S. Tilmes et al., "The Hydrological Impact of Geoengineering in the Geoengineering Model Intercomparison Project (GeoMIP)," *Journal of Geophysical Research: Atmospheres*, October 2013; quote from Andrew Freedman, "Geoengineering Could Reduce Critical Global Rainfall," online at ClimateCentral, November 4, 2013.

116, Among the many known dangers . . . "last war on earth": Fleming, "Climate Engineers"; quote from Taubenfeld and Taubenfeld, "Modification."

117, perhaps, we'll think, it's only natural: Throughout all this, the motto from Pliny the Elder (an excellent beer BTW) inscribed on the ceiling of Montaigne's library — also quoted in his essay "How Our Mind Hinders Itself" — comes to mind: "There is nothing certain but uncertainty, and nothing more miserable and yet arrogant than man."

117, "There's definitely pain involved": Pam Reed on *David Letterman*, online at YouTube, 2010.

119, He is the Master of the Spirits: Against Mircea Eliade's definition of the shaman as "the master of ecstasy," David Whitley more accurately redefines the shaman as "the master of the spirits." Whitley attempts this redefinition in the context of an argument about the relationship among shamanism, mental illness, and the origin of human religious belief. It would be unjust to summarize the argument here, as it is one of the more daring and inspired pieces of scholarship I've ever read. Rather, if you're still curious about shamanism, religion, and rock art — I assure you that this book has only scratched the surface, so to speak — I recommend you read Whitley's *Cave Paintings and the Human Spirit*.

119, "Quartz is triboluminescent": Western science discovered triboluminescence in the 1880s, but the shamans of the Cosos figured it out more than 12,000 years ago.

120, remarkable sunsets: These incidents are well documented, and a quick search will turn up dozens of articles.

120, "he who understands": Agee quoting Beethoven in *Let Us Now Praise Famous Men*.

120, "I was walking": John D'Agata, *About a Mountain*, Norton, 2010.

121, Anthony Barrett writes: These are all real YouTube user comments. Feel free to look them up and join the discussion yourself.

123, poet and essayist John Daniel: See John Daniel, *The Trail Home: Nature, Imagination, and the American West*, Pantheon, 1992. During the summer of 2009, I had a scholarship to the Community of Writers at Squaw Valley near Lake Tahoe, California. Every person who attended received a one-hour one-on-one with a published writer. John Daniel was the writer assigned to critique my nonfiction prose. He told me that my essay, "The Heart Ground in the Garbage Disposal," was a vivid and powerful evocation of childhood imagination but that unfortunately, at the crucial moment, the essay devolved into sentimentality and self-pity and ultimately failed. At that point in my writing life, John Daniel's criticism was the harshest I'd ever received. It was also among the most helpful.

125, Caldeira: The general background information on Caldeira, Hoffert, and Wood that follows comes from Chris Mooney, "Can a Million Tons of Sulfur Dioxide Combat Climate Change?" online at Wired, June 23, 2008.

126, "lifetimes of technological civilizations": Joe Romm, "Game Over: Hoffert on Unconventional Gas and Oil and Unconventional Self-Destruction of Civilization," online at ThinkProgress, June 28, 2012.

126, "near-mythological status": Hamilton, *Requiem*, quoting Jeff Goodell, "Can Dr. Evil Save the World?" *Rolling Stone*, 2006.

126, "We sat around the room": The quote comes from a video uploaded to YouTube, "Geoengineer Ken Caldeira Reveals His True Past."

127, "the bureaucratic suppression of CO_2": Fleming, "Climate Engineers."

127, "We've engineered every other environment": Hamilton, *Requiem*.

128, He ordered food: Much to my embarrassment, Caldeira had to buy my lunch. I had no cash on me and in order to pay for my chicken burrito, which we were going to walk to some cafeteria to pick up, I had to first create my own Stanford lunch account, which entailed filling out some interminable form, which I started on, sitting at Ken's computer — a fact he seemed to like no more than the prospect of paying for my lunch — only to discover after five minutes of scrolling and typing — a rather counterproductive business since the point of ordering online, according to Caldeira, was to skip the lines and save time — that it would be impossible to create an account because I had to be an employee or a student. Later that summer, I snail mailed Caldeira a postcard of abandoned Anasazi dwellings at Chaco Canyon along with a thank-you note, $6.35 burrito cash, and a vintage NOTS China Lake sticker with a rabbit riding an "EXPERIMENTAL" missile through the middle of a question mark.

130, death threats: Keith, *Case*.

131, Bill Gates' FICER fund paid for it: See McClellan et al., "Cost Analysis." Interestingly, the full Aurora Flight Sciences report refers to "military facilities" in Palmdale, California, "capable of supporting geoengineering support facilities and operations. The prevailing winds, shown as arrows, serve to further distribute the particulate around the equatorial region." The quote is supposed to explain figure 4, but there is no figure 4, no map of military facilities or of their prevailing winds. Instead, there's a patch of empty white space. Also strange is the suggestion that military facilities in Palmdale might prove useful. The only military facility in Palmdale is an aircraft-manufacturing plant called Air Force Plant 42, which shares a small runway with the Los Angeles/Palmdale Regional Airport. As far as I can tell, since any SRM system would have to run nonstop for centuries, a more secure, isolated, and massive military facility might prove useful. Such a site exists not far from Palmdale, about a hundred miles away. It's called NOTS China Lake.

136, "We do not want": This quote and the others from Caldeira that precede it are from HOR: Geo.

138, University of California trustees: The information in this section regarding George Berkeley and the history of the University of California, Berkeley, comes from my time at the university.

138, bones of tyrannosaurs and buffalo: Campanile dino bones remain a popular legend around Berkeley. In fact, the fossils are not of dinosaurs but rather of large Pleistocene mammals excavated from the La Brea Tar Pits in Los Angeles beginning in 1901.

140, let the man speak for himself: Emily Swanson and Ryan Grim, "Climate Change Poll Finds Most Americans Unwilling to Pay Higher Energy Costs," online at HuffingtonPost, November 2, 2012.

141, "a concerted Apollo-like program": Marty Hoffert, Ken Caldeira, and Gregory Benford, "Fourteen Grand Challenges," online at IEEE, 2003.

141, Hoffert said later: "The Technology Challenge: An Interview with Marty Hoffert," online at Breakthrough, March 31, 2008.

141, "If we fail": Andrew C. Revkin, "Scientists React to a Nobelist's Climate Thoughts," online at NYTimes, September 17, 2010.

146, Adam Baumgart: For fully legitimate reasons related to profound sadness, my mom asked me to change her father's first name, so I came up with another four-letter word that starts with the letter A.

147, "How far we all come": James Agee, *A Death in the Family*, Penguin, 2009.

148, the initial deities were most often feminine: I have relied on Camille Paglia's definition of the chthonic in her book *Sexual Personae: Art and Decadence from Nefertiti to Emily Dickinson*, Vintage, 1991. Other works that have informed my writing throughout this myth-based section include the chapter "Myths: Dreams, Fears, Idols" in Simone de Beauvoir's classic *The Second Sex*, translated by Constance Borde and Sheila Malovany-Chevallier, Vintage, 2011; Erich Neumann's *The Great Mother: An Analysis of the Archetype*, translated by Ralph Manheim, Princeton, 2015; Marija Gimbutas' *The Language of the Goddess*, Thames and Hudson, 2001; Cynthia Eller's *The Myth of Matriarchal Prehistory: Why an Invented Past Will Not Give Women a Future*, Beacon, 2001; and Hannah Arendt's classic *The Human Condition*, Chicago, 1998. Another helpful book was a massive shabby 1950s encyclopedia of world mythology that I found on a sidewalk in Berkeley. Unfortunately, I donated this book to the Salvation Army along with most of my belongings before fleeing Iowa in late November 2014.

148, In Native Californian mythology: All claims pertaining to origin myths and sexual symbology in Native California depend on these five scholarly papers: Daniel L. Myers, "Myth as Ritual: Reflections from a Symbolic Analysis of Numic Origin Myths," *Journal of California and Great Basin Anthropology*, 2001; Daniel L. Myers, "Symbolism among the Numa: Symbolic Analysis of Numic Origin Myths," *Journal of California and Great Basin Anthropology*, 1997; Robert M. Yohe II and Alan P. Garfinkel, "Reflections on a Possible Sheep Shrine at the Rose Spring Site (CA-INY-372), Rose Valley, Alta California," *California Archaeology*, 2012; Jay Miller, "Basin Religion and Theology: A Comparative Study of Power (Puha)," *Journal of California and Great Basin Anthropology*, 1983; and Jay Miller, "Numic Religion: An Overview of Power in the Great Basin of Native North America," *Anthropos*, 1983.

151, "To live — that means to be sick a long time": Friedrich Nietzsche, *Twilight of the Idols*, Penguin Classics, 1990.

153, "It is the manifest destiny": David H. Grinspoon, "Is Mars Ours?" online at Slate, January 7, 2004.

154, "Definitely Enceladus": Kenneth Chang, "Under Icy Surface of a Saturn Moon Lies a Sea of Water, Scientists Say," online at NYTimes, April 3, 2014.

158, They left Los Angeles a thousand strong: Information regarding the pilgrims not communicated in scene has been distilled from newspaper articles, the marchers' own blogs, randomly uploaded YouTube videos, and the Great March for Climate Action's website. In order to limit the number of references, I've confined myself to inserting only those that derive from a preexisting journalistic source.

158, Scientists described the situation: Richard Howitt et al., "Economic Analysis of the 2015 Drought for California Agriculture," online at UCDavis, July 15, 2014.

158, made mountains rise and triggered earthquakes: Colin B. Amos et al., "Uplift and Seismicity Driven by Groundwater Depletion in Central California," online at Nature, May 2014.

161, teaching prison convicts creative-writing classes online: This was how the position at the Division of Continuing Education was initially advertised. In fact, I never met my students, and while most of them seemed like unsatisfied housewives or retired high school teachers, others, judging from the contents of their essays, may very well have been incarcerated.

162, "We are on a pilgrimage": Mike Kilen, "Ed Fallon's Climate-Change Awareness Trek Reaches Iowa," online at Des Moines Register, August 8, 2014.

162, "the commitment": Terrell Johnson, "Will a 3,000-Mile 'Great March for Climate Action' Change Minds on Climate Change?" online at WeatherChannel, December 23, 2013.

168, my guide, Barry: Barry is a composite character derived from my initial tour of the Pentagon and numerous other individuals with stakes in and bets against the Pentagon's expanding military-environmental complex.

170, certifiably sustainable: By "sustainable" I mean "green"—with all the ambiguity and uncertainty these two terms imply. The US Green Building Council gives LEED awards to buildings that show "leadership in energy and environmental design." A detailed discussion of the council and its award ratings would take me too far afield. What is important here is that when you walk into the Pentagon you see images of leaves and the word "green" (classic greenwashing) and think, ah, how nice, this building is sustainable—a thought that, perhaps, couldn't be any farther from the truth.

170–71, the Thomas Jefferson Library got a bronze: Google these places and add more locations to the list.

171, The base celebrated Earth Day: NAVAIR, "AIReel: China Lake Celebrates Earth Day," online at Navy, May 5, 2010.

171, Nellis Air Force Base: "Nellis Air Force Base Solar Array Provides Model for Renewable Projects," online at Energy.gov, March 24, 2010.

171, Tooele Army Depot: Kathy Anderson, Tony Lopez, and Michael N. Meyer, "Tooele Army Depot Continues to Pursue Renewable Energy Goals," online at Army, August 18, 2014.

171, A program at NAS Corpus Christi: The DoD link I had for the figure of $2.5 million no longer works. However, Jessica Savage, "City Moves Forward with Plans to Irrigate Bill Witt Park, Two Private Golf Courses," *Corpus Christi Caller-Times*, November 21, 2012, attests to the connection.

171, All throughout the DoD: "Naval Base San Diego Opens Electric Vehicle Charging Station," online at CBS8, March 23, 2013.

172, Guantanamo Bay: Federal Energy Management Program, "Guantanamo Bay Wind Turbines Save Energy and Cut Costs," online at denix.osd.mil, 2005.

172, green torture: This little joke was suggested to me by Sohbet Karbuz.

172, annual energy use: Gregory J. Lengyel, "Department of Defense Energy Strategy: Teaching an Old Dog New Tricks," online at Brookings Institution, August 2007, and Sohbet Karbuz, "How Much Energy Does the US Military Consume? An Update," online at Blogspot, August 5, 2013.

173, "Operational energy": The DoD website where I found this quote no longer exists. See, however, Moshe Schwartz, Katherine Blakeley, and Ronald O'Rourke, "Department of Defense Energy Initiatives: Background and Issues for Congress," online at FAS, December 10, 2012, for the same facts.

173, 2011 Pentagon report: "Energy for the Warfighter: Operational Energy Strategy," online at SecNav, March 1, 2011.

173, According to Sharon Burke: Sharon E. Burke, "Powering the Pentagon: Creating a Lean, Clean Fighting Machine," online at ForeignAffairs, May–June 2014.

175, "energy-efficient U.S.": Ibid.

175, "You think about the challenges": Kate Evans, "Saugus Native Ed Fallon Walks Across Country for Climate," online at Saugus Wicked Local, November 14, 2014.

175, "We must be no less bold": These and the following quotes by Ray Mabus are from "Remarks by the Honorable Ray Mabus," online at Navy, Naval Energy Forum, Hilton McLean Tysons Corner, McLean, Virginia, October 14, 2009.

176, According to experts: Russell W. Stratton, Hsin Min Wong, and James I. Hileman, "Life Cycle Greenhouse Gas Emissions from Alternative Jet Fuels," online at MIT, June 2010.

176, "The Navy is mindful": Julia Whitty, "My Heart-Stopping Ride Aboard the Navy's Great Green Fleet," online at MotherJones, March–April, 2013.

177, "U.S. energy security": Anthony Andrews et al., "The Navy Biofuel Initiative Under the Defense Production Act," online at FAS, June 22, 2012.

177, Tewksbury spoke fondly: Dennis D. Tewksbury, United States Army, "Preemptive Energy Security: An Aggressive Approach to Meeting America's Requirements," online at DTIC, March 10, 2006.

178, "not too much American power, but too little": Thomas D. Kraemer,

"Addicted to Oil: Strategic Implications of American Oil Policy," online at StrategicStudiesInstitute, May 2006. My italics.

178, "Failing to take urgently required economic steps": John M. Amidon, "America's Strategic Imperative: A National Energy Policy Manhattan Project," Air War College, Air University, February 25, 2005.

178, "combat capability": Carin Hall, "Armed with Algae," online at EnergyDigital, May 2012.

178, "enhance its mission": Sarah E. Light, "The Military-Environmental Complex," *Boston College Law Review*, May 20, 2014.

178, The mission is the bottom line: 10 US Code § 2924, Definitions, online at Cornell, 2011.

179, The Pentagon purchases and consumes: All this information derives solely from Barry Sanders' exhaustively researched and terrifically disturbing *The Green Zone: The Environmental Costs of Militarism*, AK Press, 2009.

180, $8.5 billion: Ibid.

180, nearly $18 billion: Karbuz, "How Much Energy." See the figure titled "The US Department of Defense Oil Consumption and Costs": $362.5 \times 1000 = 362,500$ barrels per day, $362,500 \times 365 = 132,312,500$ barrels of fuel.

180, "What are you not going to do?": Whitty, "Heart-Stopping Ride."

180, greenhouse gas pollution: Sanders, *Green Zone*.

180, Executive Order 13514: "Federal Agency Strategic Sustainability Performance Plans," online at WhiteHouse, 2009.

180, President Obama: Office of the Press Secretary, "President Obama Signs an Executive Order Focused on Federal Leadership in Environmental, Energy, and Economic Performance," online at WhiteHouse, October 5, 2009.

181, "Operational energy is *necessarily exempt*": Department of Defense, "Strategic Sustainability Performance Plan," online at denix .osd.mil, 2012. My italics.

181, Secretary Mabus says: Mabus, "Remarks," Hilton.

182, "unlikely to materialize": Light, "Military-Environmental Complex." Such a global regulatory program gained substantial legs in late 2015 with the ratification of the Paris Agreement. For more on the agreement and the likelihood of limiting the global average temperature rise, see the epilogue.

182, "Droughts and crop failures": Chuck Hagel, "Secretary of Defense Speech," online at Defense, October 13, 2014.

183, "a remarkable shift": Coral Davenport, "Pentagon Signals Security Risks of Climate Change," online at NYTimes, October 13, 2014.

183, Pentagon is not only exempt: Sara Flounders, "Pentagon's Role in Global Catastrophe," online at IACenter, 2009.

183, Marshall Institute report: Jeffrey Salmon, "National Security and Military Policy Issues Involved in the Kyoto Treaty," online at Marshall, May 18, 1998.

185, Pat plucks a message: I made an audio recording (never found full video or the HBO special) of the Great March's final rally in front of the White House. It's hard to say with total certainty who is reading which written statement. I trust, however, that no one will be too bothered if I've accidentally attributed the wrong message to a reader. In general, the messages communicate the same idea — we need climate action — and I'm sure each marcher would endorse every message.

185, "serious look at the world": Press Operations, "Remarks by Secretary Hagel at the Atlantic's Washington Ideas Forum 2014," online at Defense, October 29, 2014.

186, threat multipliers: Department of Defense, "Quadrennial Defense Review 2014," online at Defense, 2014.

186, "ISIS is still gaining ground": Davenport, "Pentagon Signals."

186, "It is disappointing": Fox News, "Pentagon Calls Climate Change a Matter of 'National Security,'" online at FoxNews, October 13, 2014.

186, a hoax . . . "is to me outrageous": James Inhofe, The Greatest Hoax: How the Global Warming Conspiracy Threatens Your Future, WND Books, 2012, and Brian Tashman, "James Inhofe Says the Bible Refutes Climate Change," online at RightWingWatch, March 8, 2012.

186, "coastal installations could be vulnerable": Jim Garamone, "Military Must Be Ready for Climate Change, Hagel Says," online at Defense, October 13, 2014.

187, disrupting daily operations: Yuki Noguchi, "As Sea Levels Rise, Norfolk Is Sinking and Planning," online at NPR, June 24, 2014.

187, "the data wins": Benjamin Dills, "National Security and the Accelerating Risks of Climate Change (Report Launch)," online at NewSecurityBeat, June 16, 2014, and Caitlin Werrell and Francesco Femia, "Military Leaders Applaud Quadrennial Defense Review's Approach to Climate Change," online at ClimateAndSecurity, March 5, 2014.

187, "I do not seek": Mabus, "Remarks," Hilton.

188, "single largest purchase of biofuel": Secretary of the Navy Public

Affairs, "Navy Secretary and USDA Secretary Announce Largest Government Purchase of Biofuel," online at Navy, December 5, 2011.

188, $150 a gallon: Reuters, "Pentagon Paid $150 per Gallon for 'Green' Jet Fuel to Promote Alternative Energy," online at RT, May 8, 2012.

188, $12 million: Ibid. And see William Cole, "Environmentalists Knock Navy Plan to Sink Navy Ships," online at Military, June 29, 2012. Colby Self of the Basel Action Network's green ship recycling campaign points out another potential problem, beyond the price of biofuels, with the RIMPAC's green demonstration: "The hypocrisy of the Navy's new ecological 'Great Green Fleet' demonstrating its 'greenness' by sinking ships containing globally banned pollutants off the coast of Hawaii is particularly ironic. But the realization that this choice by the Navy to dump poisons into the marine environment is not only unnecessary, but also is costing Americans hundreds of green recycling jobs, makes this SINKEX [ship sinking exercise] program both an environmental and an economic insult." See Center for Biological Diversity, "Navy's 'Great Green Fleet' Will Pollute Ocean with PCBs, Other Toxins in Ship-sinking War Games," June 28, 2012.

188, "All systems performed at full capacity": Navy Region Hawaii Public Affairs, "Navy in Hawaii Makes Strides Toward Energy Security," online at PaCom, November 15, 2015.

188, 37 million gallons: Michael Bastasch, "Navy Looks to Purchase 37 Million Gallons of Biofuels," online at DailyCaller, July 25, 2014.

188, John McCain: Noah Shachtman, "Senate Panel Cuts Off Navy's Biofuel Buys," online at Wired, May 24, 2012.

188, James Inhofe: James M. Inhofe, "Inhofe Cautions against Wasting Limited DoD Funds on Green Energy," online at Senate, May 10, 2012.

188, Ray Mabus: NPR, "Environmental Outlook: The Military and Alternative Energy," online at Navy, July 5, 2011.

188, "Mabus' statement is utterly ridiculous": Thomas Pyle, "The Navy's Use of Biofuels Is Inefficient and Costly," online at USNews, July 19, 2012.

188, "being timid": Mabus, "Remarks," Hilton.

190, Mabus says it: Ray Mabus, "Remarks by the Honorable Ray Mabus," National Clean Energy Summit 4.0, Las Vegas, Nevada, online at Navy, August 30, 2011.

190, Burke says it: Sharon E. Burke, "National Security and Fuels of the

Future: The Importance of Sec. 526," online at WhiteHouse, July 15, 2011.

190, Gates says it: Brendan F. D. Barrett, "Militaries Have Peak Oil in Their Sights," online at UNU, June 1, 2011.

190, The cheapest biofuel: Figures from T. A. Kiefer, "Twenty-First Century Snake Oil: Why the United States Should Reject Biofuels as Part of a Rational National Security Energy Strategy," online at AU.AF, January 2013.

190, world is running out of oil: I am grateful to Sohbet Karbuz, director of hydrocarbons at the Mediterranean Observatory for Energy, for talking to me about the Pentagon's green energy revolution and giving me the courage to write this difficult section. Months of reading his insights helped confirm some of my doubts about DoD biofuels, and his broad and unstinting blog is still the best source I've found for up-to-date information about and analysis of US military energy consumption and security.

190, "As a nation": Mabus, "Remarks," Hilton.

191, "people that may not be our *friends*": Mabus, "Remarks," Las Vegas. My italics.

191, "dependency on foreign oil": Whitty, "Heart-Stopping Ride."

191, "tether of foreign oil": Ray Mabus, "Seeking Alternative Energy Sources Key to Navy Mission," online at DoDLive, Summer 2012.

191, comes from the United States: This was true in 2012, prior to Mabus' reference to "the tether of foreign oil" (see Corey Flintoff, "Where Does America Get Oil? You May Be Surprised," online at NPR, April 12, 2012). In 2015, however, according to the US Energy Information Administration (see the EIA's FAQ section), the primary federal government authority on energy statistics and analysis, "24% of the petroleum consumed by the United States was imported from foreign countries, the lowest level since 1970." In other words, 76 percent of the petroleum consumed in the United States came from the United States. For more background on this surprising phenomenon, see the US Energy Information Administration's 2011 article, "U.S. Oil Import Dependence: Declining No Matter How You Measure It."

191, University of Texas . . . "Middle East": University of Texas at Austin Energy Poll, "Topline Results," Spring 2015, and Flintoff, "Get Oil?"

191, greater Middle East combined: See the EIA's 2014 "US Imports by Country of Origin" totals, online at EIA. The OPEC countries of Venezuela, Ecuador, Angola, and Nigeria (none of which is in the Middle

East) drive the total below 25 percent. The EIA says that Persian Gulf countries accounted for only 20 percent of our gross imports in 2014 (for 2015, this figure sank to 16 percent; see "How Much Petroleum Does the United States Import and Export?" online at the EIA's updated FAQ section). Add in the remaining Middle Eastern countries from the former link, and you still don't get a value that reaches 25 percent.

191, Canada supplying . . . the United States: "US Imports by Country of Origin," 2014, online at EIA.

191, "we produce more oil here": Julie Kliegman, "Obama Says U.S. Produces More Oil than It Imports for First Time in Nearly 20 years," online at PolitiFact, January 17, 2014.

191, "net exporter of petroleum products": American Petroleum Institute, "Understanding Crude Oil and Product Markets," online at API, 2014.

192, Marion King Hubbert . . . hit in 2004: George Monbiot, "We Were Wrong on Peak Oil: There's Enough to Fry Us All," online at TheGuardian, July 2, 2012, and George Wuerthner, "The Myth of Peak Oil," online at CounterPunch, March 29, 2012.

192, "Anticipated supply shortages": Ashley Seager, "Steep Decline in Oil Production Brings Risk of War and Unrest, Says New Study," online at TheGuardian, October 22, 2007.

192, "While opinion-makers": Leonardo Maugeri, "Oil: The Next Revolution: The Unprecedented Upsurge of Oil Production Capacity and What It Means for the World," online at Harvard, June 2012.

193, Today, the lowest estimate: Wuerthner, "Myth."

193, "The lesson . . . no 'peak-oil' in sight": Maugeri, "Oil."

193, "peak oil has been predicted for 150 years": Christof Rühl was quoted in an article in EurActiv.com, a venue for "EU news and policy debates across languages." As of June 2016, however, the article no longer appears on the website.

193, "how I can look my children in the eyes": Monbiot, "Wrong."

194, The Pentagon . . . "trade one security challenge for another": Sharon E. Burke, "National Security and Fuels of the Future: The Importance of Sec. 526," online at WhiteHouse, July 15, 2011, and Elizabeth McGowan, "Congress Trying Again to Repeal Ban on Carbon-Heavy Fuels for Military," online at InsideClimateNews, July 25, 2011.

194, "The synergy": Light, "Military-Environmental Complex."

195, "The benefits of the Pentagon's drive": Burke, "Powering the Pentagon."

196, Obama reiterated: Office of the Press Secretary, "Remarks by the President on Energy Security at Andrews Air Force Base," online at WhiteHouse, March 31, 2010.

197, "bewildered herd": Walter Lippmann, *Public Opinion*, online at WWNorton, 1922.

197, "The persistent difficulty . . . lives and happiness are known to depend": Ibid.

197–98, "The Green Arms Race": Siddhartha M. Velandy, "The Green Arms Race: Reorienting the Discussions on Climate Change, Energy Policy, and National Security," online at HarvardNSJ, 2012.

200, "It is no longer possible": Lippmann, *Public Opinion*.

201, "We need to fight a war": Light, "Military-Environmental Complex."

202, "Every revolution evaporates": Gustav Janouch, *Conversations with Kafka*, translated by Goronwy Rees, New Directions, 2012.

203, "*It does not grieve . . . destroyers of all*": Ulcerate, *The Destroyers of All*, Willowtip Records, 2011. My italics.

204, $104 billion . . . "risk being canceled": Adam J. Liska and Richard K. Perrin, "Securing Foreign Oil: A Case for Including Military Operations in the Climate Change Impact of Fuels," online at EnvironmentalMagazine, 2010.

205, killed more than a million civilians: John Tirman, "In the Bush Presidency: How Many Died?" online at MIT, 2009.

205, thousands of tons . . . the written word: Sanders, *Green Zone*.

205, "Iraq holds about 18%": "Country Analysis Brief: Iraq," online at EIA, April 28, 2016.

205, "I am saddened": Liska and Perrin, "Securing Foreign Oil."

205, 4 million barrels a day: Nick Cunningham, "Iraq Shrugs Off Low Oil Prices, Boosts Oil Output to Record Levels," online at CSMonitor, January 22, 2015.

205, 60,000 gallons of jet fuel in a single raid: Sanders, *Green Zone*.

206, "Because biofuels come from plants": David Biello, "The False Promise of Biofuels," online at ScientificAmerican, August 1, 2011.

206, "use of additional conventional biofuels": Catherine Bowyer, "Anticipated Indirect Land Use Change Associated with Expanded Use of Biofuels and Bioliquids in the EU: An Analysis of the National Renewable Energy Action Plans," online at IEEP, March 2011.

206, The life cycle of corn ethanol: Kiefer, "Snake Oil."

206, "U.S. production of corn ethanol": Biello, "False Promise."

207, These taxes helped fund: Ibid.

207, The Pentagon's pursuit of biofuels: Kiefer, "Snake Oil."

207, triple the size of the contiguous United States: Biello, "False Promise."

207, The population of the world: David Biello, "Human Population Reaches 7 Billion: How Did This Happen and Can It Go On?" online at ScientificAmerican, October 28, 2011.

208, warming scenario predicted by the IPCC: Catherine Brahic, "World on Track for Worst-Case Warming Scenario," online at NewScientist, September 22, 2014.

208, drop by 40 percent over the next fifteen years: United Nations World Water Assessment Program, "The United Nations World Water Development Report 2015: Water for a Sustainable World," online at UNESCO, 2015.

208, main factor "behind the rapid increase": Donald Mitchell, "A Note on Rising Food Prices: The World Bank Development Prospects Group," online at Bio-Based, July 2008.

208, "additional demands on the food system": Food and Agriculture Organization of the United Nations, "The State of Food Insecurity in the World: How Does International Price Volatility Affect Domestic Economies and Food Security?" online at FAO, 2011.

208, "This is absolute madness": Sanjeev Kulkarni, "Nestle Chief Warns of Food Riots," online at EconIntersect, October 8, 2011.

208, "Climate change has substantially increased": David B. Lobell and Claudia Tebaldi, "Climate Experts Estimate Risk of Rapid Crop Slowdown," online at UCAR, July 25, 2014.

208, 40 percent of global corn exports: Purdue Research Foundation, "Ag 101," online at EPA, 2002, and US Department of Agriculture, "U.S. Corn Trade," online at USDA, 2016.

208, "a farm roughly the size of Maryland": Biello, "False Promise."

209, "substantial amount of energy": European Commission DG Environmental News Alert Service, "Science for Environmental Policy: Water for Microalgae Cultivation Has Significant Energy Requirements," online at Europa, November 17, 2011.

209, "A critical look": Kiefer, "Snake Oil."

209, "This model is broken": Andrew Herndon, "Biofuel Pioneer Forsakes Renewables to Make Gas-Fed Fuels," online at Bloomberg, May 1, 2013.

210, $61.33 per gallon: Kiefer, "Snake Oil."

210, "will immeasurably aid this planet": Ray Mabus, "Remarks by the

Honorable Ray Mabus," Commonwealth Club, San Francisco, California, online at Navy, August 16, 2010.

210, "a worst case scenario": Kiefer, "Snake Oil."

210, "The global corporations": Jean Ziegler, *Betting on Famine: Why the World Still Goes Hungry*, New Press, 2013.

210, 350,000 gallons: Kiefer, "Snake Oil."

210, "Leading change": Mabus, "Remarks," Hilton.

213, campaign donations from oil and gas companies: Open Secrets, "Career Campaign Finance: Senator James M. Inhofe," online at OpenSecrets, 2016.

213, she stopped speaking for 109 days: Cheryl McNamara, "When the Act of Doing Speaks Volumes: Notes from the Great Climate March," online at CommonDreams, November 1, 2014.

216, "there are a . . . control by the UN": Paul Nightingale and Rose Cairns, "The Security Implications of Geoengineering: Blame, Imposed Agreement and the Security of Critical Infrastructure," online at Geoengineering-Governance-Research, November 2014.

216, "Yes, we are rugged individuals": Barack Obama, "Presidential Economic Address to Joint Session of Congress," online at C-Span, September 8, 2011.

216, "Without a national religion": Victor Davis Hanson, "Military Technology and American Culture," online at TheNewAtlantis, Spring 2003.

216, "frontier experience . . . tranquility of the past": Ibid.

217, "Congratulations": NAWCWD Quick Facts Sheet.

217, "our manner of making war": Hanson, "Military Technology."

217, "depend on *our* natural security": Center for New American Security, "CNAS Press Release," online at CNAS, July 20, 2009. My italics.

217, "The perceptions that geoengineering": Nightingale and Cairns, "Implications."

217, Democracy is not consensus. Neither is geopolitics: In the words of Paul Wolfowitz: "World order is ultimately backed by the U.S.," and "the United States should be postured to act independently when collective action cannot be orchestrated" or when a crisis calls for swift action. See Patrick E. Tyler, "US Strategy Plan Calls for Insuring No Rivals Develop," online at NYTimes, March 8, 1992.

218, "geoengineering would have to be imposed": Instead of letting this grim picture serve as the final word, the authors opt for a more hopeful ring at their essay's end. And who could blame them? The final lines of their essay read as follows: "Instead, it is hard to avoid the conclusion geoengineering won't work, it will be un-governable . . . and will have extremely costly social and economic consequences of such a magnitude to make geoengineering untenable as a policy option." It goes without saying, however, that this perspective itself assumes a level of cooperation and rationality that the United States and other major world powers have hitherto failed to demonstrate in their tackling of human-induced climate change.

218, "being timid": Mabus, "Remarks," Hilton.

219, "Mabus puis tost alors mourra": Ned Halley, *Complete Prophecies of Nostradamus*, Wordsworth Editions, 1999.

220, "geoengineering will make weather events blameworthy": Nightingale and Cairns, "Implications."

221, Three tablespoons of crude oil: Kiefer, "Snake Oil."

221, "Going to meet our helping spirits": Sandra Ingerman, *Shamanic Journeying: A Beginner's Guide*, Sounds True, 2008. Hereafter, similar quoted fragments pertaining to the Upper World, helping spirits, whether or not all this is happening in your imagination, and so on have all been sourced from Ingerman.

224, "California has only one year of water left": Jay Famiglietti, "California Has About One Year of Water Left: Will You Ration Now?" online at LATimes, March 12, 2015. The original doomsday title of Famiglietti's op-ed was heavily criticized and has been subsequently amended to more accurately reflect the true contents of the article. "California Has About One Year of Water Stored: Will You Ration Now?" is still a frightening scenario.

225, "Experience the rituals": Petroglyph Festival, "Events," online at WordPress, 2014. This copy on this site was used to advertise the original 2014 festival. I'm surprised it's still online at this point. A more professional-looking website, rpfestival.com, has since replaced it, and the quoted copy has been scrapped.

226, "It's a different world": Chris Megerian, "Brown Orders California's First Mandatory Water Restrictions: 'It's a Different World,'" online at LATimes, April 1, 2015, and Adam Nagourney, "California Imposes First Mandatory Water Restrictions to Deal with Drought," online at NYTimes, April 1, 2015.

226, Ashley Blythe: I interviewed Kathy Bancroft, Ashley Blythe, and Greg Haverstock in Lone Pine and Bishop, California, in December 2014 and January 2015.

229, "the vulva and evil supernatural power": David S. Whitley, *A Guide to Rock Art Sites: Southern California and Southern Nevada*, Mountain Press, 1996.

230, "brought out a lot of people": Adam Robertson, "O'Neill Gives Petroglyph Update," online at RidgecrestCA, August 15, 2014.

230, "The Petroglyph Festival": Louis Sahagun, "Navy Faces Daunting Task of Counting Desert Petroglyphs," online at LATimes, June 14, 2014. My italics.

230, "50th anniversary on steroids": Jessica Weston, "Petroglyph Park Gets Ready to Go," online at RidgecrestCA, July 16, 2014.

231, "Sometimes we don't think": Robertson, "O'Neill."

231, tours remained confined to American citizens: Some of the details reported here changed during the second annual Ridgecrest Petroglyph Festival, which coincidentally I attended and reported on for *Vice* magazine. For a more in-depth glimpse of the festival, see my essay "How Ancient Native American Rock Art Is Tearing a California Town Apart," January 2016.

231, "Hotels averaged over 60 percent": Jessica Weston, "Next Petroglyph Festival Nov. 7 and 8, 2015," online at RidgecrestCA, December 9, 2014.

231, "I do several at a time": Jessica Weston, "Rock On: Olaf Doud Works on Petroglyph Park Art," online at RidgecrestCA, September 16, 2014.

233, "I've been doing it for a long time": Ibid.

233, "The park will bring everyone together": Ibid.

234, "My Life's in Ruins": See the apparel section of the Maturango Museum's website. The star t-shirt is no longer online, but at the moment they do have pictures of two fifth graders modeling other shirts while squinting uncomfortably into the sun.

ACKNOWLEDGMENTS

Thank you, Pam and Craig, for tolerating and encouraging me over the years. I never could have written this book without your unconditional love and support. Thank you, Christina, for calling me out when I'm an idiot, adoring me sometimes, loving me always, and continuing to accept me and my misguided life choices. I'd probably be working at airbnb making six figures by now were it not for the dedicated teachers who encouraged my young mind to question the world and to write. Thank you, Patrick Ojeda and Patricia Swikard, Stephen Baldwin, and Bharati Mukherjee and Clark Blaise. I am grateful for the support of the University of Iowa and its phenomenal Nonfiction Writing Program run by the tireless teacher, essayist, and friend John D'Agata. I owe Matt McGowan a major thank-you for sticking by me. I'm sorry if your power goes out. Thank you, Richard Preston, for selecting this book for publication. Along with Landon, thank you, Kyle Bruser, Steven Wilson, John Morgan, Jesús Castillo, Andrew Lincoln, and Cory Gehrich for remaining loyal friends and continuing to make art alongside me. You're all my brothers. To all my friends from the NWP, I miss you and am grateful for those years and your company. I am indebted to the myriad journalists and experts writing for the many periodicals, blogs, newspapers, and think tanks from which I quote. I could not have completed the main work of this book without such a rich and solid foundation of factual reporting to first stand upon. Thank you for helping me navigate this chaotic world. Finally, I thank the many experts who took the time to talk with me and offered their voices and perspectives to the pages of this book.